AF755382

THE FEDERAL REPUBLIC OF GERMANY AND THE EUROPEAN COMMUNITY

SIMON BULMER AND WILLIAM PATERSON

Routledge
Taylor & Francis Group
LONDON AND NEW YORK

First published in 1987

This edition first published in 2015
by Routledge
2 Park Square, Milton Park, Abingdon, Oxon, OX14 4RN

and by Routledge
711 Third Avenue, New York, NY 10017

Routledge is an imprint of the Taylor & Francis Group, an informa business

© 1987 S. Bulmer and W. Paterson

All rights reserved. No part of this book may be reprinted or reproduced or utilised in any form or by any electronic, mechanical, or other means, now known or hereafter invented, including photocopying and recording, or in any information storage or retrieval system, without permission in writing from the publishers.

Trademark notice: Product or corporate names may be trademarks or registered trademarks, and are used only for identification and explanation without intent to infringe.

British Library Cataloguing in Publication Data
A catalogue record for this book is available from the British Library

ISBN: 978-1-138-83837-6 (Set)
eISBN: 978-1-315-72630-4 (Set)
ISBN: 978-1-138-84911-2 (Volume 2)
eISBN: 978-1-315-72583-3 (Volume 2)
Pb ISBN: 978-1-138-84916-7 (Volume 2)

Publisher's Note
The publisher has gone to great lengths to ensure the quality of this reprint but points out that some imperfections in the original copies may be apparent.

Disclaimer
The publisher has made every effort to trace copyright holders and would welcome correspondence from those they have been unable to trace.

ROUTLEDGE LIBRARY EDITIONS:
GERMAN POLITICS

Volume 2

THE FEDERAL REPUBLIC OF GERMANY AND THE EUROPEAN COMMUNITY

The FEDERAL REPUBLIC of GERMANY and the EUROPEAN COMMUNITY

Simon Bulmer

William Paterson

London
ALLEN & UNWIN
Boston Sydney Wellington

© S. Bulmer and W. Paterson, 1987
This book is copyright under the Berne Convention.
No reproduction without permission. All rights reserved.

**Allen & Unwin, the academic imprint of
Unwin Hyman Ltd**

PO Box 18, Park Lane, Hemel Hempstead, Herts. HP2 4TE, UK
40 Museum Street, London WC1A 1LU, UK
37/39 Queen Elizabeth Street, London SE1 2QB

Allen & Unwin Inc.,
8 Winchester Place, Winchester, Mass. 01890, USA

Allen & Unwin (Australia) Ltd,
8 Napier Street, North Sydney, NSW 2060, Australia

Allen & Unwin (New Zealand) Ltd in association with the
Port Nicholson Press Ltd,
Private Bag, Wellington, New Zealand

First published in 1987

British Library Cataloguing in Publication Data

Bulmer, Simon
The Federal Republic of Germany and the
European Community.
1. European Economic Community – Germany (West)
I. Title II. Paterson, William
337.1'42 HC241.25.G3
ISBN 0-04-382045-X
ISBN 0-04-382046-8 Pbk

Library of Congress Cataloging-in-Publication Data

Bulmer, Simon.
The Federal Republic of Germany and the
European Community.
Bibliography: p.
Includes index.
1. European Economic Community – Germany (West)
I. Paterson, William. II. Title
HC241.25.G3B86 1987 341.24'22 86-25909
ISBN 0-04-382045-X (alk. paper)
ISBN 0-04-382046-8 (pbk: alk. paper)

Typeset in 10 on 11 point Bembo by
Computape (Pickering) Ltd, North Yorkshire
and printed in Great Britain by
Billing and Sons Ltd, London and Worcester

Contents

Tables	*page* ix
Preface	xi
Abbreviations	xiii
1 *The Federal Republic and the European Community*	1
The relationship between national systems and the EC	2
The importance of European integration to West Germany	5
West Germany's importance to the EC	14
West Germany's European policy style	14
Arguments and structure	22
2 *The Federal Government's Sectorized Policy-Making*	25
The Federal Government's European policy style	27
Ministerial responsibilities for European policy	31
Conclusion	41
3 *Government Policy: Continuity and Incoherence?*	43
4 *Interests, Interest Groups and European Policy*	85
West German interests	85
Organized interests and the EC	93
Influencing European policy	102
Conclusion	106
5 *The Evolution of West German Public Opinion and the Integration of Western Europe*	108
6 *West German Political Parties and the European Community*	123
The development of party policies on European integration	123

European policy-making within the parties 142
The impact of the parties 150
The electoral dimension 161
Conclusion 163

7 *The Legislative Dimension* 165

The role of the legislature 165
The implementation of EC policy 173
The relationship between EC law and German domestic law 179
Conclusion 182

8 *The* Länder, *West Berlin and the European Community* 185

The *Länder* 186
West Berlin, the Federal Republic and the European Community 198
Conclusion 200

9 *The Federal Republic of Germany and the European Regional Fund* 202

The development of a regional policy 204
Implementing the regional policy 217
Conclusions 219

10 *Special Relationships, Germany and Europe* 223

The Franco-German relationship 225
German–German relations and the EC 231
Conclusion 237

11 *Conclusion and Future Prospects* 239

References 253

Index 265

Tables

2.1 The hierarchical structure of German ministerial bureaucracy *page* 29
2.2 Junior foreign ministers with EC responsibilities from 1969 32
2.3 The European policy responsibilities of other federal ministries 39
2.4 Summary of interministerial committees for EC policy 40
4.1 West German economic performance since 1950 88
4.2 Structure of West German exports and imports, 1958 and 1984 88
4.3 Sectoral shares in West German Gross Domestic Product 1950–74 90
5.1 German views regarding the Schuman Plan 109
5.2 West German attitudes to problems of the EC 113
5.3 West German attitudes to the speed of integration 113
5.4 West German attitudes on advantages or disadvantages of EC membership 114
5.5 Attitudes towards a European currency 116
5.6 Numbers of West Germans giving integration a high priority 117
5.7 West German atittudes to EC membership 118
5.8 Opinion on the work of the European Parliament 120
7.1 The referral of EC proposals to committees in the Seventh Bundestag, 1972–6 169

Preface

The origins of this book lie in the authors' doctoral research, completed in the Department of International Relations at the London School of Economics. Although conducted in different decades, both pieces of research concerned aspects of the Federal Republic of Germany's participation in European integration. Dissatisfied with the available literature, we decided to collaborate on an embracing study of the Federal Republic's role in the European Community. Our particular concern was to explain German behaviour in the Community in terms of domestic politics. This book, which covers the period 1969–86, is the result. It is the product of extensive co-operation and exchanges between the authors but with a division of responsibilities. Simon Bulmer was responsible for Chapters 2–4 and 8–9; William Paterson for Chapters 5–7 and 10; Chapters 1 and 11 were joint efforts.

As with any such study we owe many debts of gratitude. Without the co-operation of numerous politicians, officials in the political parties, interest groups and in federal and *Länder* governments, the entire project would have been impossible. The vast majority of these interviews were conducted on the basis of confidentiality and this is respected by the authors.

We would especially like to thank the Commission of the European Communities for financial support for a study visit in 1981, the staff at the Forschungsinstitut der Deutschen Gesellschaft für Auswärtige Politik in Bonn, Inter Nationes (Bonn), Wolfgang Wessels and his colleagues at the Institut für Europäische Politik (Bonn) and Eva Evans of the University Association for Contemporary European Studies. We are also grateful to Michael Holdsworth and Gordon Smith of Allen & Unwin for their interest in the project at the early and later stages respectively.

Simon Bulmer would like to thank his former colleagues in the Department of Economics at Heriot-Watt University and his present colleagues in European Studies at UMIST. He is grateful to Geoffrey Roberts for comments on parts of the manuscript. An award from the Nuffield Foundation helped the research get off the ground and this is gratefully acknowledged. He is especially grateful to Inge and Friedel Alef for providing a 'home from home' in Alfter near Bonn.

William Paterson would like to thank the Social Science Research Council for providing him with an award to spend the autumn term of 1982 in Bonn, and Wolfgang Wessels for making the Institut für Europäische Politik available as a base. He is grateful to Jutta Baden, Werner Post and Margaret and Fraser Cameron for their hospitality. Last but not least, our thanks are due to Susan Spence, Joyce Spencer and Mrs Dorothy Foster for typing the manuscript. Of course, any factual errors or inaccuracies of judgement are the responsibility of the authors.

Simon Bulmer
Manchester

William Paterson
Warwick

June 1986

Abbreviations

BDA	*Bundesvereinigung der Deutschen Arbeitgeberverbände*, Confederation of German Employers' Associations
BDI	*Bundesverband der Deutschen Industrie*, Federation of German Industry
BGA	*Bundesverband des Deutschen Gross- und Aussenhandels*, Federation of German Wholesale and Foreign Traders
BPA	*Bundespresseamt*, Federal Press Office
BR	Bundesrat
BT	Bundestag
BVG	*Bundesverfassungsgericht*, Federal Constitutional Court
CAP	Common Agricultural Policy
CDU	*Christlich-Demokratische Union*, Christian Democratic Union
CEFIC	European Council of Chemical Industry Federations
COCCEE	Committee of Commercial Organizations of the European Community
COPA	Committee of Professional Agricultural Organizations
COREPER	Committee of Permanent Representatives
CSCE	Conference on Security and Co-operation in Europe
CSU	*Christlich-Soziale Union*, Christian Social Union
DBV	*Deutscher Bauernverband*, German Farmers' Union
DGB	*Deutscher Gewerkschaftsbund*, Federation of German Trade Unions
DIHT	*Deutscher Industrie- und Handestag*, German Conference of Chambers of Industry and Commerce
DM	*Deutsche Mark*
Drucks	*Drucksache*
EAGGF	European Agricultural Guidance and Guarantee Fund
EC	European Community
ECJ	European Court of Justice
ECSC	European Coal and Steel Community
EDC	European Defence Community

EEC	European Economic Community
EFTA	European Free Trade Association
EIB	European Investment Bank
EMS	European Monetary System
EMU	Economic and Monetary Union
EP	European Parliament
EPC	European Political Co-operation
EPU	European Payments Union
ERDF	European Regional Development Fund
ESPRIT	European Strategic Programme for Research and Development in Information Technology
ETUC	European Trade Union Confederation
Euratom	European Atomic Energy Community
EUREKA	European Research Co-ordination Agency
EUROFER	European Confederation of Iron and Steel Industries
EWG	*Europäische Wirtschaftsgemeinschaft*, see EEC
FAZ	*Frankfurter Allgemeine Zeitung*
FDP	*Freie Demokratische Partei*, Free Democratic Party
FEWITA	Federation of European Wholesale and International Trade Associations
FRG	Federal Republic of Germany
GATT	General Agreement on Tariffs and Trade
GDP	Gross Domestic Product
GDR	German Democratic Republic
GNP	Gross National Product
GNRP	Gross National Real Product
MCA	Monetary Compensatory Amount
MEP	Member of the European Parliament
MFA	Multi-Fibre Arrangement
MP	Member of Parliament
NATO	North Atlantic Treaty Organization
NICs	Newly Industrializing Countries
OECD	Organization for Economic Co-operation and Development
OEEC	Organization for European Economic Co-operation
SDI	Strategic Defence Initiative
SPD	Social Democratic Party
TA-Luft	*Technische Anleitung zur Reinhaltung der Luft* (technical instruction on air pollution control)
UA	Unit of Account
UNICE	Union of Industries of the European Community
US(A)	United States (of America)

USSR	Soviet Union
VAT	Value Added Tax
VCI	*Verband der Chemischen Industrie*, Association of the Chemical Industry

1 *The Federal Republic and the European Community*

The Federal Republic of Germany (FRG) is the strongest national economy in the European Community (EC). For many years, however, it played a much less important political role in the EC than its economic strength suggested. This split identity of 'economic giant' but 'political dwarf' was to be explained by the burdens of the past and the constraints resulting from the division of Germany. The legacy of that period has begun to decline so that the Federal Republic has also come to play a significant political role in the EC of the 1970s and 1980s. Our study centres on the role and behaviour of the FRG during that period. We concentrate on the period from 1969, the year in which the Social–Liberal coalition came to power under Brandt's chancellorship and in which the EC was relaunched at the summit meeting in The Hague.

How should the FRG's role in the EC be examined? In view of the influence of German history on present day politics in the Federal Republic some comments are necessary concerning the original motivation for participating in European integration. This dimension can then be used to explain the present importance of the EC, and of the related political co-operation process, to German interests. Understanding the Federal Republic's role requires an assessment which is not merely restricted to outlining the Bonn government's policy or to the governmental machinery involved. Underlying influences must also be explained. These include the country's economic structure, policy-making structures and the resultant policies. What are the attitudes of political parties, public opinion and socio-economic interests towards European integration generally and, more specifically, to individual EC policies? How far does the federal structure of West Germany become a factor in EC policy-making?

In this way we aim to outline the limits and possibilities of the FRG's role in the EC. How far will the FRG be able to build upon its status as the EC's dominant economy to become its political pacemaker as well? Is the EC about to become an international extension of West German interests, as a wider context for *Modell Deutschland*?

In this introductory chapter we look at four aspects of studying the Federal Republic's relationship with the EC. The first of these involves some preliminary comments on the nature of relationships between member states in general and the EC. The second component relates to the importance of European integration and the EC to West Germany. The third component considers in brief terms the significance of West Germany to the EC. Finally, we set out our methodological approach to the study along with signposts to the subsequent chapters.

The relationship between national systems and the EC

The importance of domestic politics to the EC has been particularly evident over the recent years. Reform of the EC Budget and of the Common Agricultural Policy (CAP) have been extremely tortuous due to the need to keep all member states broadly satisfied. The modesty of progress during 1985 on the intensification of integration (European Union) again indicates the importance of national reservations. Against this background it is clear that more attention should be paid to the examination of member states' behaviour in the EC than has been the case hitherto. Conditions at the national level have major significance for the prospects of agreement in the Community.

Over recent years there has been a growing number of such studies. They have concentrated on Britain and the FRG, with minimal coverage of France and Italy (Hansard Society, 1977; Wallace, W., 1980; Rideau *et al.*, 1975; Vannicelli, 1974; Kohl and Basevi, 1980; Feld, 1981; May, 1982; Hrbek and Wessels, 1984a; Simonian, 1985). However, divergent approaches have been employed to analyse the role of the member state concerned. Given the prevalence of edited volumes, diverse approaches have also been pursued within individual studies. The bumper 1983 harvest of literature covering Britain's relationship with the EC illustrated the variations in approach (Jenkins, 1983; El-Agraa, 1983; Gregory, 1983; Cohen, 1983). Analysis was overwhelmingly sectoral, thus limiting an overview of the general relationship. Similarly, by using *either* an economic assessment *or* the policy-making machinery as the focus of analysis, an overall view of Britain's relationship with the EC failed to emerge.

A central difficulty has thus been the absence of an agreed framework for analysing member states' behaviour in the EC. Economic analyses of the costs and benefits of EC membership run into difficulties over the static and dynamic effects. Moreover, they can give little indication of the political costs and benefits. Political frameworks of analysis have been very limited in number and of a preliminary and schematic nature (Wallace, H., 1981; Bulmer, 1983b; Feld, 1981).

One particular conclusion is that there is little value in examining a member state's European policy in isolation from its other policies. European policy is conditioned *by much the same set of factors which shape domestic policy*. Many of the same actors are involved in policy formulation: a factor which distinguishes European policy from 'traditional' foreign policy where the issues and actors tend to be much more restricted. The main difference is that some additional elements are introduced into the system by virtue of the involvement of the EC Commission and other member states.

Each member state has a distinctive position in the international economy, reflecting what Haas has termed the 'differential enmeshment of the member states in the world economy' (1976, p. 196). Hence the West German economy's dependence on foreign trade is a key factor in the FRG's European policy. The situation extends beyond the economic dimension to include policy-making characteristics and political sensitivities. Thus the decentralized nature of the political system has an impact on European policy. The Federal Government may on occasion present contradictory positions in EC bodies due to the strong tradition of ministerial autonomy. It may be a rather 'vague' actor in EC negotiations. This is because it may not have fixed views of its own because it is acting as proxy for the federal states (*Länder*) which have strong powers in certain EC policy areas. Alternatively, the Federal Bank may present obstacles to EC policy-making, reflecting its autonomy from the Bonn government (Dyson, 1981).

In the context of political sensitivities the FRG's relations with Eastern Europe, especially East Germany, impose certain constraints on EC policy-making. The wish to maintain peaceful coexistence with the East has played a role in West Germany's behaviour in European Political Co-operation (EPC), the foreign policy framework of the EC member states. This situation might be seen as undermining our emphasis on *domestic* politics because it relates to foreign policy. However, strong arguments have been made that, due to Germany's distinctive political past and geo-political present, foreign and domestic policy are virtually inseparable in the FRG (Hanrieder, 1967; 1982).

For these reasons we employ domestic politics as an explanatory factor in German European policy. 'Domestic politics' thus serves as a shorthand term for identifying national concerns which impinge upon European policy. The FRG's *Deutschlandpolitik* is one determinant of its behaviour in EPC; the commitment to domestic monetary stability is a determinant of policy positions in the European Monetary System (EMS); the commitment to sound budgetary control at the federal level is reflected in the Finance Ministry's attitude to the EC Budget. There are many other examples, too.

Another aspect which must be taken into account is the fact that the economic and political components are virtually inseparable. It has almost become a convention to propose that West Germany's economic strength translates into international political influence. The extent to which this argument can be stretched has been illustrated by Lankowski. He has argued (1982a, p. 114) that the FRG has instrumentalized the EC 'to the point where it is impossible to think of the EC in any other terms than as a regional extension of the West German state'.

This argument assumes a somewhat sinister policy on the part of the Federal Government. In this respect it is worth quoting Hanrieder's caveat 'that the dynamics of the German political economy stem from purposes that are simultaneously political and economic, domestic and foreign, amenable as well as resistant to governmental direction' (1982, p. 59). These dynamics will be seen to have equal validity for Germany's role in the EC. Thus an emphasis on any one side of the three separate equations – such as that given by Lankowski – is likely to give a misleading picture. Arguing that the Federal Government adopts a cool and calculating approach to exploiting EC membership for its own ends assumes a single-mindedness which the Bonn government does not have, as well as assuming blissful ignorance of this exploitation on the part of other member governments in the EC.

Before setting out an approach to analysing West Germany's role in the EC, it is vital to give an overview of the Community's importance to the FRG and, equally, to identify the reasons for West Germany's significance in the EC.

The importance of European integration to West Germany

European integration had an importance for the FRG right from its creation in 1949. It soon became apparent in the aftermath of the Second World War that a united Germany could not be established due to disagreements between the allied powers (Balfour, 1982, pp. 128–38). With Germany's division it was evident that a new trading system would be needed due to the loss of the primarily agricultural territories in the East. The merger of the zones in the West and their eventual transformation into the FRG went hand in hand with integration into Western economic and political structures. Dismantling of industry in the Western zones was replaced by a wish to see the establishment of an economically strong West Germany. This change had been brought about by the worsening climate of East–West relations in the emerging Cold War. What role did European integration have for the newly created Federal Republic?

Integration was adopted as one of the foundations of the West German state. Numerous motives lay behind this (Morgan, 1981, pp. 61–6; Hrbek and Wessels, 1984b, pp. 45–54). Of greatest importance were various political considerations. First and foremost, the new state had to establish its credibility and reliability in international politics. This could be achieved to some extent through relations with the occupying powers. In the early years the Federal Republic had limited sovereignty over foreign affairs and defence. Thus it had to look beyond the short term to a situation where it might obtain all the trappings of a sovereign state, including full control over its industrial production. Integration had received widespread support in the Parliamentary Council which drafted the West German constitution, the Basic Law. Hence Article 24 explicitly provides for the transfer of sovereignty to international organizations.

It was in this general context that German willingness to participate in the Schuman Plan must be understood. There was the wish to put an end to the turbulence of Franco-German relations; there was a recognition that sovereignty could be *gained* (for instance, over the coal and steel industries); and the prospect of recognition as an equal negotiating partner within the European Coal and Steel Community (ECSC) was appealing. These aspects, along with the presence of like-minded Christian Democratic leaders in other participating states, made the Schuman Plan attractive to the German chancellor, Konrad Adenauer, as a basis for international rehabilitation.

Another international aspect of ECSC membership was rather more speculative. This concerned how far it would prove to be a framework for West German security. Although the ECSC had no defence component – and the proposed European Defence Community failed to be ratified – a security motivation played a background role. Its significance was rather indirect during this period. The link derived from the 'extremely strong pressure for European integration which was exerted by Germany's main military ally, the United States' (Morgan, 1981, p. 64). It was only in the 1970s, following the establishment of EPC, that West Germany could contribute in a more direct way to a European security policy. For the 1950s, by contrast, achievements were limited to the establishment of a 'security community' of the type identified by Deutsch (1957). In other words, close relations between the six states participating in European integration excluded the possiblity of any military conflict between them.

Participation in European integration brought not only benefits to the international standing of the new state, but also acted as a pillar of the West German political system itself. The fragility of the Weimar Republic had provided many lessons on the necessary conditions for a democracy to thrive. These ranged from specific matters like the mechanics of coalition formation to a supportive international economic and political environment. Close West German integration in a supranational European Community was seen as an important aid to the new democracy. In fact its willingness to accept a federal European framework placed West Germany at the head of the supporters of European federalism. The fact that the FRG had less sovereignty to lose than the other five member states and familiarity at home with federal political structures meant that this motivation was ultimately unfulfilled due to its partner states' reservations. For example, the direct election of the ECSC's assembly, provided for in Article 21 of the Treaty of Paris, did not come about.

Hrbek and Wessels express the importance of integration to the new state's stability in terms of a 'community of values' (1984b, p. 48). Support for basic human rights, democracy, social justice and the rule of law among key politicians in the Bonn Republic found a strong European echo as the Cold War intensified and refugees arrived from the East. Although much of the European concern with these values was focused on the Council of Europe, supranational integration among the Six was seen as a further support, as was the Atlantic Alliance.

In only one area was the commitment to European integration apparently at odds with West German objectives: over the question of re-unification. Western European co-operation and integration were part and parcel of the emerging postwar division of the Cold War. By its participation in integration the FRG further reduced the already minimal prospects for re-unification. Yet this did not prevent Adenauer and his government from ensuring that various EC treaties left the German question open in terms of international law.

In political terms, therefore, European integration was central to the FRG's existence. The new state could pride itself as the paragon (*Musterknabe*) of support for supranational integration. The literal translation of *Musterknabe* as 'model boy' gives the other side of the coin by presenting the FRG as a fledgling state, with a turbulent national past, trying to gain recognition among its more established partners in the postwar international order. Under these circumstances 'good behaviour' was expected from the FRG; leadership status was not envisaged.

We can make a clear distinction between the political importance of European integration as an *arena of co-operation* and its economic importance as an *arena of competition*. West Germany had to show its ability to manage co-operative relations with the European powers, especially with France. Friendship with the USA would be insufficient. Membership of the North Atlantic Treaty Organization (NATO) would similarly be inadequate because all the West Europeans were ultimately reliant upon the USA. Without European integration as a political arena of co-operation West German economic performance would have been perceived as a threat. Thus co-operation with other West European states provided a political basis for full use of the European Communities as an arena of competition.

In more specific terms the ECSC played an important part in satisfying West German requirements in the reconstruction of industry and trade. Attributing a specific measure of importance to the ECSC is impractical due to the plethora of economic developments taking place in the early postwar years. Currency reform, (qualified) membership of the Organization for European Economic Co-operation (OEEC) and of the European Payments Union (EPU) had a greater general impact on the West German economy than membership of the ECSC. Even more fundamental was the Petersberg Agreement of November 1949, in which the Western allies agreed to cease dismantling industry in return for West German recognition of the International Ruhr Authority (Lankowski, 1982b, pp. 156–60). This measure received support from both sides of industry but not from the

Social Democratic Party (SPD), which also opposed membership of the ECSC (Paterson, 1974a).

West Germany's full participation in the ECSC from its very outset had an important psychological effect on the FRG's international economic standing. In more practical terms the increased demand for machinery and, hence, steel production that resulted from the outbreak of the Korean War, coincided with the growth of West German productive capacity in this sector. Although economic benefits to the FRG grew following the creation of the common market for industrial goods in the European Economic Community (EEC), the importance of the ECSC should not be underestimated. The early 1950s were the formative years in the creation of the West German economic structure and its social market principles. Thus membership of the ECSC ensured that integration became a key part of postwar economic and political values in the FRG.

Three decades or so later West Germany has evolved into the main economic power in the European Community. The EC itself is a more broadly based organization, having added the EEC and the European Atomic Energy Community (Euratom) in 1958. Moreover, from 1970 the political co-operation machinery associated with the EC – but with a separate procedural basis – has added a new dimension. Although now recognized as an equal partner in international politics – despite having only joined the United Nations in 1973 – the FRG has found EPC to be a particularly important device for presenting its own foreign policy. The extent of economic integration in the EC has intensified. In both economic and political terms the EC has proved the key reference point for West German opennness and interdependence.

Political importance of the EC and EPC to the FRG

The openness of the Federal Republic's political system is unparalleled among the other EC member states. By openness we mean the extent to which third countries can influence West German politics. There has been a conscious decision by West German governments not to exclude external influence. In defence policy the FRG is dependent upon the umbrella provided by the Atlantic Alliance and, in particular, by the United States of America. As a corollary to the situation regarding defence, foreign policy is conducted much less exclusively through the medium of the nation state than is the case for Great Britain or France. Instead there is extensive use of multilateral channels, such as EPC. This situation has been summed up by Saeter:

> the Federal Republic is vitally interested in forms of 'complex interdependence' which can help provide security with a stronger non-military basis, and which can at the same time be suitable instruments for converting the FRG's great economic potential into foreign policy influence. (Saeter, 1980, p. 9)

In terms of policy scope the European Community is the most encompassing multilateral channel available to the FRG.

The interest in 'complex interdependence' is, in effect, the result of a recognition that national governmental omnipotence, the primacy of the national interest and the importance of retaining national sovereignty – all the characteristics of traditional power politics approaches to international relations (Webb, 1983) – were rendered inappropriate to West Germany by their abuse during the Nazi regime.

Apart from the EC, the other main multilateral channel for West German foreign relations is the North Atlantic Treaty Organization. In broad terms membership of the two organizations has proved quite compatible. Only in the early 1960s, when Adenauer briefly flirted with President de Gaulle's vision of a Europe 'from the Atlantic to the Urals', did the compatibility with NATO membership come into question (Hanrieder and Auton, 1980, pp. 81–3).

In the 1980s West Germany has shown itself increasingly willing to contemplate the inclusion of security and perhaps even some aspects of defence in the co-operation among EC states. There was support for including security matters in EPC and this was formalized in the Solemn Declaration on European Union, agreed in June 1983 at the Stuttgart session of the European Council (*Bulletin of the EC*, 1983, no. 6). Hitherto no practical developments have occurred in line with this agreement despite the interest of France and Great Britain. Nor has there been a revival of Western European Union as an alternative forum for such co-operation. West Germany remains interested in *European* security co-operation, however, especially for as long as an icy climate prevails in East–West superpower relations, for this undermines efforts to maintain peaceful coexistence in relations with East Germany.

As one of West Germany's two pillars of integration into the West, the European Communities continue to have the objective of superseding the nation state through non-military means. This represented – and still represents – an ingredient in the thinking of

West German governments. We therefore reject the argument that German objectives did not include the construction of a supranational entity, that is a politically integrated Europe (Lankowski, 1982b, pp. 133–4). He states his argument in the following terms:

> Every key element in Germany's power block in the 1950s and 1960s perceived European regional cooperation as a means to maintain a liberal trading and payments area in Europe and to use progress in this area in Europe to further trade and payments liberalization at the global level. (op. cit., p. 134)

This assertion clearly disregards Hanrieder's caveat (identified above) that a balance must be kept between political and economic dynamics in the German political economy (Hanrieder, 1982, p. 59). Lankowski would appear to consider Adenauer not to have been a 'key element in Germany's power block'. To be sure, the argument that Erhard's 'Atlanticism' prevailed over Adenauer's 'Gaullist' European policy does support the view that economic objectives dominated (Lankowski, 1982b, pp. 170–85). But it also supports the argument – rejected by Lankowski – that the FRG was committed to supranational integration. There was opposition to de Gaulle's proposals on Political Union, that were supported by Adenauer, because they were prejudicial to the supranational integration of the EEC, preferring instead a power politics conception of Europe as a third force in international relations.

The use of traditional foreign policy methods based on the West German state is held to be inappropriate because of the Nazi past. An assertive foreign policy would arouse fears of revanchism amongst neighbours, both in the West (notably France) and in the Eastern bloc. Thus with the creation of EPC in 1970 the Federal Republic was able to broaden its international role by drawing upon some of the benefits which Adenauer had sought in his alliance with de Gaulle during the Political Union episode. At the same time as EPC was being established the Brandt–Scheel governments were placing relations with the East on a sounder footing through the *Ostpolitik*.

Both EPC and West Germany's *Ostpolitik* have been closely related to the emergence of interdependence as a characteristic of international relations. EPC is essentially a civilian foreign policy. When used, sanctions have been of an economic nature; military force is only used by national governments, not by EPC. A similar situation prevails in West Germany's relations with East Germany. Economic policy instruments have been employed in order to maintain close coexistence especially during the more hostile period of superpower relations in the early 1980s. Significantly, the idea of peaceful relations through economic interdependence was a driving force in the Conference on Security and Co-operation in Europe (CSCE), the testing ground for EPC.

Although it would be misleading to argue that West German foreign policy and its relations with the East are conducted primarily through EPC, a higher priority is attributed to the multilateral level than in the British or French case. The Nazi period and the division of Germany have rendered the concept of national sovereignty less useful as a determinant of policy. This factor, along with the use of economic instruments for foreign policy goals, reinforces the point that the EC's importance to West Germany is characterized by a blurred division between, on the one hand, domestic and foreign policy objectives and, on the other, between economic and political goals (Hanrieder, 1982, p. 59).

Apart from Eastern Europe another key area of West German foreign policy interest is the Middle East, on whose oil supplies the economy is dependent. Here again EPC has proved to be a useful mechanism for West Germany, especially because of the burdened relationship with Israel due to Nazi atrocities. The nature of these sensitivities was displayed during Helmut Kohl's visit to Israel in January 1984 which was characterized by unease between the hosts and the visiting delegation.

The cases of the Middle East and Eastern Europe show the extent of West Germany's economic interdependence. In fact recent governmental policy has deliberately sought to maintain such economic interdependence with the East. The cases also show how policy is rooted in multilateral frameworks. One commentator has argued that the 'solid anchor' of EPC is needed for the Federal Republic's negotiations with individual East European countries (Czempiel, 1980, p. 93). EPC is thus of major importance to the FRG as a force working for international stability. It has served as 'a multilateral tool for a political dwarf' (Rummel, 1980, pp. 85–7; Rummel and Wessels, 1983, pp. 34–47). The same applies for the EC and integration generally, as argued in the previous section.

Economic importance of the EC

The Federal Republic has evolved into an open economy with a high degree of trading interdependence. This situation has two facets. First, the FRG sees the EC as a multilateral force working for global trade liberalization in its foreign economic policy. Second, the FRG seeks to ensure that economic liberalization is pursued *inside* the EC's internal market. The first dimension reflects West Germany's export dependence, with one third of Gross National Product (GNP) accounted for by the export of goods and services (Economist Intelligence Unit, 1983, p. 27). As Markovits has pointed out 'with one of every four jobs dependent on exports, the FRG has had to develop a great sensitivity to the ebbs and flows of the international economic system' (1982b, p. 5). The second dimension stems from the fact that the EC states are the major trading partners. In 1981 45.7 per cent of exports went to other EC states, while 47.4 per cent of imports came from those states (Economist Intelligence Unit, 1983, p. 29). Both figures are for the EC of nine, thus excluding Greece, Spain and Portugal.

Taken together the two dimensions make the EC of vital interest for the Federal Republic. Over the last decade or so trade has increased as a share of GNP. The maintenance of liberal trade is therefore fundamental to continued sound economic performances in West Germany. The EC is an important negotiator on international trade and it is scarcely surprising that successive governments have sought to play an influential role in negotiations on such matters.

As regards the internal policies of the EC, West Germany is favoured by the strong correspondence between its own economic order and that of the Community. The social market economy, which has prevailed since the establishment of the Bonn Republic, has become the 'dominant economic philosophy' in the FRG (Smith, 1979, pp. 194–202). Its emphasis on economic liberalism, but with some social policy cushioning, has also been influential in the principles applying to the EC. The CAP is a clear exception to this market-oriented approach but, for historical reasons, this exception has also applied in the FRG. As will be seen, West German economic policy in the European context has been aimed at the continuation of this compatibility of principles. In consequence, there has been opposition to an interventionist industrial policy and opposition to the use of subsidies in the EC's industrial market-place, to take two examples.

The fear of inflation, based on the negative experiences of the Weimar Republic, has engendered a commitment to close control over the money supply. In the EC context this has led the FRG to wish to restrain its contributions to the EC Budget. It has also led to certain preferences in the mechanics of monetary co-operation in the EC.

Exchange rate stability is obviously vital to stability in the terms of trade with the important EC markets. With the collapse of the Bretton Woods system of monetary relations, disruption was caused to German trade with its EC partners. The restoration of some currency stability through the EMS was thus a logical step and one advanced strongly by Helmut Schmidt in 1978 and 1979 (Ludlow, 1982). However, in both the EMS and the earlier initiative towards Economic and Monetary Union (EMU), exchange rate stability was not acceptable irrespective of cost. The mechanisms had to include adequate safeguards against imported inflation.

The main area in terms of the extent of EC policy integration is agriculture. Here, one would not expect West Germany to derive great benefit. Such a conclusion is in fact too superficial. To be sure, the EEC traditionally has been interpreted as a trade-off between France, seeking a market for its agricultural products, and West Germany, seeking a market for its industrial goods. However, the Federal Republic has actually suffered less from the CAP than was anticipated originally. And, unlike the situation where Great Britain is concerned, no cheap alternative to the CAP existed in the past. The Federal Republic's main interest in this sector rests with the CAP's reform so that pressure on the EC Budget (and German contributions to it) may be limited. This line has often been resisted by the federal agricultural ministry, which is very protective towards its farming constituency.

Overall, the European Community and European Political Co-operation serve important functions for the Federal Republic. They provide key policy frameworks for a state burdened with the turbulent history of the German nation. Over the years since the ECSC's establishment the relationship between the Federal Republic and the EC/EPC has developed into one of 'complex interdependence', both in economic and political terms.

The FRG's reliance on the EC has been characterized by general support from the political elite and a permissive consensus in public opinion. Only in the 1980s has a fundamental critique of EC membership become apparent in West Germany. This has been associated with the growth of the 'silent revolution' and post-materialist sentiment, as reflected in the rise of the Greens as an alternative political party (see Chapters 5 and 6 below). There has also been a mood of *Europa-Müdigkeit*, i.e. disillusionment with the EC, over recent years. This had led to a growth of German-language studies concentrating on the extent to which the EC is vital to West German interests (May, 1982; Hrbek and Wessels, 1982; 1984a). The last two studies may be interpreted as efforts by pro-Europeans attempting to counter the mood of *Europa-Müdigkeit*.

West Germany's importance to the EC

This dimension is of less importance for the study as a whole and some aspects are clear from the preceding section. Thus we mention the significant factors from the EC viewpoint in comparatively brief terms.

Of greatest significance is the fact that the Federal Republic is the EC's economic powerhouse. The EC is a much more potent force in the international economy with German membership. Without it, there might be a shift in the EC's economic values away from the liberalism promoted by West Germany. There is also a heavy dependence on West German contributions to the EC Budget. Without them, many of the EC's policies would wither away. The CAP could not be sustained without major surgery.

These comments are based on the totally hypothetical idea of German non-participation: a situation which cannot be envisaged for the most consistently enthusiastic supporter of the EC and of integration among the major member states. Although a greater sense of realism entered European policy during Helmut Schmidt's chancellorship (1974–82), West Germany has continued to provide a major stimulus to European action, especially with the EMS initiative. In political terms, therefore, the Federal Republic is an important ally of the European cause. This situation seems assured in the 1980s within a Franco-German context. Major policy initiatives stand little chance of acceptance if they are not acceptable to France or West Germany: a distinction from Britain, as the EMS case showed. Hence because West German interests in the EC and EPC are so great, these vested interests make it a vitally important member of both European bodies.

West Germany's European policy style

We may summarize our conclusions thus far in the introduction as follows. First, domestic political factors will remain key determinants of political developments at the European level in the foreseeable future. Much greater attention should therefore be devoted to the relationships between member states and the EC. As the strongest national economy in the EC, the Federal Republic is an obvious candidate for this treatment. But what *analytical* treatment is appropriate? No answer was immediately available on this point.

The second conclusion was that the Federal Republic has had a major interest in European integration and this continues in the present day with the EC and EPC. In some ways the Federal Republic and European integration are like twins: neither can remember an existence independent of the other. In both economic and political terms the fate of one has a major impact on the other. This is a situation characteristic of interdependence (Keohane and Nye, 1977). Although there were signs of this interdependence being unhinged by the stagnation of integration during the second half of the 1960s, the situation has recovered since the 1970s. This came about with the weakening of American leadership in the world political economy (Keohane, 1984) and was a spur to the development of EPC and the EMS.

These two conclusions assist in setting out a framework for analysing the Federal Republic's role and policy in the EC. It is clear that any framework must recognize interdependence as the nature of West Germany's relationship with the EC. This means that we must reject the state- or government-centred assumptions of the 'power-politics' approach. Its intergovernmental assumptions that sovereignty will be defended, that policy will be defined by a national interest and that a single, coherent governmental European policy will prevail, cannot adequately explain the West German case (if any). Nor can the neo-functionalist perspective, with its assumptions that states readily yield sovereignty to the EC, that interest groups are major actors at the EC level and that a European interest will prevail. In preference to these models, interdependence can explain that interest groups and the government may have different degrees of importance in different policy areas. It can account for the hybrid nature of EC policy-making, part foreign policy and part domestic policy. It can account for the fact that German relations with the EC are conducted through both political and economic transactions.

Interdependence emphasizes the fact that West German European policy cuts across the divisions between foreign and domestic, between economic and political, while also emphasizing that governmental authority is restricted by both national and international forces. In order to take account of the complexity of interdependence it must be recognized that there is no single policy-making structure responsible for European affairs. There are strong tendencies towards sectorized (or compartmentalized) policy conducted through 'standard operating procedures' in the relevant ministerial bureaucracies. These tendencies have been identified by political scientists concerned with both domestic and foreign policy-making (respectively: Richardson, 1982; Haftendorn *et al.*, 1978).

The distinctive features of West German European policy have three sources. First, there is the structure of the German economy and its interdependence with the EC. Secondly, there is the broad political context of West German membership of the EC. Then thirdly, there is a set of determinants over European policy that relate to policy-making structures. It is in these structures that economic interests and the attitudes of political actors are pulled together and converted into negotiating positions which are defended at the EC level. These structures introduce nuances into the policy content. Thus the particularly 'German' aspects of this conversion process may be used to explain the distinctive features of German European policy.

Displaying the distinctiveness of the Federal Republic implies taking a comparative viewpoint. It should not be too surprising, therefore, that we employ an analytical approach drawn from comparative politics, namely from 'policy style' literature. The policy style concept is able to identify the different relationships between government and socioeconomic interests on a comparative basis. Such a study was recently conducted into domestic policy-making in several West European states (Richardson, 1982). There is a further advantage to the policy style approach, in that it facilitates the identification of different policy networks *within* individual countries.

A further advantage of using an analytic approach drawn from comparative politics is that it relates much more accurately to actual power structures than any of the approaches thrown up by integration theories. The neo-functionalist school has suggested that European integration has had a harmonizing effect on member states and thus treats domestic politics as a residual factor. The intergovernmental school of thought, by contrast, plays up the importance of national interests in EC policy-making but, at the same time, implicitly emphasizes the centrality of national governments or 'the state'. The weakness of the former body of work is that national policy-making processes do not follow the logic of integration but, rather, that integration follows the logic of national policy processes (Heumann, 1980, p. 43). Moreover, national policy-making is not dominated by cohesive governments in the manner that intergovernmentalists seem to think. For constitutional or electoral reasons their authority to override the sectional demands of interest groups may be rather constrained. There are many such constraints on the Bonn government's European policy and these will be examined in due course.

The problem of assuming that domestic politics have a residual nature is not by any means exclusive to the work of integration theorists. In international economic relations such problems as the oil crises and monetary instability have not led to similar responses in various advanced industrial states. Katzenstein, for example, has argued that 'analysis of contemporary foreign economic policies is inadequate as long as it focuses only on the "internalisation" of international relations; the "externalisation" of domestic structures is also important' (1976, p. 2).

This argument can also be made in the EC context. By indicating the distinctiveness in the content and consistency of German European policy, we implicitly leave a bench-mark against which other member states may be measured. Using the FRG's economic structure and its particular political concerns as the 'raw' determinants of its European policy, we can go on to measure its consistency and content through the concept of 'policy style'. This concept is defined as 'the interaction between (a) the government's approach to problem-solving and (b) the relationship between government and other actors in the policy process' (Richardson, Gustafsson and Jordan, 1982, p. 13).

In many ways examining West Germany's European policy style is akin to investigating the country's policy style as a whole. This stems from the broad range of issues on which the EC has – or seeks to have – a policy. Agriculture, the environment, exchange rates, foreign policy, trade and competition policy are examples of areas where the Community (in its various manifestations) functions as a multilateral framework. However, the fact that the EC level is common to all these policy areas does not impart a unifying logic to the domestic policy-making structures involved in formulating the German attitudes to them. Instead the structures follow a pre-existing logic of their own.

An important characteristic of this 'logic' is the decentralization of executive power which we can describe in shorthand as 'institutional pluralism' (Bulmer, 1983a). There is no federal governmental agency with a comprehensive mandate for formulating a coherent European policy on all issues. This would be quite alien to the decentralization of power and decision in the FRG.

The establishment of the Bonn Republic went hand in hand with a specific anti-centralist trend in the structure of government to reverse developments under Bismarck and Hitler (Morgan, 1981, p. 66). This decentralization was desired by the allies at a time when no one envisaged a strong international or security role for the West Germans. Decentralization took both a vertical form, in federalism, and a horizontal one, among federal-level institutions. The federal system of government is thus characterized by a dispersion of power between the different tiers of government. Added to this there is the constitutional autonomy of the Federal Bank. The weakness of the principle of collective cabinet responsibility and the continued existence of coalition governments are further features of German government which impinge upon European policy.

We have already referred to the historical factors which prevent West German governments from acting in a manner which might arouse neighbouring countries' fears of renascent nationalism. Under Chancellor Kohl there has been a rhetorical emphasis on the German nation and on national values but this has been primarily directed towards the East. No government has hitherto contemplated carving out a defined 'national interest' for European policy, even though the academic debate has moved in that direction (May, 1982; Hrbek and Wessels, 1984a). Avoidance of articulating a 'national interest' has reflected the same historical circumstances which promoted the governmental system's 'institutional pluralism'.

To these two must be added a third decentralizing factor which derives from the events in the 1950s when ministerial responsibilities for European integration were being shared out. As will be seen (Chapter 2), the Foreign Office was in a rather weak position at this time – it had only been established in 1951 – and failed to gain overall governmental responsibility for European integration.

These three anti-centralist factors in the FRG's European policy are specifically *German* phenomena. But other EC member states have experienced their 'externalization' when different German ministers or ministerial officials have presented different, even contradictory, statements in the Council of Ministers, the Committee of Permanent Representatives (COREPER) or working groups. A typical example of this was provided during the establishment of the European Regional Development Fund (ERDF) (Chapter 9). Sasse found the chain of events during the ERDF's establishment showed how Germany's decentralized policy-making on EC matters could have an impact upon other member states and upon the rate of integration in general. 'The polyphony of the ministries can all too easily lead to the confusion of the listeners on important issues, and can also result in delays in deciding in which key the musicians should play' (Sasse *et al.*, 1977, p. 19).

The main characteristic of Germany's European 'policy-style', therefore, is precisely the fact that there is no single pattern of policy-making. The procedure depends on the subject matter. The array of discrete policy networks is merely a reflection of the situation in German domestic politics.

Policy networks may vary between, at one extreme, those where a federal body acts authoritatively with virtually no interest group involvement. Examples of this are the Foreign Office's clear responsibility for drawing up a set of foreign policy goals which are to be pursued in the framework of European Political Co-operation. There is also the Federal Bank's single-minded pursuit of domestic and external stability in the value of the *Deutsche Mark* (DM). Elsewhere, however, the position is rather different. In environmental policy, agricultural structures and regional policy, the EC dimension is grafted on to the existing layered policy communities involving the federal and state (*Länder*) governments. Only minimal changes have been made to the extensive network of existing policy-making committees.

At the other extreme there are those policy areas where there are close links between the Federal Government and interest groups. Typical of these is the close working relationship between the Federal Agriculture Ministry and the German Farmers' Union, the DBV. Other relationships exist at a more discreet level between ministries and industrial branch associations, exporters' interests and the central organizations (*Dachverbände*), especially those representing the employers (BDA) and industrialists (BDI). For example, a close relationship exists on EC policy between the chemical industry and the economics ministry in Bonn (see Chapter 7).

The relationships thus bear considerable similarity to those identified in a survey of West Germany's ('national') policy style (Dyson, 1982a). However, the EC does not yet have a policy on all issues so that the mirror image is incomplete. A further distinction is that the Federal Republic's European policy scarcely develops the active, anticipatory dimension argued to exist by Dyson, for example, in the tripartite Concerted Action framework (1982a, pp. 19–20). The reason for this is that European policy proceeds overwhelmingly in the form of reactions to the initiatives introduced at the EC level, mainly by the Commission. The reactions are framed by using domestic policy as the benchmark for evaluating EC proposals and the members of the appropriate domestic policy-making network as those to be consulted. Dyson's references to the decline of 'regulation' as a policy style in West Germany do not extend to European policy. Especially in the agricultural sector there are strong elements of regulation regarding the Federal Government's relations with interest groups in various product markets.

Perhaps the only time when an 'active' European policy is pursued falls during the preparation of the six-month period of German presidency of the EC (which only occurs every six years in a Community of Twelve). This period necessitates some stocktaking and causes the government to ask itself what its objectives are in respect of European integration. Other participants submit their views (Ungerer, 1983). Frequently – and regardless of the member state concerned – an activist approach to the Community is stymied by the short-term necessities of crisis–management, typically involving the EC Budget and the CAP. And with one or two exceptions, such as the 1983 Solemn Declaration at Stuttgart, this period of active European policy-making is quickly passed off as gratuitous navel–contemplation.

In consequence of these factors Germany's European policy style is locked into three developments which have been identified as general trends in West European policy style (Richardson, Gustafsson and Jordan, 1982, pp. 9–14). The first of these is 'sectorization'. Policy responses are framed in individual German ministries in a specialist manner using 'standard operating procedures'. Coherence with the policy perspectives of other ministries involved only emerges later, often during intra-governmental crisis-management.

The second trend in European policy-making is 'incrementalism'. This refers to the tendency of governments to make successive marginal changes to existing legislation rather than undertaking a comprehensive revision. This pattern frequently occurs in technical legislation emanating from the EC Commission. By contrast with the Foreign Office, the 'technical' ministries do not have an embracing overview of developments at the Community level. Thus their immediate reference point for new legislative proposals from the EC is existing domestic legislation. However, EC legislation is for implementation in twelve member states. Thus, by referring to domestic legislation, technical ministries are not acting with the necessary degree of enlightenment for progress in integration. Yet such enlightenment is necessary, along with a political commitment from the ministerial level, in order to break out of the 'muddling through' approach and initiate a committed European policy. The federal chancellor is best placed to combine the political 'clout' and the access to a less 'routinized' staff (in the Chancellor's Office): two prerequisites for an active European policy. However, a further precondition is necessary here: that the chancellor has a strong personal commitment to European integration or to using the EC as a framework for his sectoral policy interests, as in Schmidt's attempt to improve international monetary stability through the European Monetary System.

The impact of the two trends of sectorization and incrementalism upon European policy is to cause the disengagement of two integral components. The Foreign Office's overview of the limits and possibilities for German policy in the Council of Ministers represents one strand. The other is to be found in the technical ministries' preference for Community policies which satisfy pre-existing (domestic) policy models. Yet without these two policies coming together German policy is unlikely to be successful at the EC level. Frequently the two strands only come together when the chancellor (or the Cabinet) assumes a trouble-shooting role.

A recent example of this sectorization occurred during the Spring of 1985. With the Foreign Office keenly promoting European integration in the run-up to the Milan European Council, the agriculture minister, Herr Kiechle, decided to make a dramatic use of the veto over cereals price reductions (Schmuck and Wessels, 1985, pp. 99–100). The timing could scarcely have been worse for undermining the coherence of the government's European policy.

The third trend in policy-making is that towards consensual relations within policy communities. These relations build up between policy-makers and interest groups at the specialist level. Certainly there is evidence of close relationships existing at the specialist level in EC policy between federal and *Länder* civil servants and interest groups (Bulmer, 1986, Chs 7 and 8). However, this bureaucratization of policy-making – its separation from the ministerial level – is linked in part to the absence of substantive party conflict on many economic policy issues. At the general level of the German party system this situation has been expressed in several ideas: the 'politics of centrality' (the vital importance of the median voter), the 'dominant economic philosophy' and 'restricted ideological space' (Smith, 1976; 1979).

The impact of these three party system features on the European policies of the German parties is outlined below (Chapter 6). However, they have also affected the overall European policy style of the FRG. The ideal of 'centrality' reflects the clustering of political parties around the middle ground of politics. The pre-history of the Federal Republic and the proximity of East Germany have virtually excluded ideological parties of both Right and Left (Smith, 1976, pp. 402–6). The FDP's balancing act at the centre of the party system has continued during the Kohl chancellorship, even if to the chagrin of Franz Josef Strauss. The 'dominant economic philosophy' – the social market economy – has been the basis for an economic consensus in the FRG that seems to be surviving the testing period of the recession. In general terms the EC's policy proposals have not threatened this consensus. Certainly there have been occasional clashes, such as over the management of steel-producing capacity, but these have remained at the margin. The overall picture, therefore, is that there is a 'permissive consensus' concerning the Community.

This feature of German attitudes towards the EC complements the 'institutional pluralism' in creating a uniform European policy style in West Germany. In summary, therefore, this policy style's characteristics are decentralized policy responsibilities, a routinized decisional process, consensual relations at the specialist level in discrete policy communities, the absence of 'active' policy and the co-ordination and agreement of policy at a late (crisis-management?) stage.

Arguments and structure

Throughout this study we argue that the FRG has not established a clear framework of action reflecting national interests. The underlying reasons for this are the constitutional, political and historical-psychological factors identified above. West Germany has achieved the *arena of co-operation* which it needed to establish credibility and reliability. Having achieved this, the political interest remains rather in the background. The broad commitment to the EC among policy-making elites has ensured that little dissent has been heard on this matter until the arrival of the Greens as a significant political force.

As a consequence of this, West German interests in the EC have focused on the specialist dimension of economic policy. The EC has thus served as an *arena of competition* for West German industry. Decision-making is based at the technical level and may thus ignore overall national interests. The clearest example of this has been the agriculture ministry's ability to defend the interests of (mainly) high-cost German producers in the CAP. Overall governmental policy, however, has favoured reduction in CAP expenditure in order to reduce the FRG's contributions to the EC Budget. How situations like this come about is to be explained in the following chapters.

In Chapter 2 we examine the policy-making framework in the West German Federal Government and show how decentralization of policy has led to considerable sectorization of procedures. Chapter 3 outlines the impact of these procedures on governmental policy in the period since 1969.

Chapter 4 examines the structure of the West German economy and how this is reflected in interest group policies. We argue that interest groups have developed close relations at the specialist level, taking their cue from the organization of the Federal Government.

Chapter 5 centres on the relationship of public opinion to EC membership. In particular we examine how a permissive consensus was created on EC membership. We also examine the signs of falling support for the EC and analyse the reasons for this.

Chapter 6 focuses on the political parties. What is their role in policy-making? We argue that interparty agreement on the EC has been at such a rarified level that it contributed little to debating key EC issues. The emergence of the Greens has prompted some limited change on this but only at the margins. The 1984 European election showed that the parties – perhaps because of the consensus – are failing to mobilize the electorate on EC matters.

The involvement of the West German legislative bodies and of the constitutional court are dealt with in Chapter 7. It is argued that their involvement in policy-making is mainly as a function of political parties or of regional (*Länder*) interests. The constitutional court and questions of implementation have shown up some interesting developments.

In Chapter 8 the impact of the EC on the states (*Länder*) and on West Berlin is studied in some detail. Here it is argued that the federal dimension to EC membership has further decentralized policy-making to the specialist level, presenting still further difficulties of policy co-ordination.

Chapter 9 takes the European Regional Development Fund (ERDF) as a case study showing how West German policy rhetoric dissolves into extremely specialized technical views once the details are entered into. Clear evidence is found of incoherence in European policy with, significantly, an impact on the EC as a whole.

Chapter 10 returns to the theme of interdependence, raised earlier in this chapter, and examines the extent to which other 'special relationships' of the FRG impinge on its European policy. The two cases examined are relations with East Germany and the Franco-German partnership.

Chapter 11 concludes the study with an assessment of future developments in light of the emergence of the Greens and of the current debate on European Union within the enlarged EC of twelve member states.

2 *The Federal Government's Sectorized Policy-Making*

In the first part of our survey of the Federal Government's role in the European Community we focus upon the relevant policy-making machinery. There are two reasons for adopting this approach. The first relates to the objective of explaining government policy in terms of domestic factors. How is it shaped? Where do interest groups put forward their demands? The second reason relates to the impact of procedures upon policy content. This assumes significance in Germany because of the absence of fundamental conflict over EC membership and the desirability of integration. But this 'de-politicization' of European policy, shown in the continuity of government positions after the 1982 change of coalition, introduces other variables into policy-making. The government's political leadership may leave European policy on the back burner. This in turn may lead to policy becoming loosely organized and governed by the administrative routines of the ministerial bureaucracy. European policy may become sectorized as various interest groups co-operate with ministries over specific policy areas. In their totality, these sectorized policy areas may bear an inadequate relationship to the government's stated European policy.

It is precisely the muted nature of party conflict over European policy in the FRG which promotes a policy-making style based on detailed discussion. Interest groups, the political parties, parliament and the *Länder* operate according to a 'procedural code' whose terms are set by the Federal Government. This procedural code is what we term the FRG's 'European policy style'.

What exactly is 'European policy', however? There are three elements covered by this term. The first strand is the government's strategy towards European integration. What are the government's long-term objectives in integration? Does it know? Where do its priorities lie regarding the Community's many activities both within and outside the treaty framework? To be sure, these questions are not constantly uppermost in the government's mind. They receive concerted attention prior to, and during, the member state's six-month period holding the presidency of the EC's 'inter-governmental' institutions (Regelsberger and Wessels, 1985). These particular aspects of European policy fall into the category of 'integration policy' which is treated by the Federal Government primarily as a political matter.

The second strand is also viewed as a political matter and consists of the viewpoints put forward within the framework of European Political Co-operation. In many cases these viewpoints are simply abstracted from the foreign policy agenda. For historical reasons the FRG has been keen to make full use of EPC as a multilateral framework for its European policy. As with integration policy, EPC is not as purely political as some would like to think. The use of economic sanctions by the Community to underpin EPC decisions regarding the Iranian hostages crisis (1980) and the Argentinian invasion of the Falkland Islands (1982) indicated this clearly enough.

The third strand is represented by the diverse economic and social activities of the EC. There are many separate – but ultimately interrelated – policy areas which are involved: from the specifics of songbird conservation to the global issues of international trade within the General Agreement on Tariffs and Trade (GATT). Most of these matters are economic in nature or derive from the existence of a common market. The sum of progress in all the individual policy areas gives a snapshot of the state of political integration at a given time. It is a recurrent feature of the EC that superficially insignificant, technical issues may become major issues of political principle or of national prestige in the Council of Ministers.

There is a clear interrelationship between these three types of European policy. Moreover, economic and political aspects of integration are frequently quite indivisible. Nevertheless, it is worth noting that it is only really on economic and social policy issues that interest groups become involved in close negotiations, primarily with the 'technical' ministries. EPC matters and integration policy are the concern of the Foreign Office although even they are compartmentalized into two different divisions. This devolution of responsibilities is apparent throughout the government's structure in respect of European policy. Indeed, the Federal Bank's (autonomous) responsibility for monetary policy is a case of executive devolution outside the Federal Government.

This decentralization of policy responsibilities is by no means an isolated instance within the EC. Membership of the Community has required all states to confront the ramifications of interdependence. One of the key consequences has been that domestically oriented ministries have found their work increasingly involving foreign relations. However, in the case of the FRG the impact of EC membership on the governmental structure has compounded two pre-existing decentralizing features: the dispersion of authority along federal lines, and the unwillingness to treat relations with East Germany as foreign policy so that they are also deemed to be domestic policy.

Given these circumstances, it is pertinent to ask whether the FRG's decentralized policy style is a help or a hindrance to conducting a coherent European policy. To this end we focus initially on the Federal Government's overall 'European policy style'. Attention is then turned to the individual ministries' European responsibilities, along with that of the Federal Bank. In a final section we examine the nature of interministerial co-ordination concerning European policy. Our conclusions regarding the Federal Government's European policy style are then employed as the basis of examining the post-1969 European policy of the Federal Republic in Chapter 3.

The Federal Government's European policy style

It is perhaps appropriate to make early reference to the constitutional foundations of the German government's organization, given the respect for legal principles in the Federal Republic. There are three organizational principles which form the basis of the government's structure and are set out in Article 65 of the Basic Law (Rausch, 1976, pp. 180–200). The chancellor principle identifies the chancellor's *Richtlinienkompetenz*, his responsibility for setting the guidelines of government policy. In European policy – just as in any other – the chancellor has the authority to set out the guidelines of government action. However, there are many policies competing for chancellorial attention so that it ultimately depends on the individual incumbent whether he accords European policy great attention.

To the extent that the chancellor neglects European policy, the principle of ministerial autonomy (*Ressortprinzip*) assumes greater significance. Under this principle individual ministers are granted considerable independence to conduct (EC) policy as a matter of their own concern. This encourages the development of 'house policies' where an individual ministry sees European policy through its rather subjective 'conceptual lens'. Where these individual views within the Federal Government fail to come together in a national form of 'kaleidoscopic convergence' (Puchala and Lankowski, 1976), a problem-solving framework is needed.

The third principle (*Kollegialprinzip*) assumes this function. It is concerned less with preventing the development of conflict than with resolving it *ex post facto*. Hence while the routine of co-ordination of European policy is conducted at the administrative levels of government, the political authority for resolving disagreements comes from the ministerial level, in the Cabinet.

To these constitutionally-based principles must be added the postwar prevalence of coalition governments in Bonn. Although these increase the *potential* for policy disagreement within government, there has not been any significant party conflict over EC matters since the differences between the 'Atlanticists' and the 'Gaullists' at the end of Adenauer's chancellorship and throughout that of his successor, Erhard (Hanrieder and Auton, 1980, pp. 82–8). Since this divergence of views was resolved in the mid-1960s, inter- and intra-party divisions over European policy have either been matters of emphasis only, or rhetorical conflicts among the established parties. A circularity has developed wherein the permissive consensus over European policy militates against an electorally-motivated party policy on the EC. This reinforces the permissive consensus. This situation is discussed elsewhere in further detail (Chapter 6). In the context of government policy, however, the impact is to weaken the commitment to an active European policy. This is not to deny that there are occasional active European policy initiatives (Schmidt's promotion of the EMS; Genscher's proposals for a 'European Act'). However, the electoral dimension is largely secondary, through a party figure gaining prestige as an international statesman.

By extension, the lack of party conflict over EC affairs also works in favour of disjointed policy within individual ministries. The political leadership (i.e. the ministers) does not have the same extent of engagement in those policy areas which have less party political salience. This stems from the fact that it is impossible for each minister to be involved in all his department's activities. For better or for worse, delegation is a ministerial necessity. 'Thus the function of the political leadership is reduced, in the final analysis, to drafting guidelines, controlling their bureaucratic translation and acting in many cases as crisis-manager' (Krause and Wilker, 1980, p. 151). A minister's commitment to European policy – like that of the chancellor – is dependent upon his

Table 2.1 *The hierarchical structure of German ministerial bureaucracy*

	Minister (*Minister*)	
State Secretary (*Staatssekretär*)	Parliamentary State Secretary/Minister of State (*Parlamentarischer Staatssekretär/Staatsminister*)	**Upper level**
	Division Head (*Abteilungsleiter*)	
	Sub-Division Head (*Unterabteilungsleiter*)	**Intermediate level**
	Section Head (*Referent*)	**Specialist level**

Note: Ministers of State are confined to the Chancellor's Office and the Foreign Office. The term 'bureaucracy' is used throughout in its social science meaning and not as a term of abuse!

Source: Bulmer, 1987, p. 52.

personal set of priorities rather than on any party political necessity.

To the extent that the upper (political) level of the governmental bureaucracy is not immediately involved in EC affairs, the intermediate level, consisting of division and sub-division heads, is given greater control over policy and its elaboration at the specialist level (see Table 2.1). The vertical division of responsibilities within the ministries is fairly clear-cut. Thus the intermediate level takes on the function of overseeing the preparation by specialists of tasks pursuant to the guidelines set by the ministerial leadership (Mayntz and Scharpf, 1975, pp. 63–94). Horizontal communication is far less straightforward, however, especially across ministerial boundaries. In view of the extensive decentralization of EC affairs in the Federal Government, an effective machinery for co-ordination is vital for attaining policy consistency.

Mayntz and Scharpf (1975) and Krause and Wilker (1980) have made important contributions to the evaluation of German policy-making along the lines of the 'bureaucratic politics' model developed by Allison and Halperin (1972). In the present context we are restricted to noting that there has been an increasing tendency towards bureaucratized European policy (*verwaltete Europapolitik*) in the Federal Government and that this has gone hand in hand with the reduction in party political significance of EC affairs. In the specialist ministries there is, on the one hand, a danger that the (inevitable) imperfections of EC draft legislation are rejected by a technically-oriented bureaucracy which has a 'high degree of problem sensitivity, of expertise, and of competence to deal with the problems arising in a small specialised area' (Mayntz and Scharpf, 1975, p. 71). But is there not, on the other hand, a danger that these specialists, in pursuing legislative perfectionism, lose track of the government's commitment to integration? Or is the government's commitment to integration of little more significance now than as a statement of faith?

A global view of the government's European policy suggests that it is overwhelmingly *reactive* in nature. In EPC, policy has tended hitherto to be a reaction to international events. In economic and social policy areas it is the Commission which is the centre of *active* policy-making. Its proposals are then referred directly to the specialists in the German ministries. They miss out the stage, which is relevant to purely domestic policy, where the ministerial level sets the terms of reference for policy. Yet an active integration policy (with ministerial involvement) is rather artificial when other parts of European policy are conducted reactively and with minimal involvement by ministers. At its worst it is like having a telephone answering machine in the Bonn Foreign Office that daily recites a different passage from the ill-fated Tindemans Report. At its best it makes an impression on the Community, such as was the case with Genscher's 'European Act' proposal, which resulted in the June 1983 Solemn Declaration on European Union made at the European Council in Stuttgart.

In line with its responsibilities for integration policy the Foreign Office takes a rather more global view of European policy and a more enlightened one, too. An indication of the Foreign Office's positive attitude towards European policy was given to one of the authors in July 1983 upon his inquiry about the ministry's mood (*Stimmung*) after the passing of the Solemn Declaration. Despite there having been considerable scepticism in the press about its actual impact upon integration (*Economist*, 25 June 1983, p. 60), the reply was: '*Die Stimmung ist immer gut im Auswärtigen Amt*'. This positive response seems to capture the flavour of the Foreign Office's position on European integration; it would be heretical for an official to adopt a negative viewpoint. However, there is no guarantee that this positive approach will influence government policy when it comes to more technical matters (see case study on regional policy, Chapter 9). This, of course, is quite independent of the many difficulties which may be encountered in negotiations with other member states in the Council of Ministers.

Ministerial responsibilities for European policy

The origins of the decentralized nature of European policy in the Federal Government date from the 1950s when the Economics Ministry took responsibility for matters relating to the European Coal and Steel Community (Taussig, 1970). It was only in 1957 that the Foreign Office became involved, following an agreement between Economics Minister Erhard and Foreign Minister von Brentano (Taussig, 1970, p. 75). Under this, the Economics Ministry was entrusted with 'day to day' European policy while the Foreign Office was entrusted with integration policy. Since that time the division of labour has become much more complex, especially with the extensive integration in the agricultural sector.

1 *The Foreign Office*

Foreign Office responsibilities are essentially twofold. As agreed in 1957, it is in charge of integration policy. This involves not only the framing of a medium-term strategy but also monitoring all developments within the treaties in order to assess their implications for integration. The second function relates to European Political Co-operation and dates from the procedure's establishment following the Luxembourg (or Davignon) Report (Allen, Rummel and Wessels, 1982). It is symptomatic of the decentralization of responsibilities in the government that the Foreign Office's two functions are conducted in separate divisions of the ministry. Integration policy is incorporated in Division 4, which deals with foreign economic policy, whilst EPC is viewed as 'pure' foreign policy in Division 2.

Since the change of government in 1969 the Foreign Office has been led by two Free Democratic Party (FDP) ministers; Walter Scheel 1969–May 1974; Hans-Dietrich Genscher May 1974– . Genscher's retention of the post during the 'caretaker' government of Helmut Kohl and following the early elections of March 1983 made for considerable continuity in policy. Genscher has been very active in the EC, especially in trying to encourage

Table 2.2 *Junior foreign ministers with EC responsibilities from 1969*

Period	*Office-Holder*	*Party*
1969–72 (December)	Katharina Focke (Chancellor's Office)	SPD
1972–4 (May)	Hans Apel	SPD
1974–6 (December)	Hans-Jürgen Wischnewski	SPD
1976–81 (June)	Klaus von Dohnanyi	SPD
1981–2 (October)	Peter Corterier	SPD
1982–5 (April)	Alois Mertes (deceased)	CDU
1985 (September)-	Lutz Stavenhagen	CDU

Note: All were parliamentary state secretaries until August 1974 when the post was re-designated minister of state.

greater integration through his 'European Act' proposals (Weiler, 1983), and in support for technological co-operation in 'EUREKA'. The government has also always had a 'European junior minister'. Until 1972 this was Katharina Focke who conducted this duty from the Chancellor's Office (see Table 2.2).

In 1972 this ministerial post was transferred to the Foreign Office and was placed in the hands of Hans Apel of the Social Democrats (SPD). Since that time the parliamentary state secretary – since 1974 minister of state – with European responsibilities has always been from the senior coalition party (see Table 2.2). The importance of this post has varied over time, depending upon the incumbent's style, his relations to his chancellor and his importance in his political party. It probably assumed greatest importance under Hans Apel due to his strong party position as a Cabinet ally of Helmut Schmidt (but during Brandt's chancellorship) and as a leading figure on the right wing of the SPD's parliamentary party. His outspokenness on similar themes to Schmidt (Commission 'inefficiency', weak financial accountability, etc.) gave the post a public profile, particularly by introducing the question of whether Germany should be the EC's 'paymaster' (*Zahlmeister*).

The primary function of the post is to co-ordinate the government's European policy. This involves rather more than integration policy because *new* policy areas, including detailed matters under negotiation, tend to fall within the remit of the Council of Foreign Ministers. And it is frequently the case that the junior minister deputizes in this body.

At the domestic level, the junior minister is chairman of the Committee of State Secretaries for European Affairs and may report on EC developments in the Cabinet. In this sense he forms a bridge between the elected politicians and the top level of civil servants who may be 'political' appointments (Dyson, 1977).

The two state secretaries in the Foreign Office have different functions regarding European policy. The senior post (*Staatssekretär* des *Auswärtigen Amts*) includes EPC in its responsibilities. The incumbent is the 'political director' who, with his eleven EC counterparts, prepares the agenda of the Conference of Foreign Ministers. The junior post (*Staatssekretär* im *Auswärtigen Amt*) is responsible for economic and social policy areas. For example, Herr Lautenschlager was sent as junior state secretary on a 'shuttle diplomacy' tour of other capitals to work out a package deal for resolving the British budgetary issue at the Stuttgart session of the European Council in June 1983. During the Kohl governments the junior state secretary, a political civil servant, has represented the foreign minister on several occasions in the EC Council of Ministers: a development some partner governments might (erroneously) interpret as a reduction in the European priorities in West German policy (Regelsberger and Wessels, 1984a, p. 488).

The exact division of responsibilities within the Foreign Office's two affected divisions is outlined elsewhere (Bulmer, 1987, pp. 60–1). Increasingly, the two strands of their work are becoming intertwined, especially in the context of preparing sessions of the European Council. Nevertheless, there have still been tensions between the two divisions. As Regelsberger and Wessels have noted, the *ad hoc* group of civil servants responsible for transforming the Genscher–Colombo European Act into the Solemn Declaration at Stuttgart consisted of two civil servants from each member state (1985, p. 80). This derived from difficulties in the German Foreign Office as to who would participate. In the event one civil servant participated from each of the two divisions.

In a comparative study Helen Wallace identified three functions of foreign ministries regarding the EC:

> the diplomatic representational one; that of giving political coherence to their government's positions in the internal policy-making of the Communities; and, lastly, that of helping to shape a Community identity. (Wallace, H., 1973, p. 40)

To these must now be added the fourth function regarding EPC business. Of the four, the German Foreign Office is less than fully committed to the second function, because it is shared with the Economics Ministry which co-ordinates routine matters.

Inside the Bonn government the Foreign Office acts to some

extent as a Europeanist lobby or 'institutional interest group' (Caporaso, 1974, pp. 55–6). Sometimes foreign observers may obtain a false impression of government policy if this is not taken into account. Foreign Office civil servants are not always familiar with the technical details of policy nor do they have to contend with the demands of interest groups. Nevertheless, the Foreign Office's 'Europeanness' reflects the pro-integration standpoints of the established political parties.

2 *The Economics Ministry*

The Economics Ministry established its European responsibilities at the time of the European Coal and Steel Community. Under the 1957 agreement it was entrusted with the co-ordination of routine policy. It is also involved in several policy areas in its technical capacity. Under the 1957 agreement a European Division was charged with the integration of the West German economy into the EEC market. Division E, as it is also known, has a central role within the ministry; indeed, it serves as a hub for EC communications involving the whole government. It deals with the Permanent Representation in Brussels – a task normally undertaken by a foreign ministry – and distributes EC documents at the domestic level: to other ministries, to parliament and to the *Länder* Observer. Its co-ordination also involves chairing two interministerial committees on EC affairs. The Economics Ministry's co-ordinating responsibilities are indicative of the FRG's decentralized power: the Permanent Representative in Brussels is a Foreign Office diplomat who receives instructions from the Economics Ministry!

Although it is a separate division in the ministry the *Europaabteilung* is enmeshed in the work of other divisions through the fusion of posts (Bulmer, 1987, p. 65). This leads to further decentralization of Community matters. The subject areas which the ministry deals with include EC competition policy, the 'internal market' (EC term for customs union business), EC trade agreements and the various attempts at an EC industrial policy outlined by Fendel (1981). These include steel policy and various efforts to collaborate over information technology, aerospace, shipbuilding and other sectors. Almost without exception, the Economics Ministry has opposed or stymied all proposals which fall under the heading of 'industrial policy'. Moreover, the very idea of an industrial policy – whether on a national or Community basis – is heretical in the Federal Republic. Such interventionism is anathema to guardians of the social market economy like the economic liberal, Count Otto Lambsdorff, who was the FDP minister 1978–84. There is an element of rhetoric about the ministry's persistent free market lobbying since the economy does have elements of interventionism, especially in agriculture.

In essence, it is the support of 'market principles' and free trade that characterizes the ministry's EC and domestic viewpoints alike. The FRG's export dependence and its need to maintain its international competitiveness are the economic reasons for this policy.

3 *The Ministry of Food, Agriculture and Forestry*

The impact of the European Community has been greatest on this ministry. Agriculture is the most closely regulated policy area of the EC, one observer estimating that 96 per cent of the EC's regulations concerned the agricultural market (Schwarz, 1975, p. 89). Additionally, the EC has its rather modest agricultural structural policy and its fisheries policy, established in January 1983 after much delay. The ministry has undergone several re-shuffles in its organization to accommodate EC affairs as their impact has changed (Taussig, 1970, pp. 38–54). Since 1973 the organizational framework has remained fairly constant, however. A sub-division co-ordinates EC affairs, such as legal matters, but detailed policy is integrated with national policy throughout the ministry (Bulmer, 1987, pp. 68–70).

During the Social–Liberal coalition period, 1969–82, the Agriculture Ministry was headed by an FDP minister. However, after serving during the caretaker Centre-Right government until March 1983, Josef Ertl was obliged to relinquish his post partly due to the FDP's loss of votes in the federal election. His replacement was Ignaz Kiechle of the Bavarian Christian Social Union (CSU), a dairy farmer from Kempten in the Allgäu.

Ertl's long period in office was punctuated by reports, particularly in the British press, that he was securing benefits in Brussels for German farmers to enhance the FDP's electoral support (*Economist*, 5 November 1977; Hu, 1981, pp. 47–54). It is not surprising that agriculture ministry officials reject these claims (in interviews), putting forward their belief that the ministry is impartial between consumer and agricultural interests. These two contentious views will be reviewed in greater depth below (Chapter 6). Suffice it to say at this stage that the ministry's role in the government is characterized by its sponsorship of the agricultural economy.

4 *The Ministry of Finance*

The Finance Ministry's importance in German European policy has increased in line with three developments: the EC's attainment of financial autonomy through the introduction of an 'own resources' budget (Wallace, H., 1980); the increase in German contributions to the EC Budget; and, more recently, concern about the deficit in the Federal Budget. Helmut Schmidt, finance minister from 1972–4, was in the van of this development with able support from his successor Hans Apel. Hans Matthöfer (SPD) and, since October 1982, Gerhard Stoltenberg of the Christian Democrats (CDU) have continued this policy under conditions of increasing financial stringency in German budgeting.

New EC expenditure (in new policy areas) is treated with a throughness as if it were part of the Federal Budget. The Finance Ministry is represented at all Council of Ministers' sessions which have financial implications. The ministry's influence on the government's European policy derives from this aspect of its work. But it has other functions. These concern tariff matters, harmonizing taxation methods (notably Value Added Tax) and monetary co-operation (shared with the Federal Bank in Frankfurt).

As with most other German ministries, its activities are co-ordinated in a single sub-division while detailed policy is dispersed to subject specialists throughout the 'house' (Bulmer, 1987, p. 71). The Finance Ministry seeks to ensure that it has a position paper on all EC proposals with financial implications at an early stage, presumably in part to prevent the Foreign Office making overly positive statements on potentially expensive policies.

Due to the Federal Government's operation, in particular ministerial autonomy (the *Ressortprinzip*), it is easier for the Finance Ministry to control expenditure on new policies than to check increased spending on existing ones. This is because one ministry is unable to interfere in the affairs of another without the active engagement of the chancellor. This factor helps explain why the Finance Ministry took a very cautious stance towards the creation of a small regional policy, while apparently remaining inactive over agricultural expenditure. It also helps to explain why even the federal chancellor may have difficulties in controlling established expenditure. During his chancellorship, Schmidt was sympathetic with Britain's case for budgetary reform but this had little impact on policy. CAP expenditure was established and under the control of the agriculture minister. To have challenged agricultural policy would have been to risk a serious coalition dispute on the matter. As will be seen in Chapter 3, there has been coalition conflict of this nature.

5 *Interior Ministry*

Initially the Interior Ministry had rather marginal importance to EC affairs. It was responsible for miscellaneous functions such as co-ordinating anti-terrorist measures with other member states and, as the ministry responsible for electoral law, drafting the necessary domestic provisions for the direct election of the European Parliament (EP). In the 1980s, however, environmental issues have taken on much greater salience in relation to the EC. In domestic terms the impact of the Greens on the West German political system has been to sensitize governmental elites to the importance of environmental issues. Many measures in this policy area cannot be resolved adequately at the national level. In consequence, the EC has become increasingly involved in establishing guidelines for such questions as exhaust emission control (see Chapter 11). The 1986 Single European Act, which sets out proposals for amendments to the EC treaties, includes the formal incorporation of environmental affairs into Community activity. The Interior Ministry appeared set for further extension of its involvement in EC policy-making. However, in June 1986 Chancellor Kohl announced plans to establish a new ministry responsible for the environment, thus removing this policy area from the Interior Ministry.

6 *The Chancellor and the Chancellor's Office*

As we noted at the start of this section the chancellor has a central role in European policy. He may set the tone of policy through his *Richtlinienkompetenz*; he may pursue an active European policy in a technical policy area in which he has a particular interest (Schmidt and monetary stability, EMS); or he may keep a close control over individual ministries' European policy to ensure compatibility. One thing is certain. Whether he likes it or not, the regular sessions of the European Council held since 1975, require his involvement (Bulmer and Wessels, 1987, Ch. 2). The Chancellor's Office performs a role commensurate to the chancellor's European interests and, at the very least, briefs him extensively for meetings of the European Council.

During Brandt's chancellorship the *Ostpolitik* took priority, especially in his first term, 1969–72. Focke's co-ordination of European policy in this period enhanced the role of the Chancellor's Office (Paterson, 1974b). In the second term, when Focke's functions were transferred to Hans Apel in the Foreign Office, Brandt took a closer interest in Community affairs, announcing that European Union was the government's priority (Paterson, 1977, p. 199). However, this coincided with the EC's upheaval due to the first enlargement and with a period in which the member states had many divergent interests, as reflected at the 1972 Paris Summit (Bulmer and Wessels, 1987, pp. 30–2). In consequence, Brandt's impact was largely at the rhetorical level.

At this time Helmut Schmidt and his fellow-thinkers were in ascendancy: both in the government and in the SPD. Schmidt was not exactly given to visionary speeches looking forward to a united Europe. He implicitly preferred an intergovernmental Europe to one with a major role for the Commission. 'According to Schmidt, Europe and its present condition can only be advanced through the will of statesmen and not through thousands of regulations and hundreds of sessions of the Council of Ministers each year' (*Frankfurter Allgemeine Zeitung* [henceforth *FAZ*], 30 October 1975). Thus Helmut Schmidt's concept of Europe was quite different from Brandt's visionary approach.

A further aspect of Schmidt's style was the centrality of Franco-German relations – in particular his friendship with President Giscard d'Estaing – to his European policy. Also important was action and mobilization. He was not interested in Genscher's proposed European Act but he was able to ensure the acceptance of his EMS proposals despite considerable internal opposition in the FRG (Regelsberger and Wessels, 1984a, p. 482).

Helmut Kohl's position on European policy is difficult to fathom. It seems to have a chameleon-like quality, telling the CDU party conference in May 1983 of the need for a reduction in German contributions to the EC Budget; lecturing other government heads on the critical decisions before them at the Brussels European Council in March 1983 (*Europa Archiv*, 10 May 1983, pp. 243–6); and acting as 'honest broker' in the complex negotiations at the Stuttgart European Council in June 1983 (*Economist*, 25 June 1983, pp. 59–60).

Experience thus far suggests that Helmut Kohl's influence on European policy will be primarily at the declaratory level. His experience of international affairs before becoming chancellor was much less than that of Brandt or Schmidt. He lacks an adequate grasp of technical policy details necessary for policy initiatives such as Schmidt's on the EMS. Given the importance of the European Council to EC policy-making and its preoccupation with highly technical issues, especially in 1980–4, his strength appears to be as a consensus-builder. There has been criticism of the quality of his advisers in the Chancellor's Office on European policy (*Die Zeit*, 30 November 1984, p. 7).

7 *Other ministries*

Several other ministries are involved in EC business but to a lesser extent than those already examined. Table 2.3 gives examples of this involvement. The main ministries not concerned at all are those for inter-German relations and defence.

Table 2.3 *The European policy responsibilities of other federal ministries*

Ministry	*EC responsibilities*
Economic Co-operation	EC development aid
Research and Technology	Euratom matters, EUREKA
Transport	EC transport policy
Labour and Social Affairs	Social security, European Social Fund
Justice	Legal aspects of harmonization, European patents
Youth, Family and Health	Foodstuffs legislation

8 *The Federal Bank*

The *Bundesbank*'s role in European policy is related to the EC's activity in monetary co-operation: initially in the 'Snake' and, more recently, in the European Monetary System. The *Bundesbank*'s position is distinctive in the EC because it has a legally endowed autonomy from the government under the 1957 Federal Bank Act. This autonomy assumes significance on the European level in four areas of central bank co-operation:

(a) co-operation on international currency matters;
(b) co-ordination of monetary and credit policy;
(c) exchange rate policy in the 'Snake'/EMS;
(d) Community borrowing facilities. (Gleske, 1980, pp. 87–101).

In connection with these tasks the Federal Bank participates in several EC committees and is represented in all Council of Ministers' sessions involving monetary matters (Bulmer, 1987, pp. 76–8).

9 *Inter-ministerial co-ordination of European policy*

In order to pull together these different policy-makers and shape a coherent German policy, extensive co-ordination is needed. But does this occur?

There are four committees in which co-ordination should take place (see Table 2.4). Of these, neither the Tuesday Committee nor the Group of European Specialists deals with items of major political substance, nor does either have the political authority to resolve inter-ministerial disagreements. The Finance, Agriculture, Economics and Foreign Ministries - the 'four musketeers' – are permanent members of the two committees; the Chancellor's Office is a member of the latter only. Other ministries are represented as the agenda dictates. Both committees are chaired by the Economics Ministry.

Table 2.4 *Summary of inter-ministerial committees for EC policy*

Body	*Level*	*Frequency*	*Nature of issue*
Cabinet	Ministerial	Agenda items as necessary	Important political matters or disagreements
Committee of State Secretaries for European Affairs	State or Permanent Secretaries	As necessary (approx. monthly)	Political issues
Group of European specialists	Division/Sub-Division Heads	About quarterly	General or long-term policy developments
'Tuesday Committee'	Section Heads	Weekly	Detailed administration

Source: Bulmer, 1987, p. 78.

The 'four musketeers' plus the Chancellor's Office are also represented on the Committee of Permanent Secretaries for European Affairs, which is chaired by the Foreign Office minister of state. The committee is typically responsible for preparing initial rounds of ministerial-level negotiations in the EC but, when problems arise or package-deals become necessary, either the Cabinet's authority is required or *ad hoc* ministerial meetings are. The Foreign Office minister of state acts as a useful bridge between these two bodies. Although the Cabinet is involved in the preparations or de-briefing associated with the European Council, it failed to meet to discuss governmental strategy during the West German presidency of the Council of Ministers in 1983. This was due to the March 1983 election and other time constraints (Regelsberger and Wessels, 1985, p. 78).

The various forms of co-ordination within the Federal Government still leave a loose and sectorized European policy. In fact, effective co-ordination comes mainly from crisis-management in the Cabinet, the increasing awareness of the interlinkage of policies through the EC Budget and from the Finance Ministry's caution about Community expenditure.

The composition of the German Permanent Representation in Brussels is also characterized by sectorization of policy responsibilities with the Foreign Office and the Economics Ministry each having only about one quarter of the senior staff. Loyalties are to the appropriate ministry in Bonn rather than to a collective European policy.

Conclusion

In outlining the various branches of the federal executive and their European policy responsibilities the objective has been to answer the question: who is important and why? Our findings may be summarized on two levels. First, from a global perspective, the ministerial bureaucracy has a major involvement in European policy, suggesting the existence of *verwaltete Europapolitik*' (bureaucratized European policy). This derives partly, it is true, from the overwhelmingly technical nature of the European Commission's proposals. Of equal importance, however, is the permissive consensus amongst the established German parties concerning European integration. Ministerial engagement (*active* policy) tends to favour other, more party-politically salient issues. Thus in European policy ministers frequently perform a representational role: defending policy positions developed at the specialist level. An actively Europeanist minister, such as Genscher, can cut through this proceduralization of policy to some extent but it would require a Europeanist chancellor - and not just in the rhetorical manner of Willy Brandt or Helmut Kohl – to transform the entire framework of German European policy.

From a second, more specific, perspective the 'four musketeers' (Agriculture, Economics, Finance and Foreign Ministries) are the key participants due to their 'domestic' responsibilities: the Economics Ministry's defence in the EC of the social market economy and international free trade; the Finance Ministry's hawkish approach towards extra public expenditure; the Agriculture Ministry's cocooned position *vis-à-vis* the free market principles operative in other branches of the economy; and the Foreign Ministry's role of reminding other ministries of the centrality of *Westpolitik* to the FRG's international economic and political strength. Identifying the influence of these ministries will be one of the objectives in examining the *content* of German European policy in the next chapter.

3 *Government Policy: Continuity and Incoherence?*

What have been the characteristics of the Federal Government's European policy? How consistent has it been over time? How coherent is it? How far is policy content shaped by the specific institutional framework of the Federal Government? These are the questions to be tackled in this chapter.

In addressing these questions we cover the period commencing with the formation in 1969 of the Social–Liberal (SPD–FDP) coalition. We also cover the developments in policy following the 1982 change of government which resulted in the Centre–Right coalition of the CDU, CSU and FDP under Chancellor Kohl.

We argue that the answers to all the questions are interrelated. Thus the Federal Government's European policy has been formulated overwhelmingly at the technical level with limited involvement of ministers. This has led to the prevalence of sectorization as a policy-making characteristic; co-ordination of policy has been weak. Due to this and the broad inter-party consensus on European policy (excluding the Greens), continuity has also been a key feature, with the 1982 change of government making little impact on substantive policy content. The weaknesses in policy coherence have resulted from the institutional and constitutional characteristics of government outlined earlier in the previous chapter.

These characteristics of the Federal Government's European policy present some difficulties in deciding where to start with the coverage of developments. For some member governments there would be more logic in examining initially the overall integration policy before concentrating on its integral components. However, such a centrally steered policy does not exist in the FRG due to the decentralization of governmental authority. At best the specific policy areas are satellites under limited central control. At worst the satellites perhaps set the limits of integration policy, rather than vice versa. For this reason integration policy is examined in a final section in order to evalue its compatibility with the specialist policy areas.

Some background comments are needed by way of introduction. First, by dividing up policy into a number of branches there is a danger of separating out interrelated subject areas. For example, many EC policies are connected because they make competing claims on the budget and are thus linked from the standpoint of the Bonn Ministry of Finance. Second, we must point out that external conditions shape the priorities given to policy over time. The *Ostpolitik* dominated several years of Chancellor Brandt's government so that *Westpolitik* and the EC were on the back burner. Issues such as monetary co-operation or energy have been given impulses by extra-Community developments, although with varying results. Third, some EC policies – such as on tariffs – had been established during the early 1960s and thus have not required much attention during the period from 1969. This applies to the core elements of the first policy area to be examined: that of the EC's internal market.

The FRG's growth has been based on its competitiveness as a producer of industrial goods. With the large-scale reconstruction of industry in the postwar period and the creation of a new trading pattern, the FRG was particularly attuned to the conditions of the postwar international economy. There was no need to shift trading patterns away from earlier colonial markets during the 1950s and 1960s, as was the case with France and the United Kingdom, because the FRG had established Western Europe as its main market-place in the immediate aftermath of the Second World War. Following the establishment in 1958 of the EEC, West German industrial growth was given a stronger European basis.

Four key factors lie behind West Germany's economic strength in the EC (Schlupp, 1980, pp. 53–4). First, there is the economy's specialization in industrial goods, especially capital goods. Second, there is the export orientation of the economy which is especially geared to the advanced industrial states, such as those in the EC. Then there is a centralization of capital and a financial system which is supportive of industry. Finally, there is a relatively acquiescent labour force. These four features – explained in detail by Schlupp (1980) – provide the general economic foundation upon which the Economics Ministry's European policy is based.

The link between these economic conditions and the political framework of the West German state is close. Kreile summarizes it in the following terms: 'Export-led growth created full employment and prosperity which, in turn, guaranteed popular support for the market economy and the system of democratic institutions' (1978, p. 192).

From the 1960s West German trade with its EC partners began to grow at a more rapid rate than with non-members. Compared with the other member states, the FRG has become 'the European Community's foremost exporter' (Story, 1981, p. 60). Despite this achievement and a persistent surplus in the balance of trade – with 1981 being an exception – there has been a continuing concern about an impending decline in export competitiveness on the part of West German industry. This view has been articulated through industrial interest groups (see Chapter 4), and has been an influence on the Federal Government's policy both concerning international monetary relations (including in the EC) and concerning the EC's internal market.

The guardian of the FRG's economic competitiveness, in both domestic and EC policy, is the Economics Ministry. Although certain representational duties are undertaken by the Foreign Office and financial responsibilities are primarily with the Ministry of Finance, it is the Economics Ministry which takes overall charge. Its commitment to the free trade principles of the social market economy has been a continuing feature of 'house policy' on the common market in industrial goods. This liberal doctrine ('*reine Lehre*') has become especially entrenched in the ministry's planning division (*Grundsatzabteilung*), where civil servants sympathetic to the FDP have been seen as lobbyists for free market principles.

Commencing with the first minister of economic affairs, Ludwig Erhard, the priority of policy has been to create the conditions whereby unrestricted competition may prevail in economic activity. This priority applied to conditions in both the FRG and the EC. Erhard was sceptical about the utility of achieving this objective within the narrow confines of an EEC of six states. He preferred instead a wider framework involving all OEEC countries. A speech in 1959 to that effect led to a reprimand from Adenauer, who had been instrumental in committing the Federal Republic to EEC membership (Adenauer, 1967, p. 519). It is worth noting that at this stage the Federal Government's European policy still had an overall coherence, with the political objective of achieving an arena of co-operation within Western Europe taking precedence. However, the tensions between this policy and that of utilizing the EEC as an arena of (economic) competition had begun to emerge.

When Schiller became minister of economic affairs in 1966

there was a slight tempering of the free market orthodoxy with the introduction of policy instruments *capable* of facilitating some Keynesian management of the economy. Use of these instruments has been very limited indeed. From 1972 a series of FDP ministers ensured that liberal economic principles remained during the economic turbulence which confronted the Social–Liberal coalition and, from 1982, its Centre–Right successor.

1 *The internal market*

The dismantling of customs barriers on intra-EEC trade was set out in clear terms in the Treaty of Rome. Hence the period from 1969 has not involved much policy-making in this area. From 1970 the EC itself became responsible for concluding trade and tariff agreements so that the Economics Ministry has ceded control in this area. Instead attention has focused on non-tariff barriers to intra-EEC trade. Government policy has been to lobby inside the EC for the removal of all such barriers so that a completely uniform internal market may exist. Not only has this policy run up against divergent priorities on the part of some other member governments but it has also been undermined by certain practices in the FRG itself.

The main countervailing force against economic liberalism in the EC has been the FRG's close partner, France. State intervention and neo-mercantilist trade policy have a long history in France. These tendencies began to reassert themselves as dimensions of French policy after Mitterrand's election to the presidency in 1981. The most dramatic case was the ploy of requiring all imports into France of video cassette recorders to be made via the town of Poitiers. This step, directed primarily against the Japanese, was greeted with horror in West Germany because it was seen as symptomatic of the type of non-tariff barrier which might undermine the achievements of the common market.

Related to this divergence of attitudes between the French and West German governments over the internal market was the question of attitudes towards international trade. By contrast with West Germany's commitment to international trade liberalization, France again has a more restrictive attitude. The French government saw the possibility of offering greater liberalization within the EEC in return for some measure of protectionism against Japan and the newly industrializing countries (NICs). Indeed, the French government argued that the Poitiers exercise was primarily geared towards drawing attention to the need for greater protectionism in the EC's *external* trade policy (Pearce and Sutton, 1986, pp. 65–66). French policy was thus based on the idea of opening up the internal market in return for greater external protection, sometimes known as 'Europrotectionism'.

The Federal Government's response to this was clear. Free trade should be pursued *both* within the EC *and* in the EC's commercial relations with the 'outside world' (Franzmeyer, 1984). Leaving aside the theoretical justification for this viewpoint, it is also supported by the fact that in 1983 77.6 per cent of West German exports went to the advanced industrial countries of the West and 48.1 per cent to the EC (Ten). So, although the EC is a major trading partner, so are other European countries together with the USA.

Although a firm believer in a liberalized internal market for goods, a close examination of West German practices indicates the existence of certain unintentional non-tariff barriers which contradict this rhetoric. This situation is explained by Franzmeyer (1984), who draws attention to the extensive use of standards which restrict the competitiveness of EC partners in the West German market. The German wish for high standards ('*Normenperfektionismus*') is typically justified by considerations of public health and safety.

A prime case in this context is the standard set for beer (and effected through the taxation regime on beer). The Federal Government, working in close co-operation with interest groups, created a strong climate of opposition to EC proposals put forward in June 1970 and aimed at harmonizing beer standards. As a result the Commission proposal was never put to a vote in the Council of Ministers and the trade barrier remains (Bulmer, 1987, Ch. 7). Following a 1979 decision of the European Court of Justice on the *Cassis de Dijon* case there was concern amongst West German brewers that the protective 'law of purity' might be overturned by legal means but the Federal Government resolved to protect them from the cheap competition of imports (Franzmeyer, 1984, p. 84).[1]

The extensive use of standards did not go unnoticed by the French during the early years of the Mitterrand presidency. Criticism of these standards led to a commitment by the West German Economics Ministry to take some action in reducing their impact on internal trade (Pearce and Sutton, 1986, p. 66). However, it became clear that only some of these standards are in fact established in legislation and therefore amenable to change. Others are actually established and administered by manufacturers' associations and are thus argued to be outside the control of the Federal Government.

These examples show that West German policy on the internal market does not always tie up in practice with the economic liberalism preached by the Economics Ministry. Two further cases showing deviation in practice from free market rhetoric are considered later in this chapter: international textile trade (external relations); and management of surplus steel-making capacity (industrial policy).

Despite these exceptions the basic governmental position on the internal market for goods is one of very positive support because of the policy's clear compatibility with the underlying liberal economic philosophy and because of the West German economy's extremely competitive position in key industries. But it is worth noting that there has been noticeably less enthusiasm in the FRG for liberalizing the internal market for services, as sought by the British (Conservative) governments from the 1981 presidency of the Council of Ministers onwards. To take the question of airline competition, the lack of a significant competitive framework for West German scheduled airlines – unlike the situation in the United Kingdom – is revealed as a further anomaly in German free market ideology. This is one factor behind the West Germans being less interested than the British in de-regulated civil aviation in the EC. Specific factors such as this, along with the lack of a highly export-oriented service sector like that in the City of London, have doubtless contributed to the lukewarm response of the Federal Government to the liberalization of services in the EC's internal market. As will be seen in later sections of this chapter, many of these inconsistencies can be traced to the form of co-operation between federal ministries and interest groups, together with views held by the latter.

2 *The EC's external relations*

A major component of the EC's external relations concerns international trade. Government policy on this shows considerable consistency with that on the internal market. In both policy areas national governments have lost the main policy instruments, namely tariffs and quotas, to the EC level. This again means that the Economics Ministry and the central interest group organizations take their campaign for free trade to the EC: to the Council of Ministers and European-level interest groups respectively. It is important to emphasize that the West German trade union federation, the DGB, is committed to the free trade philosophy, while several of its counterparts in the EC, for example the British Trades Union Congress, have adopted a more protectionist stance (Franzmeyer, 1984, p. 82).

With the West German economic miracle having been based on a *global* free trade policy, there is a clear divergence from the situation regarding France. The latter's postwar foreign trade was oriented initially towards the protected markets of its colonies. Thus whilst the FRG's trade was chiefly with industrial countries, France's tended to be with countries in the Franc zone, i.e. developing countries. West Germany's foreign trade grew during the 1950s while that of France stagnated. Although France's trading relations became much more oriented towards industrialized countries following the EEC's creation, there have been continuing tensions between the two member states about EC foreign trade policy.

Tensions became especially pronounced from the beginning of 1982 when the French government proposed in a memorandum that measures should be taken against unfair trading practices employed by third countries (those outside the EC). The memorandum basically proposed a strengthening of the Common Commercial Policy (Pearce and Sutton, 1986, pp. 45–6) and has also to be seen in the context of proposals to liberalize the EC's internal market (see previous section). The French proposals included the provision of policy instruments enabling the EC to take swift countermeasures against unfair practices employed by third countries. The Federal Government clearly regarded the French proposals as an attack upon international free trade. It emphasized the view that a liberal internal market was not an alternative to a liberal external trade policy (Franzmeyer, 1984; Menyesch and Uterwedde, 1982). The Federal Government also argued that there were already instruments for trade retaliation by the EC without introducing new legislation. In the event this argument, although supported by Denmark, the Netherlands and to a lesser extent Britain, was unsuccessful. Other governments argued that the EC's procedures made it very slow at agreeing retaliatory measures compared, for example, with those of the USA. As a result a compromise was reached in 1984 and some new policy instruments were brought in (Pearce and Sutton, 1986, p. 46).

Some commentators, notably Wolfgang Hager, have argued that the continued adherence by the Economics Ministry to a global liberal trade policy is mistaken (Hager, 1980; report of Hager's address to the European University Institute in *Frankfurter Rundschau*, 30 September 1981). Instead he has pointed out that the FRG's main export markets outside the EC are the European

Free Trade Association (EFTA) countries and the USA. In the case of trade with EFTA countries there is essentially zero-tariff trade in industrial goods by virtue of an agreement with the EC. Exports to these EFTA countries are almost as great as those to all other non-EC industrial countries combined, including the USA, Canada, Japan and Australia (Hager, 1980, p. 11). Thus Hager argues that the EC (and the commercial relationship with EFTA) is the dominant framework of West German trade, if one leaves aside relations with Eastern Europe, which clearly are not based on free trade.

Taking these factors as the database for his argument, Hager argues that the liberal EC *external* trade policy propounded by the Federal Government is not so vital to German interests. He bases this argument on two factors. First, the ideological component of the government's free trade policy can have a destabilizing effect on international trade. He cites as examples of this the government's free-trading stance on the North–South dialogue and on stabilizing export receipts for raw materials supplied by Lomé Convention countries. Following ideological principles in these cases is, according to Hager, likely to cause damage to trade by prolonging instability. A further danger is presented to the EC's internal market. Not all the EC member states have as adaptable an economic structure as the FRG. Yet the liberal trade sentiments of the Economics Ministry take a perfectly adaptable economy for granted. In consequence, Hager argues that there is a danger that other member states may fail to adapt and, as a result, come under domestic political pressure to 'break the discipline of the common commercial policy and even introduce trade barriers *within* Western Europe (as Italy did in 1974)' (Hager, 1980, p. 18). The Franco-German tensions of 1982–3 were, to some extent, evidence to support Hager's argument.

His arguments have not yet caused much impact on the basic position of the Economics Ministry, namely that of support for free trade. Protectionism is not seen in a positive light but rather as a means to economic self-destruction. Yet, just as in its internal market policy, exceptions to this rule have occurred in external trade. On both textiles and steel policy the Federal Government has been obliged to agree to some protectionist measures. Some comments are made here on the first of these two cases.

The Multi-Fibre Arrangement (MFA) has been created as a derogation from the rules of GATT with the purpose of 'managing' trade in textiles and clothing (Farrands, 1983). In particular it has enabled the EC to restrict low-cost imports from the NICs and other states. The first agreement came into effect in 1973 and a second in 1978 which continued until 1981. With this approaching expiry, the economics minister, Count Lambsdorff, came under much pressure in the FRG to work inside the EC for a renewal of the arrangement. During the negotiation for the second MFA, Lambsdorff had been a major critic of its protectionism. Despite his continuing crusade for free trade Lambsdorff was to find pressure for renewal irresistible. This was because demands came upon him from all sides of the textile industry.

In December 1980, as part of this pressure, the textile and clothing union held a one-hour protest strike which, while part of a European campaign, made specific reference to the 'completely unreal and anti-social policy of the German Economics Minister' (quoted in *Die Zeit*, 5 December 1980). For his part, Lambsdorff deflected the criticism on to the EC Commission, the competent negotiating agency. The inaction on renewing the MFA was, according to Lambsdorff, the result of the impending changeover of EC commissioners. To be sure, this was a factor but there was also an element of convenience in placing the blame on the Commission. Lambsdorff was content with the delay in negotiating what he considered to be a distasteful policy.

Major restructuring had had to take place in the West German textile and clothing industries during the 1970s. Major reductions in the work-force had occurred so that the industries had become the most technically advanced in the EC (Farrands, 1983). Despite this both the trade union involved and the textile and clothing industries pressed for an extension of the MFA in order to permit further industrial adjustment so that the low-cost imports could be challenged on a competitive basis.

The textile and clothing industries represented a strong lobby for continuation of the MFA and their predominantly small- or medium-sized (*mittelständisch*) enterprise structure provided the Economics Ministry with an even stronger case. Industries with this type of enterprise structure appear to be able to strengthen their lobbying by presenting themselves as the standard bearers of the social market economy (and therefore as eligible for a derogation from its principles!). Confronted by the serried ranks of the relevant interest groups, Lambsdorff was able to make an exception to his free trade ideology. In a *joint statement* with the textile industry, the minister agreed to press for a renewal of the MFA. However, this reluctant acceptance of Europrotectionism in a special case was combined with calls for *less* protectionism against products of the heavily export-dependent West German textile and clothing industries.

This somewhat incongruous negotiating position of agreeing

to Europrotectionism while pressing for more liberalization in the internal market required something of an intellectual somersault from Bonn's '*Freihändler vom Dienst*', Count Lambsdorff. It will be recalled that only in the following year he was rejecting the French proposal of greater Europrotectionism in return for a more liberal internal market. What, then, was the explanation for this?

The answer lies in the context of special pleading by the textile and clothing industry as opposed to the generalized system proposed by the French. As Deubner (1984) has graphically demonstrated, the MFA has given the West German clothing industry a highly competitive edge in the EC. German firms have acquired subsidiaries and suppliers in the low-cost countries to carry out the labour-intensive stages on products which are then completed in the FRG. The result is that 'German' goods are highly competitive in the EC's internal market because the labour costs of EC competitors are undercut while, simultaneously, the 'real' low-cost producers are excluded from the European market by courtesy of the MFA.

It should be clear from this case that the West German textile and clothing industries have done rather well from the MFA, taking advantage of low-cost imports, a practice known as 'outward processing' (Pearce and Sutton, 1986, Ch. 6). This practice has resulted in tension with some other producing countries, especially Britain. There has also been concern on the part of some member states that West Germany is able to gain significant supplies of low-cost semi-finished goods from Eastern Europe because of its refusal to recognize goods supplied from East Germany as 'imports'. This is because of the political nature of the German question (discussed in Chapter 10). Some states have questioned whether all products entering the EC through this loophole are in fact East German and therefore eligible for tariff- and quota-free entry.

Despite the special case of textiles the overwhelming pattern of West German policy is to support free trade. In the final analysis, the German economy has the least to lose on this basis. In other sectors, such as watches and shoes, free trade has been retained despite pressure for exceptions to be made. Some indication of West German support for free trade principles can be obtained from the number of occasions it has sought special national measures limiting specified imports. 'In 1982 France and Italy had quantitative restrictions on 121 items, Britain on 65 and Germany on 31' (Pearce and Sutton, 1986, p. 41).

Of the large member states West Germany is the main lobbyist for a more liberal external trade policy. It can be expected to pursue this role in any new GATT round. Given that agriculture is likely to play a key role in the latter, West German policy will be interesting because of the need for co-ordination with the protectionist agricultural community.

3 *Industrial policy*

Responsibility for industrial matters, as for the preceding two policy areas, resides in the Economics Ministry. Thus it should be no surprise that the market-oriented philosophy of that ministry again assumes primacy. In practical terms this means that there has been strong opposition to anything resembling an industrial policy. Market forces are preferred to interventionist policies as the means to structural adjustment in the economy. This applies both in domestic policy and, by extension, to positions taken on EC initiatives on industrial policy.

Industrial policy is usually defined as governmental action geared to the optimal use of resources for industrial production. EC activities under this heading have been characterized by

> a somewhat chequered history of piecemeal initiatives which have been put forward by the Commission under the rubric of industrial policy, and which have frequently been submerged or ignored in the wider debate within the Community about the future course of integration and the division of initiative and responsibility between the public and private sectors. (Hodges, 1983, p. 265)

As a consequence of the piecemeal approach, initiatives have been limited to individual sectors rather than assuming an overall framework of the type suggested in the Commission's first proposals in this area in 1970. The sectors involved have included steel, shipbuilding, synthetic fibres, textiles, aerospace and telecommunications (Fendel, 1981). However, even within the Commission, there has not been overwhelming support for these initiatives. As 'crisis sectors' steel, textiles and shipbuilding have received especial attention.

In all these activities the Federal Government's position has been one of stalling progress because of an ideological aversion to industrial policy. Once again the Economics Ministry has acted as the standard bearer of economic liberalism in the EC Council of Ministers. But it has also been confident of support for its position from the Finance Ministry in the event of any interventionist policy being agreed upon. Such a policy would clearly require financial commitments from the EC Budget and these would be opposed by a ministry which shows all the zeal of an enthusiastic bank manager for reining in the expenditure of a disreputable customer.

Only two allies could be found in the Federal Government by the protagonists of an EC industrial policy. At a technical level there was some support from the Ministry for Research and Technology for limited intervention in forward-looking sectors like data processing. There was also some support from the junior Foreign Office minister, Dr von Dohnanyi (SPD) during his term in office. When Lambsdorff's attacks on EC proposals were at their loudest, in the period immediately after he took office in October 1977, it was noted 'that [EC industry commissioner] Davignon repeatedly contacted minister of state von Dohnanyi, when he required German support' (Fendel, 1981, p. 303). Both these sources of limited support were weak in the hierarchy of the Federal Government because the Economics Ministry was in charge. However, this situation did ensure the familiar incoherence in West German European policy.

The arguments and tactics used by the Federal Government to stem the tide of industrial policy initiatives were various. They included the reasoning that such initiatives conflicted with the internal market and foreign trade policies of the EC; or that industrial policy should be achieved through the EC's competition policy; and if these arguments failed then the familiar liberal economic philosophy could be deployed. As regards tactics, elections were invoked as preventing discussion of proposals; and successive German presidencies delayed initiatives in the Council of Ministers and COREPER by 'massaging' the agenda. At the end of each presidency, however, the Federal Government sought to draw a positive balance, including on the industrial policy which it so disliked![2]

The specific case of steel is worth exploring in some detail because it illustrates the relationship between declaratory and operational policy in the Federal Government's dealings in the EC.[3] It should be recalled that steel is an exceptional case in 'industrial policy' because the EC's powers are clearly set out in the ECSC Treaty. This gave the EC authority for tackling the over-capacity in the European steel sector during the 1970s and 1980s.

In his 1977 proposals, the industry commissioner, Viscount Davignon, introduced a procedure whereby the Commission established minimum prices for some products for which the markets were particularly depressed and 'guidance prices' for all steel products. These measures proved to be insufficient for an orderly EC steel market, however. In 1978, therefore, the Commission introduced voluntary production quotas which were negotiated with the leading producers. For a time these quotas proved a more effective instrument than the previous controls, partly because they were less easy to evade and partly due to a revival in demand. However, by mid-1980 prices began to collapse despite a fall in production levels.

West German reaction to increasing difficulties in the steel sector during the 1970s involved a whole battery of policy instruments. Despite its aversion to interventionism, the provision of government aid was increased. This took a number of forms. Direct aid was provided by the 1979 programme for anti-pollution subsidies, by a number of research and development programmes, the payment of the construction costs of new plant in Dortmund and the Saar and the provision of financial aid to firms for negotiated programmes of adjustment, including the payment of the social costs of restructuring. Steel was subsidized indirectly through aid paid to the coal industry, the main energy source for steel-making. A further indirect subsidy was provided by subsidizing the shipbuilding industry, a major consumer. Not all these measures were undertaken by the Federal Government; some involved the *Länder* governments.

Another aspect of government policy was the tacit acceptance by successive governments of quasi-cartellization by the steel producers. *Kontore* (agencies) were established in the 1960s to control the sale of rolled steel in the FRG. Four agencies controlled between them almost 90 per cent of sales on the German market. They encouraged a process of rationalization through the specialization and management of market shares rather than through formal mergers which might have provoked intervention by the Federal Cartel Office. The *Kontore* played a further role by subsidizing direct exports to non-EC markets. In consequence, the FRG was the only EC state whose exports of steel to non-EC markets increased substantially, even during the late 1970s.

Alongside these measures West German producers also took other steps to protect themselves, such as by close co-operation with producers from other member states. Nevertheless, it was a German producer, Klöckner, which caused the actual collapse of voluntary quotas due to its dissatisfaction with its own target. Based, like all the quotas, on 1974 production figures, its target did not take account of restructuring then in progress. Nor did it take account of the massive new plant in Bremen which had not commenced production in 1974. After unsuccessful attempts to renegotiate its quota within EUROFER, the European producers' group, Klöckner withdrew, thus threatening collapse of voluntary restraint.

Under these circumstances another German producer, Spethmann (a director of Thyssen and a prominent steel industrialist), asked the EC Commission in 1980 to invoke Article 58, ECSC Treaty, thus setting compulsory quotas. The British and French governments made similar representations. When the Commission sought to institute proceedings under Article 58, requiring consent from the Council of Ministers, it became clear that the Federal Government (along with that of Italy) would oppose. Indeed, at the Council session of 7 October 1980 the Commission proposal was obstructed by the German government (*FAZ*, 8 October 1980). Why was this the case? The Federal Government was not opposed to regulation of the market, despite its free market principles, but it clearly opposed *compulsory* quotas. Regulation by the producers themselves could be tolerated but not intervention by the Commission or by national governments. In view of its toleration – even encouragement – of the *Kontore*, along with the subsidies to the steel industry, this 'position of principle' seemed rather hollow. A series of delaying tactics was used by Lambsdorff and the Federal Government to try and gain time. However, their obstructionism was on weak ground because Davignon and others argued that the Article 58 procedure, the declaration of a 'manifest crisis', was not subject to any veto; decisions would be taken by majority vote.

Although at the Council of Ministers' session on 30 October 1980 the Federal Government was obliged to agree to the declaration of a manifest crisis, a large number of concessions were secured. These arose as a product of the negotiating tactics of the government and because of the size of the German steel industry. It was also probably an advantage to the FRG that it was represented by a powerful economics minister (and part of a government re-elected earlier that month) rather than - as was the case with several states - by a (more protective) industry minister, often of relatively junior status in his government.

The major concessions granted in return for Lambsdorff's agreement were:

- a limitation of the quota system to a period of six months. However this was later extended (Hodges, 1983);
- a strict control of national subsidies to steel which would be effected by the Commission. In March 1981 ministers agreed

that no further subsidies should be introduced after the end of 1985. This concession reflected Lambsdorff's concern that relatively efficient German steelmakers were in 'competition with the finance ministers of the partner countries' (quoted in Kramer, 1982, p. 416);
- the restructuring of the entire EC steel industry so that efficient producers could flourish;
- the exclusion of special steels from the quotas.

With the problems of the European steel industry still unresolved, negotiations have continued in this vein. The Federal Government's role in the talks during 1980 allows us to draw a number of conclusions which relate to its role in European policy as a whole.

First, contrary to West German public perceptions, which regard the government as not pushing its own interests in the EC, the Economics Ministry pursued a rather obstructive policy with great vigour and a considerable amount of success. Agreement to a 'manifest crisis' and the associated obligatory quotas was only reached once a series of important concessions had been obtained from other governments and from the Commission.

Secondly, in a situation where domestic interests were at stake there were few concessions to Europeanist rhetoric or practice. With the Federal Government out of step with its partners, a Europeanist posture would have implied handing over a share of shrinking production quotas to competitors in other member states. Thus the rhetoric of the declaratory policy was that of market forces but, given the amount of indirect subsidy provided to the steel sector, it may be best regarded as a veil to cover a self-interested defence of the German steel sector. Steel policy, like industrial policy, may present the Federal Government with challenges to its economic philosophy. However, economic interests will ultimately prevail over ideological principles if these are not identical (as is generally the case in EC policy on the internal market and foreign trade).

To summarize on industrial policy, the Economics Ministry is strongly in favour of a 'hands-off' approach, characterized by economic adaptation at the level of the firm. This is clearly preferred to governmental intervention. This position led to criticism of the French memorandum which proposed using the EC level to enable member states to keep up with the third industrial revolution, currently being dominated by Japan and the USA (Richonnier, 1984; Pearce and Sutton, 1986, Ch. 6).

There was agreement that the EC's industry lags behind the technological development of its counterparts in the USA and Japan (although Germany has the most advanced industry in the EC). Disagreement emerged, however, over tackling the symptoms. The Economics Ministry adopted its ideological posture of rejecting intervention in industry. Pearce and Sutton express this as follows:

> Just as the role of the government is only to ensure appropriate framework conditions for industry, so the role of the Commission is not to initiate projects but to construct a real common market and to promote free cooperation and competition which is not distorted by subsidies. (1986, p. 77)

A formal EC industrial policy is effectively ruled out by this situation but this does not exclude a policy response completely. On the contrary, the emphasis is shifted towards research and competition policies.

4 *Research and competition policies*

The Federal Government's willingness to tackle the technological challenges of economic innovation has excluded the use of industrial policy (with some exceptions), as has been outlined above. It has been prepared to offer encouragement to industry by two other means, however. On the one hand, it has been prepared to encourage verbally European-level mergers to create industrial enterprises which are competitive internationally. On the other hand, it has been prepared to support European-funded research projects provided that the funds are allocated to research bodies rather than companies. Following the latter course of funding would be perceived as industrial policy. Protecting the development of new technology in firms in this way is seen in a negative light because it may make them dependent on further financial protection.

Taking the competition policy context first, the West German position, as presented by the Economics Ministry, is that the use of national subsidies in industrial policy should be phased out. In addition, the liberalization of the internal market should be extended. Other measures desired include creating a free capital market in the EC to enable risk capital to be raised more easily and the liberalization of public purchasing on an EC-wide basis. Once progress was being achieved in these areas it would then be desirable to make changes in the practice of competition policy in order to facilitate co-operation in research between firms with a view to making them more effective at the international level (Grewlich, 1984).

Thus far the Federal Government has not been prepared to allow European industrial objectives to overrule German competition policy. Permitting the formation of internationally competitive concerns through mergers may involve a reduction in competition within the West German market. Such a development is not favoured by the FRG's competition law, however. This was demonstrated by developments in 1982–3 when the Mitterrand government encouraged the French industrial concern Thomson-Brandt to link up with the German firm Grundig to create a more internationally competitive concern (Pearce and Sutton, 1986, Ch. 12). It became clear in 1983 that the Federal Cartel Office, which is responsible for judging the effects of takeovers and mergers on market shares, would not approve this link-up. Even though the Economics Ministry had the power to set aside such a decision it was concerned about the development on other grounds. It was worried because Thomson-Brandt was a nationalized industry. The result was that the project was aborted and the opportunity to create a European firm of the magnitude to challenge the Japanese in the electronics industry was lost.

Support for research policy is rather more straightforward. The specialist ministry concerned in this area is the Ministry for Research and Technology. It does not follow the strong ideological position favoured by the Economics Ministry; to emphasize the role of markets in the economic process would be to undermine its own role. Instead research and technology are regarded as being in a 'pre-competitive' domain of the economy. They may therefore be promoted by public funds, provided that the application of research is carried out by industry itself. This pre-competitive stage is ensured in the European Strategic Programme for Research in Information Technology (ESPRIT) which, in line with German policy, requires research to be in excess of five years from commercial application.

Grewlich (1984, pp. 257–8) sets out the key principles enumerated by the FRG regarding the acceptability of specific EC research programmes. They must be subject to close cost-benefit analysis; they must be most efficiently pursued at a collaborative rather than a national level; and the funding of the projects must be controlled efficiently and according to clear criteria. These are in addition to the requirement that research is pre-competitive and of a temporary nature, thus fitting in with GATT conditions. Finally, publicly funded research must not penalize those companies who are able to pursue research and technology at their own expense.

The conditions for approval of EC research and technology policy are thus set out in reasonably clear terms. And although the FRG is the economy best placed for technological innovation *without* public support, there is a recognition of the need for European collaboration. The Ministry for Research and Technology is supported by the Foreign Office's positive attitudes towards European co-operation and integration. The EUREKA initiative has also received strong support from Chancellor Kohl ('Kohl tells Eureka delegates: technology is our destiny', Report from the Federal Republic of Germany, 6 November 1985).

The (economic) policy areas examined hitherto display a considerable degree of consistency at the abstract, theoretical level. This is because the principles of the social market economy form the underlying reference point. The emphasis upon free trade principles, increased market integration and competitive forces is clear. Nevertheless, there are exceptions to the rule, such as steel and textiles, and the high level of free market rhetoric is designed in part to emphasize that these cases must remain exceptions rather than reference points for other industries. There is also clear evidence that the political desirability of European integration is not an end in itself. Further substantiation of this is provided by the case study on regional policy (see Chapter 10). The EC is regarded much more as a framework of economic competition for West German industry and trade.

The desire to maintain market principles as the dominant reference point for economic policy lies at the root of the West German view of the EC as an arena of competition. However, there is a useful convergence with other West German interests. For example, there is concern to limit the influence of the Commission over industrial matters because of a fear that market principles might be diluted. There is also a clear recognition that any EC-funded policies on industry or research would necessarily involve disproportionate costs for the FRG, due to its role as the largest net contributor to the EC Budget. In the final analysis the FRG is the best placed of the twelve economies for coping with the future international challenges *without* interventionist policies. This clearly places the Federal Government in an even stronger position in resisting costly interventionist policies run by the EC.

The importance of the Economics Ministry's liberalism to West German European policy is great. One commentator has gone so far as to 'consider Germany's liberal, pro-market attitude its most important positive contribution to, and influence on, the Community' (Steinherr, 1980, p. 131). Perhaps the clearest statement of this pro-market attitude was made in the 'Memorandum of the German Delegation on Structural Policy in the Market Economy'.[4] This identified the following components of German policy:

- structural change is primarily a task for enterprises themselves;
- neither the EC nor the member states may determine for enterprises what the 'correct' industrial structure is;
- the task of keeping open and extending markets must be pursued vigorously at the national, EC and international levels;
- the development of advanced technology may be pursued at the EC level;
- EC regional and social policy measures may assist structural change provided that they promote improvements to infrastructure, replacement jobs and labour mobility;
- scarce public funds should not be employed for measures preserving (outmoded) industrial structures;
- in very limited exceptions fixed-term transitional arrangements may be permitted on the grounds of serious employment problems if they assist a self-help approach.

Adherence to these ideas has been an important feature of governmental policy, a factor which sets the FRG apart from the shifting policies of French and British governments over the last two decades. Thus, although we have concentrated primarily on recent developments in these policy areas, the same views have been propounded since 1969 and, indeed, since the 1950s. But what of the view of federal governments towards the EC's activity in financial and monetary matters?

5 *Monetary co-operation*

In the Federal Government monetary co-operation falls within the remit of the Ministry of Finance, which is also responsible for matters relating to the EC Budget.[5] In monetary policy ministerial authority is limited by the powers which the Federal Bank has in connection with the money supply and exchange rate policy. It is worth dwelling upon the rationale for the Federal Bank's autonomy because this will be seen to have a wider impact on German European policy. The experience of hyperinflation in 1922–3 in the Weimar Republic made an indelible impression on the German people by virtually destroying the value of financial assets. A similar development occurred under quite different circumstances with the currency reform of June 1948 (Kloten, 1980, pp. 179–81). The response of the political elite (and of the allied powers) was to ensure that the West German central bank be independent of government in order to underpin institutionally a commitment to sound monetary practice. As Wadbrook puts it:

> Powerfully influenced in its institutional shape and through its personnel by memories of Germany's two great inflations, the Bundesbank has consistently seen defense of the DM's domestic value and international parity as the primary goal, not only of its own, but of all economic policy. (Wadbrook, 1972, p. 251)

The wider impact upon European policy has been twofold. First, there has been a clear concern on the part of the Federal Bank not to sacrifice domestic price stability on the altar of European integration. Secondly the central bank has resolutely opposed the ceding of any of its powers to the supranational level.

These two concerns assumed relevance from 1968 when pressure began to increase for monetary co-operation at the Community level. The causes of this pressure are well documented and included the decline of the Bretton Woods system of international monetary relations (including the failure of the United States to initiate any remedial action) and the disruptive effects of this upon intra-Community trade and upon common pricing in the CAP (Tsoukalis, 1977). It was at the EC summit meeting at The Hague in 1969 that the first effort to tackle this instability was aired in the proposals for an Economic and Monetary Union (EMU). Already at this stage differences of strategy towards EMU became evident in what was later referred to as the dispute between the 'economists' and 'monetarists'. The former group consisted of those wanting the initial emphasis to be on economic policy convergence with monetary union representing the final stage. By contrast, the monetarists wanted this process to be in reverse; the first step of creating a monetary bloc would necessitate economic convergence in order that exchange rate fluctuations remained within the permissible margins.

Chancellor Brandt's proposals at the 1969 summit fell squarely in the economist camp and this applied to the Federal Government's thinking throughout the EMU debate. Why was this the case?

Underlying West German support for the 'economist viewpoint' was the concern that inflation presents the main threat to political stability: a concern based upon the historical experiences outlined above. Other member states had a less committed attitude towards counterinflationary policy. There was particular concern about the primacy given to growth among French economic policy objectives and about the large deficits in its balance of payments in 1968 and 1969. Tsoukalis explains the possible impact of French economic policy on the FRG through EMU as follows:

> If the 'monetarist' strategy was adopted, then the Community might reach a *de facto* monetary union without having an effective system of economic co-ordination. The irrevocable fixity of parities, together with the existence of a European Reserve Fund or some other balance of payments aid, might lead to a situation where surplus countries financed indefinitely the deficit ones without being able to force the latter to take any corrective measures. The only other option left open to the surplus countries would be to adapt themselves to a higher rate of inflation and thus accept the burden of adjustment. (Tsoukalis, 1977, pp. 92–3)

As a result of the aversion to importing inflation in this way, West German negotiators ensured that, if progress was to be achieved on the EMU initiative, and if the 'economist' perspective was politically unacceptable to other countries, then it was essential that the principle of parallelism should apply. In other words any advances on monetary integration would have to be conditional on parallel advances on economic convergence. This was in essence the route taken in the Werner Report, reflecting a balance of the member governments' views on the programme for implementing EMU. Significantly, the West German negotiators had ensured a safeguard clause in the report, whereby the FRG could opt out of monetary co-operation at the end of a five-year period if the parallel approach had not been followed (Tsoukalis, 1977, p. 110).

In fact that option never became a reality because of the continued decline of the Bretton Woods monetary system, with its eventual demise coming in March 1973. The inauguration of the Snake in April 1972 was accompanied by further currency speculation which had a divisive effect on the participating currencies. This resulted eventually in the emergence of a slimmed-down 'mini-snake'; by April 1976 only five EC currencies remained as members. This core membership of West

Germany, Denmark and the Benelux countries as well as two associates (Norway and – until August 1977 – Sweden) formed in effect a DM-zone.

This arrangement was much less of a threat to West German interests in monetary policy because the other EC participants were closely tied by their trading patterns to the German economy, which dominated the 'mini-snake'. There had been little progress on the economic component of EMU, in the way desired by the German government, so there was little chance of proceeding further. A second phase of EMU was improbable in any case due to the limited participation in the Snake.

The 'mini-snake' served some purpose for the FRG's trade but a purpose which, in the final analysis, was limited due to several of its key EC markets not participating. As Tsoukalis notes, 'It was certainly better than no arrangement at all. It can also be argued that participation in the snake did not entail any serious additional constraints on German monetary policy' (Tsoukalis, 1983, p. 125). The wish to extend participation in monetary co-operation and thus provide German traders with greater certainty in their dealings was one of the motives underlying the 1978 proposals for monetary co-operation in what was to become the European Monetary System. The initiative, which was largely the work of Chancellor Schmidt, but with close co-operation from President Giscard d'Estaing, was first aired during the informal discussions at the April 1978 European Council session in Copenhagen (Ludlow, 1982, pp. 88–94; Carr, 1985, pp. 139–149). In terms of the earlier division regarding the strategy towards EMU, the new and less ambitious proposals followed the 'monetarist' approach. Why, then, was there an apparent 'U-turn' in the thinking of Helmut Schmidt?

A number of reasons have been identified by commentators. Two factors were of crucial interest, namely the chancellor's scepticism towards the foreign economic policy of the US president, Mr Carter, and Schmidt's increased domestic prestige especially after some successes over terrorists (Ludlow, 1982, pp. 63–4). One of the major German concerns about the French support for the 'monetarist' strategy during the EMU negotiations was that Pompidou and his government were seeking to deliver a blow to the political status of the US dollar in the international monetary system. The West German authorities were not interested in an adventure of that kind. Quite apart from the inflationary risks of the 'monetarist' strategy, the FRG's ultimate dependence on the USA's security umbrella placed a politically motivated step of this nature in contradiction to West German interests.

By 1978, however, the situation had changed considerably. The failure of the United States to play a leadership role in stabilizing the international monetary system had been highlighted by the Carter administration's benign neglect of the dollar. Other issues had contributed to undermining Schmidt's confidence in the USA, including repeated pleas to the German government to reflate the economy. The dollar's fall was promoting increased use of the DM as a reserve currency so that there was a risk of importing inflation through *inaction* rather than through integration in the shape of EMU. Neglect of the dollar was also having a differential effect on the FRG's trading partners. Ludlow speaks of 'widespread, if unarticulated, concern amongst German industrialists and public opinion at large that appreciation of the DM against other European currencies ... could not be accepted without serious risks to German exports' (1982, p. 73).

The deterioration in relations between Schmidt and the Carter administration was counterbalanced by continued improvement in the chancellor's relations with Giscard d'Estaing. Their shared views on the management of international interdependence had already spawned the creation of the European Council and Western economic summits (Bulmer, 1985; Putnam and Bayne, 1984). Now there was further evidence of convergent ideas, this time relating to economic management. Giscard's prime minister, M. Barre, had introduced an austerity programme and this had been characterized by a marked shift towards the economic policy priorities of the FRG. This convergence was matched by deflationary policies in other member states, due to the effects of the oil crisis, so that the risks of following a 'monetarist' strategy were perceived as being reduced.

The path taken by Schmidt in pursuing the EMS project is important in connection with the sectorized European policy-making machinery of the FRG. The idea was first launched in the informal after-dinner discussions of the European Council so that the routine participants from the Finance Ministry, the Federal Bank and the Economics Ministry were by-passed. Advice was sought from various confidants but there was no consultation in the Cabinet. Schmidt was well aware of the unresponsiveness of the European Community to international challenges and was thus determined to avoid the humdrum procedures of full consultation of the relevant authorities. A group of three experts was created in the aftermath of the Copenhagen European

Council to pursue the initiative. Schmidt's nominee was Dr Schulmann, the chief economic adviser in the Chancellor's Office. This group played the key role in the vital early stage of elaborating the EMS.

The independence of Dr Schulmann from the executive agencies empowered with responsibility for economic and monetary policy was crucial. It facilitated the adoption of a more rounded view of West German interests than would otherwise have been possible. The Federal Bank's brief, although important to this policy area, was constitutionally limited to considering the EMS proposal on its technical merits as a monetary policy instrument. It may not allow the desirability of European integration or other political motives to enter its considerations. The same applied to a lesser extent to the Finance Ministry. It too was concerned with the EMS's mechanisms rather than with its effect upon West German industry. For the Economics Ministry the situation was reversed.

Due to these circumstances the Chancellor's Office was best placed to avoid narrow, technical views which would dominate the other specialist federal agencies. The important question was whether the narrow institutional interests of branches of the executive could be persuaded to fall in behind the political agreement when this became necessary. Schmidt's commitment both at the political and the technical level was crucial in this context. He took charge of trying to persuade civil servants, ministers and the all-important Federal Bank of the technical merits (Ludlow, 1982, pp. 135–9). Despite major opposition on the part of the Federal Bank, some concessions were made on the mechanics of the system and agreement was reached.

Implementation of the EMS was delayed by just over two months until mid-March 1979 due to a Franco-German dispute over the exchange rate system for CAP prices (Bulmer, 1983c, pp. 581–2). Two years later the second phase of the EMS was due to commence. In fact it was only in March 1982 that some attempt was made to strengthen the system, but without success. Subsequent efforts – including at the European Council in 1985 – have met with similar failure. A major stumbling block has again been the Federal Bank. Its opposition to strengthening the EMS has been based on several factors. There has been concern that some participating governments have not taken adequate measures to ensure economic policy convergence. Another problem area relates to the creation of a European Monetary Fund as the central institution in the second phase. The Federal Bank would require its legal autonomy to be maintained otherwise its own constitutional basis would be at risk. Finally, the bank has indicated that British membership of the EMS is a prerequisite for its strengthening. A rather more optimistic German viewpoint on enhancing the EMS has been presented by the father of the EMS, Helmut Schmidt (1985).

The European Monetary System has been interpreted as one of the key recent achievements associated with the EC. Ludlow has described it as 'arguably the first major act of German leadership in the history of the European Community' (1982, p. 290). It is remarkable that such an achievement was secured by the expertise and awareness of Chancellor Schmidt in overcoming the scepticism and opposition of the German financial establishment. The EMS initiative demonstrated how the adoption of an active European policy initiative in the FRG requires an astute tactician, a self-confident technician and an electorally secure politician to occupy a key political office. Due to the institutional decentralization of West German government the scope for such initiatives is very small. This places limits on West Germany's ability to assume the leadership of the EC. A much more 'normal' role for West German ministers is that of acting as a powerful veto group in the EC. This role has arguably been perfected by the Bonn Finance Ministry in its attitude towards the EC Budget. And paradoxically it was Schmidt's period as finance minister that was decisive here too.

6 *The EC Budget*

1969 is again a useful starting point for examining West German policy for it was at the summit meeting in The Hague that agreement was reached on a self-financing (own resources) budgetary system. This came into effect from 1971 but only became fully operational in 1980. The Brandt-Scheel government's support for an own resources budgetary system was clear and was motivated by the political wish to re-launch the EC. Brandt referred approvingly to the pre-federal nature of the own resources system when it was being ratified (cited in Müller-Roschach, 1974, p. 137). Significantly the Federal Government's annual report of 1969 had already seen the need to use the budgetary changes to reduce agricultural surpluses and the costs of the CAP (Müller-Roschach, 1974, p. 133). That insufficient progress was made in curbing agricultural costs was to become a major concern of the Finance Ministry from the mid-1970s.

Concern about West Germany becoming the 'financier' of the EC was raised as early as 1973. Following a session of the Council of (Foreign) Ministers, which was discussing the establishment of an EC regional fund, Hans Apel announced: 'We are not the paymasters of the Community' (*BPA Press Release*, 18 December 1973). With these words the paymaster issue was launched, receiving wide attention in the press. More substantial analysis soon followed (Nass, 1976; *Monthly Report of the Bundesbank*, 1977, pp. 15–22).

An especially thorough analysis of the budgetary impact of the EC upon the FRG had been conducted by May (1982). His figures (based on those of the government) demonstrate how *gross* contributions to the EC Budget rose from DM 2,654m (1971) to DM 11,547m (1980). *Net* contributions rose from DM 454m (1971) to DM 4,811m (1980) (May, 1982, p. 45). The difference between these figures is accounted for by receipts from the budget, approximately 75 per cent of which are CAP payments. German receipts from the EC Budget have grown at a slower rate than contributions, rising from DM 2,200m (1971) to DM 6,736m (1980).

The main focus of attention was upon the tenfold increase in the FRG's net contributions, 1971–1980. This increase served as important evidence upon which the Finance Ministry based its extremely rigorous examination of proposed new EC expenditure. The ministry's ability to subject expenditure on *existing* policy to such scrutiny was (and is) limited because this would involve interference in policy areas for which other federal ministries held responsibility in the FRG. The principle of ministerial autonomy excluded such interference, unless undertaken at the chancellor's request.

A qualitative change in the Federal Government's approach to financing the EC Budget came about once Mrs Thatcher began pressing for a fairer deal regarding British contributions. There was a realization that any success achieved by the British government would place an even heavier burden on the West German Federal Budget. In consequence the Federal Government sought to ensure that no single member state had to bear a disproportionate share of the EC Budget, whether that state be Britain or the Federal Republic itself.

Another significant change was the increasing role of the European Council as the forum for budgetary negotiations. This had the effect of placing the chancellor in a key role in policy-making. A more collective form of governmental decision-making was required. The Cabinet was therefore brought into play to try and resolve differing ministerial viewpoints (May, 1984).

Four ministries were involved in the budgetary debate in the period 1980–4. They were those responsible for finance, foreign affairs and agriculture, together with the Chancellor's Office. Interviews in these ministries during 1980 revealed that each ministry had a different attitude towards the subject matter: a situation confirmed by May (1984). The Ministry of Finance was the principal actor involved. Its position was, unsurprisingly, one of seeking reductions in budgetary expenditure through reform of the CAP. Until such reform had been achieved, it was unwilling to contemplate an increase in the size of the EC Budget. This position was diametrically opposed to views expressed in the Agriculture Ministry where various arguments were deployed with a view to defending the CAP. No ideal solution existed regarding curtailing CAP expenditure, it was argued in the Agriculture Ministry, although the Finance Ministry clearly had just such a solution in mind! (Bulmer, 1987, p. 87). The Agriculture Ministry argued that only some limited changes to the CAP would be possible; the basic principles of the policy were sacrosanct.

The Foreign Office and the Chancellor's Office were more disinterested in their viewpoints. The view of the former was much broader than that of the Finance Ministry. There was concern about the negative impact of an inflexible book-keeping approach on the Federal Government's integration policy. For its part the Chancellor's Office was involved because the budgetary question had been placed on the European Council's agenda so that Schmidt (and later Kohl) required briefing. At least one member of senior staff in the Chancellor's Office was entrusted with monitoring the budgetary issue during the later years of Schmidt's chancellorship.

Two concrete examples of the interplay of these ministerial positions are given by May (1984, pp. 377–8). One relates to the aftermath of the May 1980 decision, reached in the Council of Ministers in Brussels, about British net contributions to the EC Budget for 1980 and 1981. This decision, agreed to on the German side by Foreign Office minister Klaus von Dohnanyi (SPD), would involve an increase over the two-year period in the Federal Republic's net contributions to the EC of ECU 1,011m, a large increase. As a result of this the Finance Minister, Hans Matthöfer (SPD), demanded a decision of the Cabinet on how this extra sum should be financed. At the Cabinet session of 4 June 1980 the Finance Ministry's view prevailed over the Foreign Office and the Agriculture Ministry. The decisions taken formed the basis of the German position during later negotiations on the Budget. The decisions confirmed support for the 'own resources' revenue system of the budget; they pressed for an examination of the burden of net contributions placed upon the FRG; and they sought the establishment of an upper limit both for net contributions and net receipts available to any individual member state (May, 1984, p. 377).

In 1983 a similar problem arose when it gradually became clear that the size of the EC Budget would have to be increased due to its virtual exhaustion.[6] This would involve raising the ceiling of Value Added Tax (VAT) receipts from 1 per cent to 1.4 per cent (May, 1984, p. 378). The CDU Finance Minister, Herr Stoltenberg, strongly opposed such a move. He had just secured a significant cut in the Federal Budget as part of the new government's economic policy strategy and was unwilling to sacrifice his ministry's hard fought achievements by reinstating much of the reduction in the form of contributions to the EC. Nevertheless, the Foreign Office had important countervailing considerations because it was holding the presidency of the Council of Ministers during the period January-June 1983. It wanted to secure a package of measures including the resolution of budgetary problems, some small CAP reforms and approval in principle of the Iberian enlargement (Ungerer, 1983, pp. 7–8). In consequence, a compromise had to be reached with the Finance Ministry so that there was some chance of success at the European Council sessions, to be chaired by Helmut Kohl (Brussels March 1983, Stuttgart June 1983). In fact, the package was only agreed twelve months later at the Fontainebleau session of the European Council (Denton, 1984). Significantly the agreement incorporated a mechanism which ensured that the Federal Republic would not have to bear the full burden of the British budgetary settlement (Stadlmann, 1985, p. 38).

Throughout the period since the introduction of an 'own resources' system, the Finance Ministry has consistently lobbyed within the Federal Government to ensure prudent housekeeping in the EC Budget and to limit West German contributions to it.[7] Its rationale for this is primarily to ensure that some member countries do not profit unduly from the distributive effects of the EC Budget, to which the FRG is the main contributor. However, a further factor in the ministry's thinking is that higher contributions to the EC Budget create a *domestic* budgetary problem (May, 1982, p. 69). All the contributions are paid from the Federal Budget; no contributions come from the *Länder* budgets which form an important tier in West German public finance (Knott, 1981). The result of this federal dimension is that the Bonn Finance Ministry has restricted scope for filling the budgetary 'hole'. Only limited forms of taxation benefit the

Federal Budget alone; many are divided between the two tiers of government and therefore offer no solution to the imbalance. There have been attempts to introduce some equalization mechanism, so that the *Länder* contribute to the EC, but these have been unsuccessful.

One final aspect of the Finance Ministry's attitude towards the EC Budget requires a mention. When the own resources system was introduced for the revenue side of the budget, the Finance Ministry was quick to see an opportunity to introduce more effective control and scrutiny of EC expenditure. The Federal Government was influential in the decision to create a new body for this purpose, the European Court of Auditors. A treaty amendment formally approved the creation of the Court of Auditors, which was set up in 1977 with its location in Luxembourg (Wallace, H., 1980, pp. 101–2). The Finance Ministry's promotion of this body may thus be seen as a parallel policy to its close monitoring of West German contributions to the EC Budget.

Apart from its interests in budgetary policy and monetary co-operation the Finance Ministry has also been responsible for West German policy in fiscal harmonization within the EC. The main steps in this direction came with the introduction of VAT and produced familiar signs of incoherence in government policy. On this occasion there were policy differences within the Finance Ministry (Puchala and Lankowski, 1976; Puchala, 1983, pp. 147–50). However, the most important stages in this policy area occurred in the early 1960s and thus fall outside the scope of this study.

7 *The Common Agricultural Policy*[8]

Agriculture has enjoyed a rather special status in the FRG. Due to a range of historical factors, including the loss of important farming regions with the division of Germany and resultant food shortages, agriculture has secured a privileged position within the West German economy. In the early postwar years protectionist measures were introduced for agriculture and these remained in force until being replaced in the 1960s by the intervention system of the CAP (Averyt, 1977, pp. 7–10; Priebe, 1980). As a result, West German agriculture has been 'excused' from the rigours of the social market economy, thereby creating a somewhat anomalous situation. Following the creation of the CAP this anomaly was transferred to the EC level where the dominant ideology of industrial competition has co-habited with a protectionist regime for agriculture.

The CAP is usually regarded in general terms as part of a trade-off opening wider agricultural markets for France, whilst the FRG gained a larger market for its industrial goods. Here we find another anomaly because the anticipated negative impact upon German agriculture has been quite small. However, for the European taxpayer the costs of the CAP have been large and have generally accounted for more than two-thirds of the EC's annual budget. As the largest net contributor to the budget under the own resources system the FRG has indirectly provided much of the CAP's finance. In addition, the Federal Government has had occasion to make 'adaptation' payments to German farmers through the Federal Budget. One instance of this was in 1984 when farmers were compensated for falling incomes due to the effects of dairy quotas and other policy changes.

Agriculture thus operates according to a completely different set of principles from those applying to industry more generally. And if the Agriculture Ministry is diametrically opposed to the Economics Ministry in terms of economic ideology, it is similarly opposed to the Finance Ministry on the grounds of the CAP's cost. Why has the agricultural sector remained impervious to the economic and financial principles which have been central to other areas of European policy? The answer to this question may be subdivided into two categories; one concerns attitudes towards agriculture, the other concerns the institutional framework of agricultural policy-making.

Popular attitudes have been broadly supportive of the protectionist regime for agriculture. Public opinion poll data indicate that the West Germans do not perceive agricultural surpluses to be at the top of the EC's difficulties (see Chapter 5). This situation is doubtless assisted by unfamiliarity with a more consumer-oriented agricultural policy, such as the deficiency payments system which operated in Britain prior to EC membership. The absence of fundamental opposition to the CAP is further borne out by the lack of substantive party conflict on the subject (see Chapter 6). Even the Greens favour a relatively high-cost agricultural policy, albeit for rather different reasons (including the potential for greater environmental benefits).

The institutional framework is, in our view, of decisive influence. The sectorized nature of policy-making in the Federal Government places the existing policy – and its protagonists in the ministry – in a strong position. The emphasis which the West German governmental system places on expertise in policy-making has a major effect at both the specialist and political levels in the Agriculture Ministry.

The specialist level is dependent upon the information which the farming lobby has at its disposal. As a result close links are inevitable between policy-makers and the *Deutscher Bauernverband* (DBV), the farmers' union. The impact would be different if there were other interested parties which could act as a counterweight to the agricultural lobby. In fact the main critics of the CAP's operation are exporters and wholesalers whose policy-making contacts are not with the Agriculture Ministry and are therefore unimportant (see Chapter 4). The important specialist level of agricultural policy-makers is thus predisposed to supporting the agricultural consensus.

At the political level within the ministry there has been a preponderance of office-holders with pro-agriculture sympathies. The last three ministers have had their political base in Bavaria, the most rural state in the FRG. Herr Höcherl, minister from 1966–9, like the incumbent from 1983 onwards, Herr Kiechle, was from the CSU, the party most positively disposed towards agriculture. If these factors are considered inadequate as suggesting pro-farmer sympathies, there is also the fact that Höcherl and Ertl came from agricultural backgrounds, whilst Kiechle himself is a dairy farmer by occupation.

This situation reflects the premium placed upon special interests and expertise in the career development of West German politicians: a factor reinforced by the dominant role of committees in the work of the Bundestag (Loewenberg, 1966). Its agricultural committee is dominated consistently by parliamentarians with pro-agriculture leanings, primarily farmers (Bulmer, 1987, pp. 196–7). This committee can be relied upon to provide strong support for the Agriculture Ministry and farmers' interests, were they to be challenged by other branches of government. Evidently the politician with merely an interest in agriculture – as distinct from a *vested* interest – is a rare breed: both in the FRG and in the EC as a whole.

The features outlined above have led to a situation where the ministry and the DBV work in close co-operation. The main intrusion upon this somewhat cosy relationship comes about when another ministry – normally either the Finance Ministry or the chancellor himself – seeks to influence agricultural expenditure. However, there are strong defences against circumstances such as these. The principle of ministerial autonomy represents an important obstacle to challenging existing policy without full Cabinet involvement. Moreover, the recent agriculture ministers, Höcherl, Ertl and Kiechle, have come from junior government partners (the CSU or FDP) and have introduced elements of intra-coalition bargaining into such a challenge. All these obstacles have rendered attempts at reforming the CAP highly problematic at the *domestic* level, i.e. before the complexities of negotiating with other EC governments have been addressed. Even the efforts of Chancellor Schmidt to press for CAP reform were unsuccessful despite his political authority and his ability to 'take on' other policy-makers in specialist debate.

The impact of these institutional features upon German attitudes towards the CAP has been to ensure considerable continuity. German farmers have been strongly defended at the domestic and EC levels, such as in the annual CAP price review. This is not to say that the DBV is entirely satisfied with the farmers' lot; it has consistently seen room for improvement (see Chapter 4). The defence of agricultural interests can be seen in two short examples in the period from 1969.[9]

The Mansholt Plan for tackling structural reform of EC agriculture serves as an example from the early period (Bulmer, 1987, Ch. 8). This proposal was launched by the European Commission in 1968 and was inherited by the Social–Liberal coalition when it came to office in 1969. The proposal was a discussion document which envisaged an approximate halving of the agricultural work-force over the decade up to 1980. This labour shake-out would go hand in hand with farm mergers so as to create larger units. In addition there would be various incentives to encourage reductions in labour along with provisions for retraining those affected.

The opposition of German farmers was entirely to be expected because of the fundamental challenge posed by the document. The DBV saw no reason why farmers should be the sacrificial lambs of European integration. The Agriculture Ministry was similarly very critical, although its arguments were less polemic. Existing domestic policy was considered much more attuned to German circumstances, in the ministry's view. Domestic policy had only just been established in a new framework as a 'joint task' (*Gemeinschaftsaufgabe*) shared between the federal ministry, on the one hand, and the *Länder* agriculture ministries, on the other. There was considerable reluctance to change a newly established policy instrument which was just being implemented.

One particular aspect of the Mansholt Plan caused particular concern among German farmers and civil servants alike. This was the idea that farms would have to be of a certain size in order to be eligible for EC aid. There was considerable scepticism about whether these large-scale farms would suit the varying regional conditions in West Germany. Farm holdings in southern

Germany are much smaller than those in the northern states and there is the further phenomenon of part-time farming, especially in Baden Württemberg. Domestic policy had been designed to be reasonably neutral in relation to these regional variations; Mansholt's proposals had not. In addition there was fierce opposition to the plan's support for farm collectivization because of East German connotations. Many had fled to the West to escape such a policy and any variation on the theme of collectivization, however voluntary, was ideologically unacceptable. A final criticism came from the Finance Ministry in the shape of opposition to the expected additional burden of expenditure. The Agriculture Ministry also adopted this criticism, a development which is rather perverse in view of their later disagreements over the CAP's cost and the need for fundamental reform!

As a result of these criticisms substantial changes were made before Mansholt's proposals were presented in the form of legislative proposals (Rosenthal, 1975, p. 84). There were also many changes brought about by criticism from other member states (Rosenthal, 1975), and those measures eventually agreed on in March 1972 required very few changes from domestic measures already implemented by Agriculture Minister Ertl (Bulmer, 1987, p. 364). The ministry and the DBV had resisted another challenge.

Our second brief example relates to two interrelated measures agreed upon in 1984. One involved the introduction of dairy quotas to the EC as a whole. The other involved dismantling the FRG's positive Monetary Compensatory Amounts (MCAs).

Dairy quotas were agreed upon by the Council of Ministers in March 1984 and involved reductions in milk production for most member states from the accounting year 1984/85. For West Germany the reduction against 1983/84 was to be 6.7 per cent rising to 7.6 per cent in following years (von Urff, 1985, pp. 99–101). Targets were set domestically for each farm so that there was some scope for making the reductions less severe for small farms. However, any farm overshooting its quota would be heavily penalized. This measure, combined with price restraint, caused major problems for German farmers (as well as others in the EC). Indeed, the issue assumed major importance in the June 1984 election to the European Parliament, with the agriculture minister coming under especial pressure from Bavarian farmers (Bulmer and Paterson, 1986).

Under circumstances of price restraint the West German Agriculture Ministry has often been able to alleviate the impact upon farmers' incomes by manipulation of Monetary Compensatory Amounts. MCAs were first introduced in 1969 when devaluation of the French Franc and revaluation of the DM caused major disruption to the common pricing of the CAP (Strauss, 1983). Although originally intended to be temporary in nature, for some states they had assumed permanency. In the case of the FRG there had been persistent use of positive MCAs, reflecting the wish of the Agriculture Ministry that the green DM should not be revalued to the level of the DM generally. The effect of this was to keep farm incomes in the FRG higher than would otherwise be the case. In addition, it meant that German farmers received an export subsidy on produce sold elsewhere in the EC. The latter effect had been a persistent annoyance to French farmers who saw the Federal Government as giving a competitive advantage to German farmers. Tension over this subject caused the delayed introduction of the EMS (Bulmer, 1983c; Hu, 1981, pp. 47–54).

Following much pressure, the German Agriculture Ministry had had to agree to the phased dismantling of positive MCAs. This decision was reached in principle at the European Council in March 1984 and was confirmed at the Council of Agriculture Ministers later that month. In consequence, German farmers were facing income reductions across the board, but especially fierce ones in the dairy sector. Already at the European Council session Chancellor Kohl had indicated that dismantling of the MCAs would be dependent on other member states and the Commission approving a package of compensatory payments to German farmers of the order of DM 2,000m (Stadlmann, 1985, p. 35).

The campaign mounted by West German farmers against the March 1984 agreements focused upon the forthcoming election to the EP in June. After coming under increasing pressure the Agriculture Ministry decided to increase the compensatory payments to approximately DM 3,000m and to bring their introduction forward from September to July 1984. In order to achieve this the payments had to receive political agreement at the European Council session in Fontainebleau on 25/26 June – only a few days beforehand! Although reluctantly approved, there was some dissent on the grounds of the increased amount involved, as compared to that mentioned in March. As Stadlmann notes (1985, pp. 38–9), Kohl's 'gain' from obtaining approval necessitated concessions on other matters under discussion at the European Council. In particular, he had to agree to the FRG bearing a larger-than-wished share of the cost of the budgetary settlement (see section 6 above). It would appear, therefore, that both decisions were obtained to the cost of the Finance Ministry.

In this section on the CAP we have argued that the Agriculture Ministry has been an especially strong defender of German interests. For many years it resisted the attempted interference in its domain by other ministries and by the chancellor. When, in 1984, the chancellor did become involved, he too became sucked into the defence of farmers' interests at the cost of German taxpayers. The agricultural sector has been able to transform its sectional interests into a vital national interest by taking advantage of the sectorization of West German European policy and by using its political influence. Further evidence of this came in May/June 1985 when the Agriculture Ministry vetoed a proposed cut in EC cereals prices during negotiations in the Council of Ministers.

8 *European political co-operation*

Unlike the policy areas considered thus far, EPC is much more straightforward as far as policy-making is concerned. Negotiations with other governments are on an intergovernmental basis compared to those policy areas discussed above, where the EC Commission is involved (Wallace, W., 1983). Of greater significance is the fact that policy-making within the Federal Government in this area is the exclusive preserve of the Foreign Office. Another distinction of EPC from EC business is the virtual absence of interest group involvement in policy formulation.

At the time of its establishment in the 1970 Luxembourg Report, EPC received considerable support from the Federal Government because of its potential as an 'emancipation factor' (Rummel and Wessels, 1983, pp. 39–40; Regelsberger and Wessels, 1984b, pp. 391–4). Not only was the Federal Republic restricted in its foreign relations by limited contacts with Eastern Europe on account of the unresolved German question, it was also hindered in its Middle Eastern policy by the burden of Nazi atrocities against the Jews. Even more significant was the fact that West Germany was not a member of the United Nations until 1973. That West Germany had become a near 'normal' member by the mid-1970s was the result of several developments, intrinsic to which was the creation of EPC.[10]

Placing relations with the Soviet Union and Eastern Europe on a more regulated footing was the principal development. This was achieved through the FRG's treaties with the East, these being underpinned by parallel developments on a multilateral basis through the Conference on Security and Co-operation in Europe (CSCE). This wider context dampened down potential fears of West German unilateralism both for countries in Eastern Europe and for Western neighbours, especially France.

It must be recalled that Chancellor Brandt's *Ostpolitik* also depended on acceptability within the Federal Republic's other key multilateral foreign policy framework, namely NATO. Ensuring the compatibility of EPC objectives with those of NATO has been a continuing objective of the government due to West German dependence on American security guarantees. Significantly it was during the West German presidency that the foreign ministers agreed on a means of keeping the United States informed of developments within EPC. The agreement was reached during an informal session of the ministers at Gymnich (a castle near Bonn) in April 1974. Similar developments – including an arrangement with Japan – were recorded during the 1983 German presidency (Regelsberger and Wessels, 1985, pp. 93–5).

In recent times the Federal Government has sought to involve security policy in the EPC framework. The rationale for this wish has been the increasing superpower tension of the mid-1980s. Not only does the government wish to keep some kind of limited European 'detente' despite superpower relations, but there has also been a wish to use EPC as a kind of caucus session for European NATO members prior to policy discussions within the Atlantic Alliance as a whole (Regelsberger and Wessels, 1984b, pp. 395–8). Once again we must note that the clearest statement of EPC's potential on security policy came during the 1983 West German presidency. The Solemn Declaration on European Union, agreed by the European Council in June 1983 at Stuttgart, placed some aspects of security policy on the agenda of EPC but not as strongly as desired by the foreign minister, Herr Genscher (Dettke, 1984, p. 434). Due to the sensitivities of other member states, such as Ireland's wish to maintain its neutralism, the German government has failed to achieve its goal thus far.

The Genscher initiative, which later became known as the Genscher-Colombo 'European Act' and culminated in the Solemn Declaration on European Union, reflected continuing strong German interest in EPC. Not only has the policy brought strong achievements for the FRG, but it has created fewer problems. Its non-binding nature is one factor, although the government would like to strengthen this. However, unlike the EC it has no direct budgetary cost to the FRG. The Genscher initiative was thus a means of maintaining the momentum of EPC and European integration without imposing additional financial burdens upon the Federal Budget. Indeed, the Genscher initiative aimed partly to counter the negative (German) press which the EC was obtaining specifically because of the critical voices being heard from the Bonn Finance Ministry. In this sense it neatly combined the Foreign Office's support for the extension of EPC with its custodianship over integration policy.

9 *Integration policy*

In this final section on the Federal Government's role in European policy-making we examine its overall policy towards integration in the period since 1969. In particular we focus on the impact which the loosely co-ordinated policy-making framework has had upon policy content. In the preceding sections we have seen how numerous discrete policy networks exist, emphasizing the sectorized nature of the government's 'European policy style'. How far does such sectorization impede the government's attainment of its medium- and long-term goals?

The Foreign Office is entrusted with formulating the government's integration policy, although the chancellor is also a key actor due to the importance of summit meetings in deciding upon the steps towards integration (Bulmer and Wessels, 1987, Ch. 5). The Foreign Office is prone to enunciate rather positive, rhetorical statements on integration. These may turn out to be untenable once specialist departments, especially the Finance Ministry, produce their assessments. Chancellors Brandt and Kohl have also tended towards rhetoric, while Schmidt preferred specific policy initiatives to sketching grand vistas for European Union.

During the Brandt–Scheel governments of 1969–74 integration policy placed particular emphasis on supranationalism. This was reflected in support for an 'own resources' budget and calls for direct elections to the EP. With the benefit of hindsight Brandt's support for British membership of the EC appears to contradict the goal of supranationalism but was one means of unblocking the stalemate which had developed in integration during the mid-1960s. Support for a European Union by the 1980s was underlined by the Federal Government's commitment to an Economic and Monetary Union. Nevertheless, implementation of that objective proved to be much more conditional, once the mechanics of EMU came under discussion.

Support for supranationalism becomes extremely cautious

where positive integration in EC policy areas is concerned. Brandt's wish for an ambitious social policy programme, as put forward at the 1972 Paris summit, was symptomatic of this. As with other proposals, for instance the regional policy (see Chapter 9), the Federal Government would be the main contributor to the extra budgetary provision required. In consequence, converting a broad political commitment into specific action became a tortuous process due to conditions attached by the Finance Ministry and other 'technical ministries'. The original political commitment was made dependent on other policy developments, such as on the second phase of EMU or on the creation of an EC energy policy. To the annoyance of some partner governments the member state with the most powerful support for integration proved to be the state with the most detailed stipulations for agreeing new policies. Among the West German public this policy incoherence had a somewhat negative effect. Pro-integration rhetoric built up public expectations which were then dashed by slow progress due to the defence of German interests.

During the Schmidt–Genscher governments of 1974–82 the contradictions of European policy were less pronounced but present none the less. The main change derived from Schmidt's unwillingness to contemplate the overall strategy of European integration. His criticisms of the Commission, the key supranational agency, were paralleled by support for more pragmatic developments.

> Let the realists who know what they are talking about look after Europe, and spare us the opinions of people who could not even run a tram company for more than two years without making a loss. (Schmidt at a 'background briefing', 23 October 1975, cited by Carr, 1985, p. 96)

Typical of this realism was his strong support for regular summit meetings (the European Council) and enhanced monetary co-operation through the EMS. Both these measures were achieved on the basis of the Franco-German friendship, which was a very important foundation for Schmidt's European policy. To be sure, there was still support for supranationalism, such as in governmental pressure for agreement to hold direct elections to the EP and in the Foreign Office's broad endorsement of the 1975 Tindemans Report on European Union. These causes were associated more with Foreign Minister Genscher than with the chancellor.

Although the creation of the EMS demonstrated the *possibilities* of chancellorial authority for promoting European initiatives, its *limits* were reflected in the inability to contain agricultural expenditure through CAP reform. Schmidt proved unable to translate his criticism of the CAP and of the budgetary burden into decisive action because of the resistance of the Agriculture Ministry. Conscious of the impact which the debate (led by SPD ministers) concerning the CAP and the budget was having upon public opinion, foreign minister Genscher launched his initiative on European Union. His initiative was able to give the FDP an electoral profile, give the EC a more positive public image, whilst extending integration/co-operation in the financially neutral foreign policy domain. In fact the initiative was only to bear fruit after the 1982 change of government.

The new Centre–Right government under Chancellor Kohl assumed office with a commitment to continuity, which was reflected in the retention of Herr Genscher as foreign minister. However, continuity has also been reflected in the persistence of divergent or even contradictory policies within the government. For instance Kohl reintroduced the fashion of rhetorical Europeanism as early as 13 October 1982, when he committed the government 'to opening new routes to European unification' (quoted in Kramer, 1983, p. 312). One important reason behind the collapse of the Social–Liberal coalition had been disagreement over the need for cuts in the Federal Budget and the form they should take. With the new government's commitment to reduce the federal budgetary deficit there were clear limits to the scope for new forms of integration. Agreement to the Iberian enlargement of the EC thus became contingent upon no additional financial burden being placed on the FRG. This position became a component of the government's policy despite unanimous support for enlargement on political grounds. Recalling the benefits European integration had brought to the emergent West German democracy, the established political parties based their support on the similar benefits envisaged for the Iberian democracies in the late 1980s. And, given the economic competitiveness of German industry, it was scarcely conceivable that the Federal Republic could lose from enlargement.

During the first six months of 1983, the presidency of the Council of Ministers was entrusted to the Federal Government. An opportunity was thus available for the Centre–Right coalition to demonstrate its new commitment to integration. Genscher presented five goals for the presidency in an address to the EP in January 1983: agreement on the Genscher–Colombo 'European Act'; the fight against unemployment; extension of the internal market; completion of the southern enlargement of the EC; and resolution of the budgetary problem (Ungerer, 1983). This was an ambitious programme in view of West German elections taking place in March and so it proved when the balance sheet was drawn. Although progress had been recorded on all objectives only the first goal had been achieved. Even so, the Solemn Declaration on European Union was rather watered down compared to the original proposals.

In the period following the German presidency agriculture has emerged as the main obstacle to the government's European policy. We have outlined above how dairy quotas and the phased dismantling of MCAs led to the introduction of national policy measures which are a challenge to the CAP. During 1985 agriculture became even more of a challenge. Kohl's wish to present a positive pro-integration package to the June 1985 Milan European Council was seriously undermined by agriculture minister Kiechle making West Germany's first full use of the veto on the question of cereals price reductions. It became clear that support for increased use of majority voting was shared only by the chancellor and the Foreign Office. The ministries with responsibility for finance and agriculture – and perhaps others – were in favour of retention of unanimity. As a result of this division of views, the government's most noticeable contribution to the European Union debate was limited to a Franco-German draft treaty on EPC.

Another persistent weakness in German integration policy has been the low calibre of the government's nominees as EC commissioners. This was again a problem in 1984 in the preparations for the change of Commission personnel in 1985 (Kramer, 1985, pp. 322–3). Attempts to secure the presidency of the new commission for a German proved unsuccessful on two grounds. First, no suitable candidate emerged until rather late in the day. Secondly, once the CDU politician Biedenkopf had been decided upon, the government was hampered in pushing his credentials at the June 1984 summit meeting by lack of support from other governments and by a preoccupation with securing the European Council's approval of compensatory payments to German farmers (Stadlmann, 1985, p. 38). The CSU's wish to have their own appointee to replace the CDU's Karl-Heinz Narjes contributed to weakening the latter's authority upon re-appointment. The SPD's nominee, Alois Pfeiffer, came from a similarly uninspiring trade union background to that of his predecessor, Herr Haferkamp.

The integration policy of the Centre–Right government has

begun to come under fire for its failure to translate pro-integration rhetoric into policy action. The stout defence of West German farmers' interests, threats of unilateral action on emission control (environmental policy) and the poor calibre of German commissioners have been viewed as weak achievements from a government with the objective of giving new impulses to European integration. Disagreements between ministries on European policy have further compounded the dissatisfaction. For instance, the disagreement between the hawkish Finance Ministry and the more flexible Foreign Ministry over defining the principle of 'financial discipline' in the post-Fontainebleau period aroused public attention (*The Times*, 3 October 1984).

This chapter has sought to demonstrate that such developments are not new but have existed since the EEC's establishment. They are a by-product of the constitutional structure of the FRG and of its 'procedural code' in policy-making. *Control* of the symptoms of policy incoherence is all that is possible; their *prevention* would necessitate constitutional reform. As will be seen in the succeeding chapters, other policy-making actors follow the Federal Government's European policy style. In the case of interest groups, to be examined next, they strongly reinforce the tendency towards policy-making at the specialist level. As a result of the close co-operation achieved between the government and interest groups, the tendency towards a 'house' policy, specific to an individual ministry, is strongly reinforced.

Notes

1 The broader significance of the '*Cassis de Dijon* case' is contained in Welch, 1983.

2 All these cases are abstracted from Fendel, 1981, *passim*. Conclusions of the presidency are drawn up by the Foreign Office.

3 The following case study is based partly on material collected by Paterson in West Germany in 1982. It is also very much indebted to the analysis in Thomas Grunert, 'Decision-Making Processes in the Steel Crisis Policy of the EEC – neo-corporatist or integrationist tendencies'. The version made available to Paterson was a preliminary draft for Mény and Wright (1985) on the EC and steel policy. Although we cover much the same ground, our perspectives are different. Dr Grunert is basically interested in looking at the crisis for what it indicates about the EC's role, whereas we are interested in the light thrown on the behaviour of West German policy-makers.

4 'Memorandum der deutschen Delegation zur EG-Strukturpolitik in der gewerblichen Wirtschaft', EC Council of Ministers R/1068/78, 3 May 1978, cited in Kohler, 1980.

5 The Economics Ministry was also involved in the negotiations regarding EMU because of the economic component in that initiative.
6 These positions are summarized from May, 1984, pp. 376–8.
7 Technically these are not 'contributions' to the EC Budget because, under Community law, the revenue is *automatically* the EC's 'own resources'.
8 The CAP is also considered in connection with party politics in Chapter 6.
9 On the integration of West German agriculture into the CAP during the 1960s see Ackermann, 1970.
10 For more extended discussion of EPC's benefits for the FRG, see Rummel, 1980, Rummel and Wessels, 1983 and Regelsberger and Wessels, 1984b.

4 *Interests, Interest Groups and European Policy*

In the previous chapter we examined at some length the Federal Government's policy in the European Community and in foreign policy co-operation, focusing on the period since 1969. The reason for concentrating in the first instance on the policy of the Bonn government was that, internal contradictions notwithstanding, it is the most articulate and immediately recognizable voice of West German interests in the Community. However, we emphatically do not wish to give the impression that the Bonn government's policy is an independent variable. It may have some dynamics of its own, such as that stemming from its sectorized organization, but policy content is, by and large, the result of interest aggregation. In broad terms the Federal Government's policy should be a reflection of West German interests.

In this chapter we first examine what West German interests are with regard to the EC and what are the important sectors of economic activity. We then consider the role of organized interests – that is, interest groups – in connection with European policy. Are there any common themes in interest group activities towards the EC? In order to avoid too many generalizations the activities of several interest groups are examined. Particular attention is paid to the 'targets' of interest group lobbying on European policy. We argue that interest groups tend to treat the substance of EC policy within their organizations as if it were domestic policy. They therefore follow the pattern already identified within the Federal Government. The effect of this is to keep open those channels of interest group–government relations which are already well proven, especially for industrial interests. The impact is also one of strengthening a sectoral explanation of West German European policy.

West German interests

What are West German interests? In order to answer this question we need to examine postwar economic development with a view to identifying the key principles of economic policy and key sectors of the economy. Four periods of economic development have been identified by Hennings (1982). Each phase provides pieces of a jigsaw representing West German interests.

The first period, covering the years 1945–50, laid the foundations of the West German economy. Initially, economic reconstruction was very fragmented and localized. It was established on a much sounder footing and as an integral part of a broader framework by means of three key developments in 1948: the inauguration of Marshall aid, the currency reform and some dismantling of wartime price controls. The creation of the Federal Republic in 1949 provided further unifying logic to the process of reconstruction. Taken together, the four developments have set important guidelines for subsequent economic evolution. It was to be on the basis of integration into the Western economy; the economy would be predominantly privately owned; industrial interests would be strongly taken into account; and combating inflation would be the priority objective of economic policy. All these factors have been seen to have had an impact upon the Federal Government's European policy.

During the second period – the 1950s – the West German economy built upon this foundation with a decade of rapid, export-led growth. Over the period the average rate of growth in Gross Domestic Product (GDP) was some 8 per cent per annum. This economic 'miracle' was based upon an abundant labour supply (including some 2.5 million refugees from the East), on an undervalued *Deutsche Mark* and on a foreign economic policy which 'has been consistent in its design to develop and expand export markets for German industry' (Kreile, 1978, p. 193). It is sometimes overlooked that important parts of industry escaped wartime destruction. One commentator has put the level of destruction and dismantlement of industrial capacity as low as one quarter (Lawrence, 1980, p. 15). A further contributory factor to economic growth was the high rate of industrial investment: partly a product of governmental policy.

The 1960s represented a period of some 'normalization'. Average growth in GDP declined to just under 5 per cent per annum and the economy became noticeably subject to cyclical fluctuations. Even so, the balance of trade remained in surplus, partly because of the continued undervaluation of the DM; exports continued to contribute an increasing share of GDP. The emergence of a cyclical pattern to West German economic activity led to the 1967 Stability and Growth Act, which was an attempt to provide the policy instruments to counteract this pattern through demand management (Smith, 1983, pp. 110–11). Linked to the new policy instruments was the creation of the Concerted Action framework (*Konzertierte Aktion*), bringing together both sides of industry, representatives of government and the Federal Bank. Although wage restraint on the part of the quiescent labour force continued to make an important contribution – along with low inflation – to export growth, the trade unions became more assertive at the end of the decade. Pressure built up for more equitable income distribution and increased social policy provision. Dissatisfaction that incomes had not risen in line with increases in profitability led to some wildcat strikes in 1969. Some steps were taken in this direction by the new Social–Liberal coalition, which took office in 1969.

The fourth period is that from 1970 onwards. It has been characterized by low economic growth, increased unemployment and a higher rate of inflation (although still low by comparison with that in other EC economies). The high level of foreign trade dependency has exposed the West German economy to the international recession engendered by two oil shocks. This became particularly evident at the end of the decade when the balance of payments moved into deficit for the years 1979–81. The West German economy remains relatively strong in European terms but, like the EC as a whole, is falling behind Japan and the United States in the high technology sectors of the third industrial revolution. Its ability to derive international competitiveness from an undervalued currency declined from the beginning of the 1970s with the demise of the postwar system of fixed exchange rates.

The overall picture of postwar economic development (summarized in Table 4.1) is one of export-led growth which was at its peak in the 1950s but stagnated in the 1970s. The main period of economic growth was strongly linked with economic integration in Western Europe. The establishment of the ECSC and the EEC provided important growth in the FRG's markets. Nevertheless, amongst the EC economies, it is West German industry which is the most effective competition for Japan and the United States in non-EC markets (Deubner, 1984b, pp. 531–5). This is the main reason why the Federal Government, unlike its French counterpart, has been unwilling to contemplate increased protectionism around the EC as a whole. With the European economies in recession, it would be against the interests of West German export industries to risk retaliation in potential growth markets by so-called Europrotectionism. Another reason for supporting

Table 4.1 *West German economic performance since 1950 (average annual percentage increases)*

	GNRP[2]	Industrial production	Exports of goods and services
1951–60[1]	8.0	9.6	16.7
1961–70	4.7	5.4	7.8
1971–80	2.9	2.2	6.1

Notes: 1 Data for 1951–60 exclude Saarland and West Berlin.
2 Gross National Real Product.
Source: All data based on calculations of Smith, 1983, pp. 33–4.

Table 4.2 *Structure of West German exports and imports, 1958 and 1984 (as percentage of total)*

Destination/origin	*Exports*		*Imports*	
	1958	*1984*	*1958*	*1984*
Belgium, Luxembourg	6.6	7.0	4.5	7.1
Denmark	3.0	2.1	3.4	1.7
Greece	1.4	1.0	1.7	0.7
France	7.6	12.6	7.6	10.6
Ireland	0.3	0.4	0.1	0.6
Italy	5.0	7.7	5.5	7.8
Netherlands	8.1	8.5	8.0	14.1
United Kingdom	4.0	8.3	4.4	7.4
Total EC	35.9	47.7	35.2	50.0
Other European OECD countries	23.7	19.2	15.8	16.2
USA	7.3	9.6	13.6	6.6
Canada	1.2	0.9	3.1	0.9
Japan	1.0	1.4	0.6	4.0
Australia	1.0	0.8	1.2	0.4
Developing countries	22.3	13.8	24.4	15.2
Centrally-planned economies	5.0	4.8	5.3	5.9
Rest of world/unspecified	2.6	1.8	0.8	0.8
Total	100	100	100	100

Source: *European Economy*, November 1985, no. 26, p. 178.

liberalized international trade is the FRG's dependence on suppliers outside the EC for raw materials which are vital to its manufacturing industry (Pfetsch, 1981).

West Germany's trading partners are quantified in Table 4.2. This shows that its main export markets are the advanced industrial economies of the West, with the EC representing a vital part of this.

Towards a sectoral definition of German 'interests'

Which sectors of the economy have provided the main foundations for export-led growth? In general terms it has been manufacturing industry which has been vital and, within this category, the capital goods industries in particular (see Table 4.3). The traditional heavy industries, such as mining, have been of less importance. Of still less significance has been agriculture; the division of Germany left the main agricultural regions in the East. There has been further decline over the postwar period so that agriculture now represents only some 3 per cent of GDP.

These are among the most pronounced sectoral differences within the West German economy but there are many more. In an important article Deubner (1984b) has examined the unequal sectoral dynamics of industrial expansion in some depth. He has argued that the West German economy is relatively 'over-industrialized'. The share of the work-force engaged in industry – in 1982, 43.5 per cent – is significantly higher than in comparable economies (Deubner, 1984b, p. 505). 'Statistics . . . show a total export dependence of about 41 per cent for industrial production in general and more than 50 per cent for many industrial sectors' (p. 506). Apart from the capital goods industries (especially electrical and non-electrical machinery and automobiles), the chemical industry has been an important export-dependent sector (Schlupp, 1980, p. 59). Figures for the period 1978–81 indicate that these and other sectors have continued to expand, while others, such as clothing and textiles, have stagnated or even shrunk.

West German membership of the EC has been an important platform for the development of export-led growth. The development of a common market in industrial goods has been of most significance in this context. Nevertheless, the EC has caused some sectoral differentiation in its impact upon various branches of the West German economy. Of greatest importance here has been the disproportionate role of agriculture in EC legislative

Table 4.3 *Sectoral shares in West German Gross Domestic Product 1950–74 (average annual percentages in real terms)*

Sector	*1950–9*	*1960–9*	*1970–4*
Agriculture and forestry	8.3	4.8	3.9
Industry (total)	49.5	55.2	57.1
including			
energy/mining	5.4	4.4	4.2
manufacturing	37.4	43.1	45.6

Source: Data cited by Schlupp, 1980, p. 56.

activity as a whole. Between 1950 and 1979 the full-time agricultural labour force in the FRG declined from some 3.9 million to about 1.1 million. This decline in the economic importance of agriculture has been arrested politically by the dynamics of the European Community, which have made that sector central to positive integration. Furthermore, the sectorized nature of the Bonn government has provided farmers with an authoritative 'advocate' at the highest level of policy-making (see Chapters 2 and 3). In this instance economic decline has not been translated into a decline in political importance.

EC membership has also underlined some existing sectoral tendencies in the FRG. For example, there has been a tendency in some West German industries to use cartel arrangements. In the previous chapter we saw how quasi-cartellization has been employed by steel producers in order to try to manage market shares in rolled steel. It has been argued that such arrangements are a function of the high level of concentration present in the steel sector (and in a few other industries) being transformed into influence upon governmental agencies (Deubner, 1984b, p. 517). The fact that the Federal Cartel Office tolerated the quasi-cartellization of the steel agencies (*Kontore*) might be presented as supporting evidence for this view in the context of European policy.

More recently, the use of crisis cartels to attempt to solve the corporate crises associated with a series of steel producers was actively encouraged by both federal and *Länder* governments. This took place initially in the Saar (1978), then in the Ruhr (1982–3) and again in the Saar (1983) (Esser and Fach with Dyson, 1983). Although these decisions were taken essentially at the domestic level, the EC was closely related, given that the surplus in steel-making capacity was a Community-wide phenomenon. The EC's extensive powers in the steel sector – due to the more dirigiste regime of the ECSC – also made the supranational level important (Wilks and Dyson, 1983, pp. 22–4). Individual rescue plans required the Commission's consent but this was highly likely in the case of the crisis cartels because all the interested parties – the federal and/or state governments, the company, trade unions and the banks – had formed a kind of 'pact of steel' which the EC Commission could scarcely resist.

The organization of West German trade unions along broad industry lines is another potential support for sectoral differentiation in economic interests. Again Deubner offers important evidence. He argues that 'the two biggest and in effect dominant trade unions, the metalworkers and the chemical workers, see themselves as active participants in modernizing industry and in increasing international competitiveness if need be at the expense of jobs in backward sectors or subsectors' (Deubner, 1984b, p. 508). Nevertheless, it is not just these two large trade unions which are able to reinforce sectoral differences in economic policy-making. The trade union responsible for the textile and clothing sectors (*Gewerkschaft Textil – Bekleidung*) was identified in the previous chapter as having joined forces with the clothing and textile industry federations to lobby the Economics Ministry for an extension of the Multi-Fibre Arrangement.This type of pressure could not be brought to bear without a sectorally organized trade union structure. The British model of craft-based trade unionism or the ideologically divided French (or Italian) pattern would be hampered organizationally from operating in this manner.

It can be seen, therefore, that West German interests have a strong sectoral organization. Of especial importance is the fact that this coincides strongly with the sectorization of the Federal Government. Clearly it will be necessary to have a sectoral component in examining the involvement of organized interests in EC policy-making. Which interest groups are to be examined then?

The economic indicators set out earlier in the chapter are taken as the basis for giving extensive attention to business interests, especially those of industry. The organization of business interests in the FRG is intricate (Weber, 1977, pp. 87–105). There are separate central organizations for industrialists, commerce and trade but all these strands come together where employers' interests are concerned. There are also central organizations for small- and medium-sized enterprises (the *Handwerk* system) and, additionally, the chambers of industry and commerce. Of these we have selected the following organizations: the Federation of

German Industry (*Bundesverband der Deutschen Industrie*, BDI); the Confederation of German Employers' Associations (*Bundesvereinigung der Deutschen Arbeitgeberverbände*, BDA); and, from commerce, the Federation of German Wholesale and Foreign Traders (*Bundesverband des Deutschen Gross- und Aussenhandels*, BGA).

These organizations are important as representatives of broad sections of the business community but, for precisely this reason, they are insufficient for gaining an adequate overall picture. We have already argued that the sectoral dimension is of great importance. We will therefore avoid the preoccupation, which characterizes many Anglo-Saxon studies of West German policy-making, with central interest organizations and with the 'Concerted Action' level of tripartism. The sectoral dimension is accommodated by examining the role of the Association of the Chemical Industry (*Verband der Chemischen Industrie*, VCI), which is a member organization of the BDI. The VCI itself has many subsectoral member associations, such as those responsible for the agrochemical and petrochemical industries. Evidence suggests that there are in fact important differences at the subsectoral level with, for example, the agrochemical industry having close relations with the Ministry of Agriculture, while other subsectors of the chemical industry deal primarily with the Economics Ministry and, more reluctantly, with the Interior Ministry on environmental matters (see Chapter 11).[1]

Outside the representation of business interests, attention will be focused on two other groups: the Federation of German Trade Unions (*Deutscher Gewerkschaftsbund*, DGB) and the German Farmers' Union (*Deutscher Bauernverband*, DBV). These two organizations are in a rather paradoxical situation. The DGB represents a large membership of some 7.6 million (1984 figures, *Statistisches Jahrbuch*, 1985) yet plays a comparatively small role in European policy-making. By contrast the DBV, with a membership in 1985 of about 750,000 (same source), has played a major role. An important factor explaining this situation is the balance of policies pursued at the EC level. Almost all areas of agricultural activity are now subject to some measure of EC control. However, the key areas of interest to the trade unions, such as employment and social policy, or collective bargaining, are overwhelmingly under national control. Another explanation is that the DBV has no effective countervailing interest group, whereas both the BDI and BDA are lined up against the DGB. The percentage of farmers organized in the DBV is also much higher than that of the labour force in the DGB.

Several commentators have accorded a high level of importance to the role of the banking sector in explaining the West German economic model. This is a view which has been advanced by Dyson (1982b), for example. The banks are adjudged to play a major role in policy-making at the level of the firm through the idea of the 'house bank': they also have important influence either as direct shareholders or as proxies for small shareholders. According to 1979 figures cited by Deubner (1984b, p. 508), they represented on average more than 62 per cent of the vote at the general meetings of 74 key stock companies. We recognize the importance of the banks in *corporate* decision-making, while noting that there are differences of opinion on their exact significance, especially from sector to sector (Grant *et al.*, 1985). However, because the banks' influence is at the level of the firm, the relationship to European policy-making is rather indirect on general economic issues. An exception to this is in the area of monetary co-operation in the EC. At the time of the establishment of the EMS several interest groups in the banking sector were involved in lobbying the Federal Government. But this activity was not qualitatively different from that of other groups in other policy areas. The importance of the banks is recognized, therefore, but their role is not considered in detail.

What, then, has been the role of these organized interests in the context of West German European policy?

Organized interests and the EC

West German business interests are based upon four pillars of representation (Weber, 1977, p. 87). First, there are those federations representing the interests of various industries. As noted above many of these federations are members of the Federation of German Industry but commerce and trade have separate representation. None of these groups is active in collective bargaining matters or in social policy. Instead there is a second separate pyramid of groups active in this policy area; they come together in the Confederation of German Employers' Associations (BDA). This situation is thus distinctive from the norm in most other EC states, where the two functions are integrated in a single organization.[2] The third pillar of business interests is organized in the German Conference of Chambers of Industry and Commerce (DIHT). The member chambers are organized regionally and, unlike the BDI and BDA, have no sectoral sub-structure. The chambers are responsible for overseeing the implementation of some legislation, for example on vocational training, and therefore have a special legal status. Membership is compulsory for all businesses in the respective locality (Bulmer, 1987, pp. 136–8). The fourth pillar comprises small business enterprises but is not considered here.

The Federation of German Industry (BDI)

West German industrialists have been amongst the foremost supporters of European integration. In the 1950s, however, the situation was not so straightforward. This has been outlined both in the pioneering study of the BDI by Braunthal (1965) and in the recent, more specialized study of Platzer (1984). The official position of the BDI was one of support for the various initiatives on co-operation and integration, including the establishment of the Organization for European Economic Co-operation, the creation of the ECSC and, later, of the EEC and Euratom. In the case of ECSC the broad support of industrialists was based on a variety of often contradictory motives (Braunthal, 1965, p. 318). Braunthal also notes that there was some opposition among steel manufacturers and coal producers who feared competition from France and Belgium. Among the supporters of the ECSC there were those who believed that the High Authority was endowed with too many powers.

By the time of the drafting of the EEC Treaty opposition to integration had virtually disappeared. The BDI welcomed the establishment of the EEC on four key grounds. It was seen as enlarging the market for West German industrial goods; increasing living standards by facilitating a more effective division of labour; boosting the competitiveness of European industry in third markets; and enabling new forms of co-operation between the member states (Platzer, 1984, p. 51). The low level of tariff and quota restrictions already existing for the West German market enabled industrialists to feel reasonably confident about their future in the emergent common market. Nevertheless, the BDI did express some notes of caution. While welcoming the EEC as a less dirigiste framework than that of the ECSC, it noted that some provisions were still open to interpretation; the BDI would have to lobby for market principles in these cases. There was also criticism of the 'little Europe' of the EEC; industrialists preferred a broader market than that offered by the Six. In this respect they were in tune with similar views articulated by economics minister Erhard. Other criticisms concerned the treaty's failure to require economic policy co-ordination amongst the member states; there was also concern about maintaining separate institutions for the ECSC and the EEC (Platzer, 1984, pp. 52–5).

Of the four criticisms it was the wish for a wider Europe which was of greatest importance over the long term. The BDI was concerned about the division of the West European market into two camps: that of the EEC and that of the European Free Trade Association (EFTA), created in 1960.[3] The BDI remained supportive of enlargement from the first British application in 1961 right through to the Mediterranean enlargements of the 1980s.

Although these views may be regarded as functional to the interests of West German industrialists, the BDI has taken a broad view of European integration. It has become part of the West German consensus of support for European integration. For example, in the aftermath of the 1969 summit meeting at The Hague, it favoured the proposals to increase the EP's budgetary powers and to introduce an 'own resources' revenue system for the EC Budget. Neither of these proposals had a direct bearing upon industrialists' interests. Indirectly, these measures would, upon implementation, develop a momentum in integration which could potentially bring West German industrialists more tangible benefits. Thus while the first enlargement brought a wider market to West German industry, other BDI objectives, such as the achievement of an EMU, did not materialize. The BDI has been a consistent supporter of the creation of a completely integrated internal market for industrial goods (BDI, 1984, p. 186): a measure agreed to by the Twelve in the 1986 Single European Act, with a target date of 1992.

Policy-making within the BDI is at quite an abstract level, given the need to aggregate the views of thirty-seven branch associations, which are themselves further subdivided. Although large industrial conglomerates tend to be over-represented in the BDI because they belong simultaneously to several branch associations, public enterprise is of virtually no importance.[4] Small and medium-sized firms within the BDI have sought to put across their own views on EC policies (BDI, 1984, pp. 193–6).

Of all the BDI organs, it is the secretariat, located in Cologne, which plays the main role in EC policy-making (Bulmer, 1987, pp. 119–29). Its work is assisted by various specialized committees. The organization of European policy in the BDI follows a pattern used by many German interest groups; it reflects the thinking behind the Federal Government's own organization. The co-ordination office for European matters oversees general developments but consideration of specific EC initiatives is carried out by subject specialists elsewhere in the secretariat. Originally located in the foreign trade division, the co-ordination office was moved in 1981 to a more central location, directly responsible to the director general. This office performs broadly comparable functions to the Foreign Office on the integration policy of the government. The main distinction is that the BDI's co-ordination office, by virtue of its central location, is able to ensure greater coherence in policy positions. The co-ordinating function comes into play when EC proposals do not conveniently fit into the responsibilities of a single section of the specialist policy areas of the secretariat. The co-ordination office also occasionally conducts special tasks on EC policy. For instance, the office circulated all the branch member organizations in order to gain a picture of attitudes on the proposed second enlargement of the EC. This was then formulated into a BDI position paper which was presented to the hearing held by the Bundestag Foreign Affairs Committee on the subject in May 1978 (BDI, 1978). It is also important to note that the head of the EC co-ordination office is also the BDI's representative in Brussels. He is not only the BDI's listening post there but is also its representative in the Committee of Permanent Delegates in the Union of Industries of the European Community (UNICE). UNICE is the transnational interest group responsible for industrialists' and employers' interests.[5]

Much of the BDI's internal policy-making is geared not only to policy-making in the FRG but also to the transnational level, via UNICE. Opinions are formulated on almost all EC policy areas, including even relatively tangential ones, such as the annual CAP price review (Bulmer, 1987, pp. 121–3). The opinions are formulated in the BDI secretariat's specialist committees of which there are some twenty-five (including sub-committees). As is normal with West German interest groups, there is no special committee for EC affairs; Commission proposals are dispersed amongst existing specialist committees. Many of the opinions developed in this manner are co-ordinated at the transnational level inside UNICE. The importance of UNICE among the various targets of BDI pressure is discussed below.

One problem in internal policy-making concerns reaching agreement between the various branch member organizations of the BDI. There are thirty-seven such organizations and these may also be members of a transnational *sectoral* interest group. Due to the different circumstances within different sectors of industry, this exercise can present significant difficulties.

Problem-solving is usually a matter for the meetings of the thirty-seven branch association director generals, meeting in the BDI. Where a consensus proves impossible, it may be left to a branch association to reflect its minority viewpoint in its own right. It is in this context that the textile and clothing industries' support in 1980 for an extension of the Multi-Fibre Arrangement must be understood. Since the MFA represents 'managed trade', it therefore runs counter to the BDI's policy of supporting free trade.[6]

The Confederation of German Employers' Associations (BDA)

The BDA forms the second pillar of the representation of business interests in the EC. Although it covers a broader constituency than the BDI, by virtue of including commercial interests, the BDA has also been a supporter of European integration (Platzer, 1984, pp. 259–62). However, this support has been more conditional than that of the BDI. Two broad qualifications have been contained in the BDA's support for integration. On the one hand, the BDA has shown the wish that the EC should concentrate on *economic* rather than social policy integration. This position has been expressed even though the former is primarily a matter for the BDI. On the other hand, the BDA has sought to restrict possible interventionism on the part of the EC in the social and employment policy sectors. This reflects a concern about the ideological terms of integration and may therefore be compared with the BDI's concern about the interventionist regime of the ECSC. The BDA's opposition to further integration in the social policy sector derives from a fear that employers would lose out. Precisely for this reason the DGB *has* supported an expansion of the EC's role in this area.

Since the 1950s the main impact of the EC relevant to the BDA has been upon social and employment policy, co-determination, occupational training and social security. The extent of integration achieved by the EC in these areas has in fact been rather limited and this has coincided with the BDA's aims. Thus it has resisted the transfer of any collective bargaining responsibilities to the EC level. It was reluctant to endorse the efforts at EC-wide tripartite concertation in the 1970s. It has also been dubious about harmonizing national conditions concerning labour market and social policy matters for fear that this might affect the FRG's competitive position in the EC market place. In all these areas the BDA has been willing to countenance policy co-ordination but no levelling or equalization of national legislation.

The BDA's organization of European policy is conducted in a slightly different way from the normal practice amongst West German interest groups. European policy is not dispersed throughout the secretariat's work. Instead it is located in the international social policy division. The reason for this is that the EC's responsibilities run parallel to similar work carried out by the International Labour Organization in Geneva and by the OECD in Paris. Policy-making is largely a matter for the international division (one of eleven); it is assisted by about twenty specialist committees, including the 'Committee for Social Policy in the EC' (Bulmer, 1987, p. 129).

Apart from organizational differences, the BDA has other distinctions from the BDI. For example, there are no major policy divisions between branch member organizations on EC policy. This is because the EC's activity has a broadly similar effect on each of the forty-seven branch associations. Another difference is that the BDA does not have a liaison office in Brussels. However, like the BDI, it places strong emphasis upon the work of UNICE (see below).

The Federation of German Wholesale and Foreign Traders (BGA)

The BGA is an important interest organization in the Federal Republic due to the economy's export orientation. In terms of its position as a representation of the business community, it occupies a similar place to the BDI. Although it represents a narrower economic activity, the BGA has none the less no fewer than seventy-one member branch associations (BGA, 1979).

The BGA's philosophy has three pillars: the social market economy, European integration and liberal trade. EC business is thus at the heart of its activities. Like the BDI, the BGA is a fervent advocate of trade liberalization. In some ways it adopts a more aggressive policy than the BDI in this area. For example, in 1978 it published documentation showing examples of protectionism actually permitted by the EC and combined this with a press conference at which such practices were strongly criticized (BGA, 1978). Another area where the BGA has pursued an aggressive policy is on the 'costly' CAP which 'threatens to block the progress of European unification' (BGA, 1979, p. 49). The BGA has criticized many protectionist aspects of the CAP from milk marketing boards in the United Kingdom (for their monopolist role) to the subsidized sale of EC agricultural surpluses (for undermining free trade in the world market). By virtue of these and other views, the BGA acts as a kind of free market ginger group in EC policy-making in the FRG. The effectiveness of this lobbying will be examined below.

As regards internal policy-making, the BGA follows the general pattern of treating EC issues no differently from other business. The main location for EC policy-making is within the BGA's secretariat which has nine separate divisions, assisted by sixteen committees. The Foreign Trade Division has overall responsibility for EC policy but most business is dealt with according to subject matter. Like the other interest groups, the BGA is a member of a transnational organization. Until 1979 this was the Committee of Commercial Organizations of the EC (COCCEE). However, this body was found to cover too many disparate interests and this led to the creation of the Federation of European Wholesale and International Trade Associations (FEWITA). It is through this body that the BGA has had access to the EC Commission since 1979.

The Association of the Chemical Industry (VCI)

The last of the business groups to be considered is the VCI, one of the branch associations of the BDI. During the postwar period the West German chemical industry has expanded its already important position in the economy. This has been achieved through an increasing export orientation. With 46 per cent of its production exported in 1981, the FRG is the largest chemical exporting nation in the world. Of these exports 46.3 per cent were destined for EC markets (VCI figures). The industry is dominated by three giant concerns: Bayer, BASF and Hoechst. This domination also applies to the VCI but less to its thirty-one subsectoral branch organizations (Grant *et al.*, 1985).

The VCI's involvement in EC affairs revolves around several themes (Platzer, 1984, pp. 201–2; Lange, 1983, pp. 8–9). There is a general concern with the Community on account of its importance as a market place and as an actor in international trade matters generally. The VCI lobbies for free trade and pays especial attention to cases where non-EC chemical products are dumped at below their normal price in an EC market. The European Council of Chemical Industry Federations (CEFIC), the transnational interest group of which the VCI is a member, has been the body most frequently requesting the Commission to take anti-dumping measures (Lange, 1983, p. 9).[7]

A particular concern for the VCI in recent years has been the pressure for greater environmental protection in the FRG. This has caused the VCI concern that higher domestic anti-pollution standards might penalize the industry's competitiveness with its EC counterparts (see also Chapter 11).

The common ground for all these interest groups regarding policy content has been their support for the use of the FRG's social market principles in EC policy,. With the exception of the BDA (due to its lack of direct interest in the subject), all the interest groups are particularly involved in upholding liberal trading principles, both within the EC and in its (external) commercial policy. Even in crisis sectors, such as textiles, there is a recognition that derogations from liberal trade, for example through the Multi-Fibre Arrangement, should be of temporary duration. This was a view expressed by the director general of the West German textile industry association.[8] The steep decline in textile production in the FRG, which has become the largest textile import market in the world, has not modified this commitment. According to this sector managed trade through the MFA is better than the alternative, namely a protectionist free-for-all.

It can be seen that business and industry are highly organized on EC matters. Apart from having these interest groups to represent them, some of the major concerns have contacts of their own with the Federal Government. Another noticeable fact is that most West German industrialists refer to the EC as the domestic market. This is an indication of their absorption of the European market into their business routine. Many businessmen are also active in the West German European movement.

The Federation of German Trade Unions (DGB)

The DGB is the central trade union organization in the FRG. It has the task of counterbalancing both the BDI and BDA. Like other economic interest groups it has been a supporter of European integration, having adopted this position before the SPD, with which it has close relations, revoked its early opposition (Paterson, 1974a, p. 115; DGB, 1978). Nevertheless, the DGB's support is not so enthusiastic as that of the interest groups examined above. This is because of the concern that trade union interests have been neglected in the EC's policy balance. Such criticism has been voiced by the DGB, for example at the 1978 Congress, where the low priority given by the EC to alleviating unemployment came under fire (DGB, 1978, p. 29).

Attempts to shift the policy balance have had limited effect.

One key problem until 1973 was the lack of a united European trade union interest group. The DGB was arguably the keenest supporter of the establishment of this body, the European Trade Union Confederation (ETUC). However, the DGB was firmly opposed to admitting the French communist trade union as an ETUC member. Divisions within the labour movement (and within the ETUC) have impeded the European policy of the DGB, which is amongst the most integrationist of all ETUC member organizations. The DGB was very active in supporting the so-called Vredeling proposal, aimed at enabling the local labour force of foreign multinational companies to gain better access to information.

Day-to-day responsibility for EC policy within the DGB secretariat is held by the international division but much of the work is dispersed around its twenty-two specialist divisions.

The German Farmers' Union (DBV)

The DBV is the voice of West German farmers' interests and, like the DGB, sits at the top of both regional and branch organizations. The CAP permeates all agricultural activity and, in consequence, all the DBV's work. As with other interest groups, the majority of work is based on the secretariat, which is in Bonn. This has a co-ordinating office for EC matters but virtually all Community business is dispersed to specialist divisions.

The DBV's attitude towards the EC was strongly influenced by the early moves in establishing the CAP. The decisions in 1964 to reduce cereals prices in the FRG as part of creating a common pricing structure led to the DBV's adoption of a highly sceptical view of integration (Ackermann, 1970). Having previously relied upon CDU and CSU support (in return for votes), some in the DBV began to seek help elsewhere, including shortlived links with the Neo-Nazis (*Der Spiegel*, 13 February 1967, p. 22). Gradually the DBV began to become less critical of the CAP as ways of manipulating its mechanisms to the benefit of the membership became evident. This change in behaviour occurred in 1969 with the end of Edmund Rehwinkel's tenure as a charismatic president (Averyt, 1977, p. 12). It also coincided with the end of CDU/CSU participation in the Bonn coalition.

During the Social–Liberal coalition (1969–82) the DBV held a reasonably positive view of the CAP but with some exceptions. Most notable was the debate following commissioner Mansholt's 1968 plan to restructure agriculture into an efficient and less labour-intensive industry. It met with considerable criticism in the FRG (Bulmer, 1987, Ch. 8). Some analysts have sought to explain the DBV's more positive role in terms of its success in influencing the FDP agriculture minister, Herr Ertl, but we reject this as an over-simplified view (see Chapter 6).

From 1984 onwards West German farmers have again come under threat due to the effects of (limited) reforms of the CAP. The introduction of dairy quotas (1984), reductions in cereals prices (1985) and a commitment to dismantle MCAs have caused great concern to both the DBV and the agriculture minister. This has once more placed farmers' interests at the centre of EC policy-making (see Chapter 11).

Like the other interest groups, the DBV belongs to a transnational group, the Committee of Professional Agricultural Organizations (COPA). Due to the extent of the EC's influence on agricultural policy, COPA has developed into one of the most important transnational groups in the EC (Burkhardt-Reich and Schumann, 1983).

Influencing European policy

The previous sections of this chapter involved identifying West German interests, establishing how some of them are organized and examining their attitudes towards the EC. This final section assesses which channels are used in order to put such views across. We will also consider whether some groups have better access to the decision-making process than others and what the overall effect is upon governmental policy.

1 *The transnational level*

All the interest groups examined above are members of transnational interest groups. What functions can this transnational level perform for West German interests? Normally two broad roles are performed (Butt Philip, 1985, pp. 27–41).

The first function is that of acting as a listening post in Brussels. As the Commission is the official initiator of EC policy, it is vital for national interest groups to anticipate the Commission's legislative plans. This function is especially important for smaller national groups which cannot afford the luxury, enjoyed by the BDI, of a permanent representative in Brussels. This is a *passive* role for a transnational group. In other words no authority is transferred to the transnational level by member national interest groups but the latter are better informed for domestic lobbying of national ministers.

The second function is that of representing member organizations to the EC institutions. This function is encouraged by the Commission, which prefers to deal with recognized transnational groups rather than with (the much more numerous) national ones. In this function transnational interest groups have a potentially *active* role in EC policy-making. Exactly how actively this role is performed varies from case to case depending on how a number of problems are resolved.

A first problem is the long line of communications which may exist between the transnational group and the actual membership. This is especially the case with UNICE because neither it nor the two West German member organizations, the BDI and BDA, have direct company membership. This means that UNICE views may be very abstract. In this sense transnational *industry* groups, such as CEFIC for the chemical industry, offer a more direct link. Another problem, applicable to the ETUC, is the presence of members from European countries not in the EC. This has the effect of blurring the organization's image. A third problem concerns internal decision-making within the transnational group. Where unanimity is required,the transnational group may not be able even to formulate a view to lobby the Commission with. In the case of UNICE and FEWITA majority voting is possible but minority views must be recorded and presented alongside the majority opinion. This creates a strong tendency towards the practice of unanimity, thereby making opinions thus formulated rather vague. COPA and the ETUC follow qualified majority voting. A fourth problem concerns the size of the transnational group's budget and secretariat. If this level of interest articulation is to be effective, it needs to be endowed with adequate resources. The vast majority of the 500 or so groups have very small budgets and even COPA or the ETUC has an annual budget of less than £1 million (Butt Philip, 1985, p. 36). According to Butt Philip only five transnational groups have a staff of more than ten people. UNICE, COPA and the ETUC are among these – as is CEFIC, which has a larger secretariat than UNICE (Platzer, 1984, p. 205).

All these problems place significant limitations on the utility of transnational interest groups for actively representing West German interest groups, even though the latter are among the most committed to using that level of action. This commitment derives from the general support for integration on the part of German interest groups and their familiarity, through their own federal structures, with multi-tiered operations. In any case, the transnational level of operation is only really effective at the early stages of EC policy-making. Once the Commission has presented its proposals, the national level becomes of vital importance due to the significance of the Council of Ministers as the EC's key decision-making institution. Lobbying the EP and the Economic and Social Committee are usually either supportive background measures, or steps taken in desperation.

2 *The national level*

One of the common features found in the above case studies of West German interest groups' activities on European policy was the tendency to treat EC matters in the same way as domestic ones. EC co-ordination offices were not involved in substantive policy formation but acted as a kind of sorting office within the federal secretariat, as well as co-ordinating with the relevant transnational group. The specialization by policy area within interest groups has helped minimize the need for costly reorganization measures to cope with EC membership. In the context of interest groups' primary goal of putting forward members' views, the most significant effect of this has been to retain pre-existing contacts with government and other policy-making bodies. This has been further reinforced by precisely the same organizational pattern being adopted within the government's own structure. The impact of this is to reinforce the already dense network of relations between government and interest groups that characterizes West German policy-making.

Most contact is undertaken at the specialist level between staff of an interest group secretariat and the ministerial bureaucracy in Bonn. These contacts are underpinned by the official provision in the Federal Government's standing orders for the consultation of relevant interest groups. For their part, groups 'are "interested" above all in the ministerial administration where it can act in an area of relative autonomy vis-à-vis the political leadership' (Weber, 1977, p. 258). The absence of fundamental dissent on key areas of economic policy (including policy principles), and on the substance of most European policy produces the conditions enabling interest groups and the ministerial bureaucracy to search for a 'rationalist consensus'. These conditions are bolstered further by the sectorized nature of European policy-making in the Federal Government.

The sectoral dimension is again worthy of attention and may be illustrated by agricultural policy. It was mentioned above that the wholesalers and exporters (the BGA) are strongly opposed to the protectionist regime of the CAP. Why then do they have no apparent success in influencing the Federal Government's policy? The primary explanation lies in the fact that the BGA is not considered to be a 'relevant' interest group by the Agriculture Ministry. At an interview in the ministry (11 September 1980) the BGA's views were summarily dismissed as 'polemical'. Although regarded as an important and trusted negotiating partner by the Economics Ministry, being represented on thirteen advisory committees, its contacts with the Agriculture Ministry (2 committees) are at a very general level and in no way counterbalance the DBV's extensive contacts (data from BGA, 1979, p. 126). Similarly, West German consumer interests – a large but very weakly represented constituency – deal mainly with the Ministry for Youth, Family and Health, which has little influence over agricultural policy-making. The sectorization of the Federal Government thus encourages the over-representation of farmers' interests.

The agricultural policy area displays other examples of sectorization. The tendency of the Bundestag to conduct its business at a specialist level, in this case in an agriculture committee dominated by MPs sympathetic towards (or with second professions as) farmers, has also facilitated the avoidance of any broader challenge from countervailing interests. In those cases where West German farmers have considered themselves especially disadvantaged, such as after the 1986 CAP price round, they have been able to gain preferential assistance through an electoral appeal. In May 1986 this led to national measures reducing farmers' social insurance contributions; these were obtained despite the disapproval of the financial and social affairs ministers (*FAZ*, 14 May 1986).[9]

Although the specific circumstances differ, the chemical industry displays similar general conditions. The close relations between the VCI and the Economics Ministry on EC legislation concerning the introduction on the market of new chemical products led to the West German industry gaining important concessions (see Chapter 7 below). How far these close relations survive the Green's vigilance over environmental policy remains to be seen.

A further case has been the success of the brewing industry in obstructing EC efforts to open up the West German market by overturning the so-called law of purity, which severely limits the ingredients of beer sold in the FRG. The *Deutscher Brauer Bund*, the sectoral organization belonging to the BDI, and the small-business (or *Handwerk*) organization representing brewers succeeded in their opposition to the EC proposal by tailoring different arguments to three different federal ministries (Bulmer, 1987, Ch. 7). This is a further variation on the sectoral theme.

The predominant focus of West German interest groups is upon lobbying the government or, more specifically, the ministerial bureaucracy. Whether it be through links between the BDI and the Economics Ministry, or between the DBV and the Agriculture Ministry, the predominant pattern is of sectorized policy styles organized around governmental contacts with 'co-operative, trustworthy "professional" organisations which acquire privileged institutionalised status' (Dyson, 1982a, p. 19).

Conclusion

This chapter has been concerned with explaining some of the origins of West German European policy. Right from the outset the FRG's economy was based on international trade and this continues today. This explains the Federal Government's concern with liberalizing trade both within the Community and in the international economy as a whole. The high level of trading interdependence and the importance of economic integration for the economy are reflected in the thinking of interest groups, including those which were considered specifically.

Economic development and the nature of integration have not had a uniform effect across the economy as a whole. Some sectors, such as investment goods and chemicals, have benefited from the dynamics of the international economy to the detriment of others, such as textiles and clothing. The dynamics of European integration have brought other sectoral divergencies, especially by virtue of the strong representation of agriculture in the EC's policy portfolio. This has allowed an economically weak sector to mobilize additional political resources for its self-defence.

Existing political resources for influencing policy-making have been retained despite the addition of the new EC level. This has occurred because West German interest groups have absorbed Community business as domestic policy. Indeed, the fact that European policy tends to be subject to less co-ordination in the Bonn government than domestic policy has increased sectorization and given greater scope for interest group influence. Unorganized interests, such as taxpayers or consumers, have had less influence on key policy areas than the agricultural lobby, which forms a much smaller 'constituency'.

Two policy areas have been subject to little direct pressure from interest groups. These are integration policy and EPC. In these policy areas public opinion has greater significance. It is to that theme which attention now turns.

Notes

1 More detailed research on the chemical industry in the FRG is being carried out by Paterson (with Wyn Grant and Colin Whitston) as part of a wider ESRC project on government–industry relations in the major OECD countries.

2 Other exceptions are Denmark and the Irish Republic: see Platzer, 1984, pp. 102–4.

3 Unlike the other EC member states, the FRG had much closer trading links with the EFTA states. In 1960 some 30 per cent of exports went to EFTA countries (Platzer, 1984, p. 60).

4 Membership is via branches; there is no direct company membership of the BDI itself.

5 On UNICE see Platzer, 1984, pp. 102–72.

6 On the BDI's own view of the clothing and textile industries, see BDI, 1982, p. 56.

7 On the mechanisms of anti-dumping measures, see Hine, 1985, pp. 88–92.

8 Conference of the *Arbeitskreis Europäische Integration* in Frankfurt, 9–11 December 1982: paper by Dr Konrad Neundörfer, *Hauptgeschäftsführer der Textilindustrie – Gesamttextil*.

9 For more on party links with agricultural policy, see Chapter 6; and on the problems in 1986, see Chapter 11.

5 *The Evolution of West German Public Opinion and the Integration of Western Europe*

> Whatever the precise significance of the unsuccessful mobilisation might be – the integration process is so faint that only a few hear it. (Herz, 1977, p. 141)

Public support for European integration, long held to be of an extremely high order in the Federal Republic, shows signs of decreasing intensity and breadth. In this chapter we examine the initial consensus on the desirability of European integration and the grounds for its persistence over several decades. We then look at the extent to which this support shows signs of erosion and what the implications of such an erosion might be.

The early years

The West German consensus on the desirability of Western European integration really dates from the latter half of the 1950s. In the initial occupation period such fragmentary public opinion evidence that exists indicates a great breadth of support and almost no opposition to the idea of uniting Western Europe (Merritt and Merritt, 1970, p. 173). There is nothing very surprising about this. Germany was in such a parlous state morally, economically and politically that the prospect of being united with other Western European countries was almost bound to be very attractive. Respondents at this stage were reacting to the idea rather than concrete plans, so they were likely to ignore any disadvantages. It is unlikely, for instance, at this stage that many Germans envisaged that only the Western zones would be permanently involved in these creations. It would also not have been apparent at that time to German respondents that countries like Britain and the Scandinavian democracies were very unlikely to be involved in supranational institutions which would be set up. Churchill's Zurich speech of 1946, for instance, was widely misinterpreted on the mainland of Europe as indicating that Britain itself would play a part in a unified Europe.

The Federal Republic

Public opinion with regard to European integration was largely split along partisan lines in the early years of the Federal Republic. Supporters of the Christian Democrats by and large welcomed the various plans for European integration. The supporters of the SPD were opposed on the whole, though not as consistently. West Germans were still positively disposed towards the idea of European integration but were reluctant to abandon the goal of a reunified Germany. Christian Democrats following Adenauer's lead were inclined to see European integration as compatible with German reunification, Social Democrats tended to think that a prior acceptance of West European integration would rule out the reunification option.

The partisan colouring of West German opinion at this time is apparent if we look at the results of a survey on West German opinions on the Schuman plan carried out in April 1951.

Table 5.1 *German views regarding the Schuman Plan (percentages)*

Question: This plan by the French foreign minister Schuman proposes the pooling of the heavy industries of France, West Germany, and other West European nations with the aim of economic co-operation of West Europe. Do you on the whole agree with this plan or not?

	West Germany	*British zone*	*US zone*	*French zone*	*Berlin*
Yes, agree	42	39	46	46	66
No, do not agree	25	27	23	21	21
No opinion	33	34	31	33	12
	100	100	100	100	100

Source: Office of the US High Commissioner for Germany, Report no. 71, Series no. 2, 5 April 1951.

It is noticeable that opinion in the British zone, the area of greatest strength for the SPD, was markedly less favourable than in the American and French zones. In answering the questions respondents also showed that they had internalized the arguments of the contending parties. Respondents who supported the

Schuman Plan cited a number of familiar arguments put forward by the CDU/CSU, namely the expected benefits for the West European and, in particular, the West German economy, the contribution of the Schuman Plan to peace in Western Europe and the increased interdependence with other West European countries and the consequent necessity of co-operation (US High Commission Report, 1952, pp. 5–6). Those against the plan relied on well-known SPD arguments such as that West Germany would be exploited by other members of the ECSC and might not be able to retain enough coal for its own industries. There was a marked distrust of the French who were perceived as wishing to keep Germany enslaved and to use the Schuman Plan to gain access to cheap German coal.. The establishment of a consensus in public opinion was thus dependent on the cessation of partisan conflict over European integration. By 1955 the SPD had completed its transition from initial harsh opposition to support for the creation of Euratom and the EEC. The FDP, which opposed West German membership of the EEC, had accepted the main lines of the consensus by the late 1950s (see Chapter 6).

An emerging societal consensus on European integration was now underpinned by a party political consensus on European integration. It had very quickly become apparent to business and trade union elites that the attainment of formal sovereignty, and thus the capacity of the West German system effectively to bargain for itself, was dependent on the acceptance of an integration framework in both the economic and political (foreign policy) fields (Haas, 1958, *passim*). This was the only choice acceptable to Germany's erstwhile foes and new partners. This perception quickly became part of a general public opinion. It was also apparent to these same elites that the production ceilings imposed by the victorious Western allies would not be lifted without acceptance of the integration framework since France in particular would feel too threatened.

Already by 1953 at the latest there was a broad and deep consensus in West Germany of attachment to the values of the 'social market economy' and liberal capitalism. This consensus was reinforced rather than threatened by membership of the ECSC, EEC and Euratom since these institutions were based on the same values. The one major sector where the Communities avoided competition and espoused protection, namely agriculture, was also the major area on which there was a consensus in the Federal Republic that it should be spared the rigours of economic competition (Chapter 6).

The general consensus on the desirability of European integration was strengthened by the problematic nature of the political identity of the citizens of the Federal Republic. Counselled by the Basic Law to treat the Federal Republic as 'provisional' and rendered ambivalent towards German symbols and traditions by the traumatic and shaming nature of the immediate past, it was hardly surprising that a European identity proved so attractive to West Germans in the 1950s and 1960s. These feelings were initially at least reinforced by the striking progress in European integration as contrasted with the total lack of progress towards German reunification.

The 1960s

Commitment to European integration remained high throughout the 1960s despite the retirement of Konrad Adenauer, its most enthusiastic advocate. Public opinion surveys indicate that the economic prosperity and general feeling of success enjoyed by the Federal Republic rubbed off on respondents' views of the European Community.

> Economic prosperity and political stability in one's own country ensure that the institutions of the European Community receive support. This also means that measures by national governments as well as measures by European authorities lead to a positive perception of the European Community. (Herz, 1977, pp. 90–1)

The tension between the twin goals of European integration and German reunification which had been such a feature of party and public opinion in the early 1950s evolved considerably in the 1960s. The breadth of the consensus that Adenauer had managed to create is illustrated by the findings of a survey undertaken in 1959. In this survey 70 per cent of those interviewed thought that German reunification would strengthen the process of European integration and only some 27 per cent thought that membership of the European institutions would hinder reunification (Feld, 1981, pp. 90–1). As memories of the Nazi regime faded, support for German reunification rose at the end of the 1950s and in the early 1960s (Paterson, 1975, p. 31). However, developments in the international political system, especially the evident desire of the new Kennedy American administration to seek an accommodation with the Soviet Union in Europe, even on the basis of a divided Germany, and the equally clear interest of the Soviet Union in the permanent division of Germany, as shown in the building of the Berlin Wall in 1961, convinced many Germans that reunification was impractical as an objective of foreign policy. In 1956 the partition of Germany was considered 'intolerable' by 52 per cent, in 1962 by 61 per cent and in 1963 by 53 per cent. This percentage dropped further to 38 per cent in 1965 and 22 per cent in 1966 (Paterson, 1975, p. 31). At the same time the saliency of reunification also declined. Uwe Kitzinger has claimed that by 1969 reunification was considered the most important task of a West German government by only 6 per cent of the electorate (*The Times*, 30 September 1969).

The 1970s

> The consensus has been disturbed. What was considered stable – here we are talking about the years 1962–73 – was now in flux. In the Federal Republic, a country that was always regarded as the example par excellence of a pro-Community country, there are signs of exhaustion. (Herz, 1977, p. 171)

> There are no signs of real enthusiasm for the European idea, and people do not appear to be captivated by the historical moment. (Noelle-Neumann, 1980, p. 55)

These quotes indicate the almost universal opinion of analysts of public opinion in West Germany that, despite a continuing high level of formal commitment to the idea of European integration, there has been a decline in West German support for the actual practice of the European Community. This view of decreasing West German support in the 1970s is based on the findings of a number of surveys. These surveys pointed to a general decline in interest in the Community.

Table 5.2 *West German attitudes to problems of the EC (percentages)*

Question: Are you interested in the problems of the European Community?

	1973 autumn	*1975 autumn*	*1976 autumn*	*1978 autumn*
Very much so	31	23	23	16
A little	48	51	50	53
Not at all	16	23	24	25
No reply	5	3	3	6
	100	100	100	100

Source: Noelle-Neumann, 1980, p. 61.

There was also a perceptible decline in support for a faster pace for European integration. Table 5.3 is taken from a Eurobarometer survey and only in Germany did the answer 'speed up' decrease in comparison to 1973.

Table 5.3 *West German attitudes to the speed of integration (percentages)*

Question: At what speed should the development towards a united Europe proceed – should it speed up, slow down, or continue as in the past?

	1973 autumn	*1975 autumn*	*1976 autumn*	*1978 autumn*
Speed up	49	47	41	38
Slow down	4	6	9	7
Same as in the past	34	36	37	34
Undecided	13	11	13	21
	100	100	100	100

Source: Noelle-Neumann, 1980, p. 66.

A propensity to judge the EC in harsher terms than hitherto is demonstrated in the responses to the question as to whether or not membership of the EC has been an advantage to the Federal Republic (Table 5.4).

Table 5.4 *West German attitudes on advantages or disadvantages of EC membership (percentages)*

	1975 autumn	*1977 autumn*	*1978 autumn*
EC an advantage	34	15	20
EC a disadvantage	17	25	31
Neither	26	46	32
Undecided	23	14	17
	100	100	100

Source: Bogulanski, 1982, p. 13.

These changes in West German public opinion towards European integration can be explained in a number of different ways. In the very special situation of the infant Federal Republic, of a contingent dependent sovereignty and an export-dependent economy which needed access to markets, European integration offered a set of generalized advantages. Once the Communities were actually established, membership for the populations of member states became associated with a focus on specific advantages and disadvantages. In the case of the Federal Republic this balance was initially seen by public opinion to be overwhelmingly positive. A large part of the explanation for this can probably be found in the fact that these years, from 1949–73, were years of tremendous success for the Federal Republic both economically and politically. As we have noted, success at the national level appears to positively influence the citizens' perceptions of European institutions (Herz, 1977, pp. 90–1).

This very positive balance began to alter in the 1970s. It is not so much a question of difficulties in the integration process feeding back negatively into public opinion. If this were the case, then we would expect to find this occurring already in 1965 at the time of the EC institutional crisis and the French withdrawal from Community institutions. A more likely explanation is to be found in the oil price rise of 1973 which brought to an end the period of almost continual uninterrupted growth for the West German economy and heralded a period of unprecedented difficulties for successive federal governments. Just as a period of sustained success coloured citizens' perceptions of both national and European institutions in a positive manner, so a period of difficulty had the opposite effect. This argument is reinforced by evidence from opinion polls that indicate that the Community is perceived in primarily economic terms by the citizens of Europe and the Federal Republic (Noelle-Neumann, 1980, p. 63).

The oil price rises of 1973 brought a new concentration on budgetary questions at the national and EC level. At the national level 'the reform policies' of the SPD/FDP coalition were severely curtailed. At the EC level this new emphasis on budgetary questions had an impact on the negotiations for the establishment of the Regional Fund in 1973. Hans Apel's pronouncements during the negotiations sensitized public opinion to budgetary questions which then acted as a further constraint (Chapter 9 below; Simonian, 1985, p. 220). This focus on financial costs was to continue throughout the Schmidt government. The tone of governmental pronouncements which had normally concentrated on the generalized advantages of membership changed to some extent to an emphasis on financial costs and the danger of the Federal Republic being regarded by the other members as a 'milk cow'. Not surprisingly, this led to a more critical stance in public opinion.

The negative impact on public opinion of the oil price rise and its attendant difficulties was probably amplified by the fact that the governmental coalition was SPD led. The SPD had supported membership of the Communities since 1955 but it remained to some extent an affair of the head, rather than the heart. Its leading representatives could be described as '*Vernunfteuropäer*'; they recognized the necessity of membership without necessarily sharing the emotional commitment to it of many Christian Democrats. In the harsher climate occasioned by the oil price rises, they would continue to believe in the necessity of membership but they were much more ready than the CDU/CSU to discount the generalized advantages of membership. These feelings among the membership were strengthened by the pronouncements of two leading *Vernunfteuropäer*, Helmut Schmidt (finance minister and later chancellor) and Hans Apel (state secretary in the Foreign Office and Schmidt's successor as finance minister). Public opinion surveys also indicate that SPD supporters lack the strong emotional identification with Western Europe and the converse rejection of Eastern Europe displayed by CDU-CSU supporters.

'Among the Social Democrats . . . the proponents of a Europe encompassing West and East (41 per cent) are as strong as the adherents of the Western conception (40 per cent)' (Noelle-Neumann, 1980, p. 67). These attitudes were to some extent created by, but also interacted with, a new emphasis in Brandt's foreign policy, namely to search for pan-European solutions rather than rely on Western Europe exclusively (Chapter 6). The profound enthusiasm of West German elite and mass opinion for a supranational Europe, that existed in the late 1950s, reflected both the fragile provisional nature of the Federal Republic and the conditional circumscribed character of its citizens' loyalty towards it. The success of the Federal Republic, its consequent consolidation and the deepening of its hold on the loyalty of its citizens was always likely to reduce their enthusiasm for a supranational Europe. A striking illustration is provided in Table 5.5. The significance of this table and other similar findings has been well expressed by Elisabeth Noelle-Neumann. 'Although nothing seems to change on the surface, the preparedness to go supranational decreases as soon as it becomes imaginable and phrased in everyday terms' (Noelle-Neumann, 1980, p. 60).

Table 5.5 *Attitudes towards a European currency (percentages)*

Question: Would you be in favour of or against a single European currency in place of the deutschmark?

	1970	*1977*
Would be in favour	52	35
Would be against	26	49
Makes no difference	14	11
Undecided	8	5
	100	100

Source: Noelle-Neumann, 1980, p. 57.

Direct elections and after

This process of erosion at the edges of the West German consensus on the desirability of European integration did not go unremarked in the Federal Republic and considerable hopes were expressed about the possibility of a '*Wiederbelebung*' of the European idea through the direct election of the European Parliament. That this hope was stillborn was apparent even at the time of the first direct election. The electoral turnout (65.7 per cent) was much lower than normal in German federal elections. In Community-wide terms this turnout was marginally above the EC average but the findings reported by Noelle-Neumann are of greater long-term significance.

> Although the data indicate *support* there is the paradox that *interest* in the EC has steadily decreased as the first direct election for the European Parliament approached. (Noelle-Neumann, 1980, p. 58)

It was probably unrealistic to expect the direct election to have a mobilizing effect given the overwhelmingly consensual nature of the party positions on European integration. This has contributed to a situation in which, apart from the exchange of pious rhetoric, there is often very little real debate on European integration. Debates on Europe often have the character of the participants attempting to pelt each other to death with balls of cotton wool. Not surprisingly, this absence of real argument or debate contributes to a climate of declining interest.

> Up to the present, the subject of Europe has not held any potential of risk: no courage has been required to profess one view or another; the subject has not been controversial; it has had no partisan colours. (Noelle-Neumann, 1980, p. 53)

Table 5.6 *Numbers of West Germans giving integration a high priority (percentages)*

December 1979	*June 1980*	*September 1980*	*November 1980*	*May 1981*	*October/November 1981*	*May 1982*
53	46	38	42	48	41	32

Source: Noelle-Neumann and Herdegen, 1983, p. 97.

The direct election thus failed to have any perceptible impact on German opinion in the short term and all the indications are that it was similarly unsuccessful in the long term. Noelle-Neumann, in a joint article published in late 1983, pointed to a steep decline in the number who regarded the integration of Western Europe as constituting a high priority (*besonders wichtig*) (Noelle-Neumann and Herdegen, 1983, p. 97).

In the same article Noelle-Neumann and Herdegen reproduced a table of findings on the question as to whether or not respondents considered membership of the EC a good thing for their country (Table 5.7). The number of German respondents who consider it a good thing is now the same as the Community average; in 1973 it was 7 per cent above.

Table 5.7 *West German attitudes to EC membership (percentages)*

Question: Is the membership of your country in the European Community in your opinion a good thing; a bad thing; neither good nor bad?

	September 1973	*1974–80 (14 polls)*	*April 1981*	*October 1981*	*April 1982*	*October 1982*
Good Thing	63	60	49	58	54	51
Neither good nor bad	22	24	28	26	31	34
Bad Thing	4	6	9	6	8	9
No answer	11	10	14	10	7	6

Source: Noelle-Neumann and Herdegen, 1983, p. 95.

In very recent years the sensitivity of West German public opinion on budgetary contributions has increased in line with the determination and, to some extent, success of Mrs Thatcher in shifting some of the burden of budgetary contributions away from the United Kingdom. This dichotomy in West German public opinion between generalized support for the idea of European integration and a lack of underlying willingness to carry out some of the measures necessary for its achievement helps to explain the contradiction noticed by West Germany's partners in the Community between *communautaire* rhetoric and considerable caution in concrete steps. We would not wish to argue that public opinion acts directly on governmental policy but it does have significant background effects. It helps explain, for instance, why the Federal Government put so much effort into the Genscher/Colombo 'European Act' proposal. It corresponds precisely to a public opinion which, like the British, is against financial sacrifices but, unlike the British, is in favour of rhetorical declarations. The desire to switch debate away from an emphasis on budgetary questions to the level of rhetorical commitment was certainly an important motive in the launching of the Genscher/Colombo initiative (see Chapter 6).

A comprehensive picture of West German public opinion on European integration is provided by the results of a large scale survey (2,000 sample) carried out in October 1983 by Infratest for the *Konrad Adenauer Stiftung*. The results of this survey have been presented in two pamphlets, *Europa im Spiegel der Umfrageforschung* and *Politische Einstellungen zur Europäischen Gemeinschaft* (Veen *et al.*, 1984; Veen, 1983). In line with other surveys it is clear that there is still a high level of formal commitment to the idea of European integration. However the surveys also indicate areas of difficulty, declining support and a widespread feeling that West Germany ought to push its own interests harder. Only 5 per cent thought West Germany pushed its interests more than other partners in the EC (Veen *et al.*, 1984, p. 19). The number of respondents who feel themselves to be strongly 'European', in the sense of defining their identity in terms of the European Community, has declined since the first direct election from 49 per cent in 1979 to 40 per cent in October 1983. In the same period the number of those who do not identify strongly with the Community has risen from 31 to 36 per cent (Veen *et al.*, 1984, p. 1). There was also a pretty clear rejection of the supranational solution; 56 per cent were against the concept of a European government as against 27 per cent who were in favour (Veen *et al.*, 1984, p. 25). This lack of European consciousness, of a feeling of socio-psychological community, is also apparent in the finding that only a minority (46 per cent) were prepared to accept economic drawbacks in order to help the poorer countries of the Community (Veen *et al.*, 1984, p. 37). Alongside this declining European consciousness there is a clear perception that increased economic difficulties in West European countries were likely to increase tensions (Veen, 1983, p. 6). H. J. Veen sums up the public mood as regards the consequences of economic difficulties as follows: 'No high expectations are being placed at present and for the foreseeable future in the economic capabilities and development of the EC. Scepticism largely rules in relation to the economy' (Veen, 1983, p.6).

This scepticism about the EC's economic capability is, potentially at least, very damaging to support for the EC in West Germany and could in the long term undermine the generalized commitment to a European ideal. This prospect comes more sharply into focus if we look at what respondents named as a high priority for the EC; 70 per cent named the combating of unemployment as constituting the highest priority for the EC (Veen *et al.*, 1984, p. 41). Given the very high unlikelihood of the EC being able to do anything significant to reduce unemployment, the expectations uncovered by the survey pose a problem, particularly among the young who are most affected by unemployment. H. J. Veen has already indicated that among the small but growing number who reject the EC in its present form, there is a quite disproportionate number of young males (aged 18–24) (Veen, 1983, p. 7). They either have no fixed party identification or vote Green (see Chapter 6).

This scepticism about the ability of the EC to solve economic problems is flanked by a heightened pride in the identification with the Federal Republic; 78 per cent thought the Federal Republic had done most for the EC (Veen *et al.*, 1984, p. 18). This identification with the Federal Republic also emerges clearly when respondents are asked to identify disadvantages of EC membership. The clear leader with 40 per cent was the paymaster role of the FRG. All other disadvantages were cited by less than 10 per cent (Veen *et al.*, 1984, p. 18).

One very significant finding was that only 5 per cent mentioned over-production and agricultural surpluses as a problem (Veen *et al.*, 1984, p. 3). Moreover, the most often cited advantage of EC membership was better food supplies (18 per cent as against 11 per cent for trade advantages) (Veen *et al.*, 1984, p. 32). These findings indicate very little dissatisfaction with the CAP and one part of the background condition for the strength of agriculture which will be examined in the next chapter.

The Konrad Adenauer Foundation survey was undertaken in the run up to the European election of 1984 and its findings on the parliament itself were extremely grim (Veen *et al.*, 1984, p. 23). The major positive element from a European point of view in the

Table 5.8 *Opinion on the work of the European Parliament (percentages)*

	On balance positive	*On balance negative*	*Don't know*
December 1979	42	10	48
December 1982	24	29	47
October 1983	23	29	46

Source: Veen *et al.*, 1984, p. 23.

survey was the scale of support for the EC as a foreign policy actor that was revealed by the survey. Of those questioned, 69 per cent thought that the Community ought to exert a greater global influence. With regard to the exercise of this role 17 per cent thought it should be carried out in very close co-operation with the United States; 62 per cent thought Europe should remain a partner of the USA but should pursue a more independent role than hitherto; and 19 per cent felt that the Europeans should pursue a quite independent policy (Veen *et al.*, 1984, pp. 11–12).

The second European election

The gloomy view presented in the Infratest report was confirmed by the second European election on 17 June 1984. Turnout (56.8 per cent) was very low by German standards and the campaign itself had revealed little interest or support. An internal paper of the Federal Government, commenting on a public opinion survey conducted during the campaign by EMNID, referred to West Germans' feelings towards the EC as being 'characterised by considerable inner reserve' (*Tagesspiegel*, 22 April 1984). Only 37 per cent of respondents were prepared for personal economic sacrifices such as tax increases to help another member country in economic difficulties. The same survey also revealed a major ambiguity; most West Germans still give formal priority to European integration and the majority are in favour of faster progress but they are also (52 per cent) against any further loss of national independence.

Conclusion

This analysis of the evolution of West German public opinion on European integration allows us to isolate four broad public moods. In the very early years of the Federal Republic opinion was split along partisan lines though there was a groundswell of support for the idea. The years from the mid-1950s to the oil crisis of 1973 are the years of maximum support. After 1973 there are signs of erosion but support continues at a fairly high level. More recently the signs of erosion have become more pronounced and now include a small minority of the population (who normally vote Green) opposed to the Community.

There is still massive support for the idea at a very general level. However, this is balanced by a steep decline in the enthusiasm for supranational solutions and an even steeper decline in the readiness to make financial sacrifices for the EC. In other words this seems to be a public mood which could sustain the present mode of Community politics but looks like a very unsure foundation for anything other than limited departures from it. It could probably sustain 'variable geometry' integration, whereby some states press ahead with closer integration in particular sectors since this would not involve the further financial transfers to the poorer regions of the EC that would be entailed in a deepening level of integration that involved all members. A 'two-speed Europe' of an inner core pressing ahead with integration would run up against financial susceptibilities and would not correspond to a public opinion in which 'the preparedness to go supranational decreases as soon as it becomes imaginable' (Noelle-Neumann, 1980, p. 10).

It is a public opinion which, given its support for the general idea of European integration, would support the broad outline of the European Parliament's Draft Treaty on European Union and the Dooge Report on institutional reform of the EC. In view of the fact that the measures decided upon at the December 1985 Luxembourg European Council were more modest than these proposals (Bulmer and Wessels, 1987), no major dissent is likely in public opinion. Past survey evidence would strongly indicate support for the modest progress achieved on EPC at the Luxembourg summit meeting.

The duality between a public opinion which is in favour of integration (though less so than formerly) but is much less enthusiastic about concrete measures which might compromise specific German interests, provides a striking parallel to the Federal Government where the *Auswärtiges Amt* (Foreign Office) corresponds to the generalized mood in favour of integration and the specialist ministries who tend to raise difficulties about specific initiatives (Chapter 3).

One danger from the Community point of view is a further

erosion in the generalized support for the EC if it is consistently unable to act on issues of perceived high priority like unemployment or the environment. It is equally clear that, quite unlike Britain, the popular legitimacy of the EC in West Germany does not depend on doing something about agricultural surpluses.

At present, policy-making on European integration in the Federal Republic is clearly conducted by an elite actively operating within a 'permissive consensus'. Although permissive, this consensus has clear borders/constraints related to budgetary contributions and specific German interests. The reverse side of the coin is that this opinion is largely passive and that, if the policy-making elites who at present support European integration become disillusioned, then there does not appear to be a broad and deep reservoir of support which could be mobilized against such a development.

One final marked contrast with Britain is in the place of media coverage of the EC. If support for the EC has waned, it is difficult to assign any role to the press in this process. In Britain, it is quite common to argue that press trivialization of European issues weakens support. In the Federal Republic there is very extensive coverage of the EC often by seasoned Europeans and the coverage is on the whole positive.

6 *West German Political Parties and the European Community*

A contrast has often been drawn between the adversarial nature of British party politics and the consensual character of German party politics. This contrast also holds in relation to European policy where all the established parties support European integration in West Germany while the major opposition party in Britain appears, at least in theory, unreconciled to British membership.

In this chapter we start from the position established in Chapter 5, on public opinion, of this broad if slightly fraying consensus in favour of European integration in West Germany. In the first section, we examine the development of the European policies of the individual parties in the Federal Republic. In the succeeding section, we see how the parties handle questions of European policy. In the third section, we analyse the impact of the political parties on governmental policy with special reference to agriculture and in the final section we examine the electoral dimension.

The development of party policies on European integration

The Christian Democratic Union

The first two decades in the history of the Federal Republic were dominated by the Christian Democratic Union (CDU) and its Bavarian ally, the Christian Social Union (CSU). The Christian Democrats were similar to parallel groupings which appeared in other European countries but represented a new departure in Germany of a successful conservative biconfessional party. Although the party was consciously biconfessional, its core membership was preponderantly Catholic. This high proportion of Catholics in the membership and leadership of the CDU would have been likely to make the CDU take a sympathetic view of European integration. In postwar Europe Catholic political opinion, reflecting affinity between the Christian Democratic parties of the original six member states and the strong anti-communism of Pope Pius XII, was markedly in favour of European integration. This predisposition was immeasurably strengthened by the ideas and policy preferences of Konrad Adenauer who was chancellor from 1949–63. Adenauer dominated the formulation of the government's European and foreign policy (Baring, 1969). In domestic policy support was attracted to the CDU/CSU by a whole range of personalities and conceptions; in foreign and European policy there was only one conception, one policy that mattered: that of Adenauer. This position was reinforced by the decision of the SPD leadership to oppose Adenauer primarily in the field of foreign and European policy since this meant it was much easier for him to integrate the government and the CDU/CSU around his personal programme than would otherwise have been the case.

Adenauer was equally dominant in relation to the CDU which throughout his period as chancellor remained organizationally undeveloped and mortgaged to his electoral success. In looking at the early history of the CDU and European integration, we are really looking at Konrad Adenauer.

Adenauer's Europeanism revolved around a deep but narrow complex of sympathies and antipathies. His Europe was a Western Catholic Europe radiating out from his beloved Cologne. Symbolically, from Adenauer's house in Rhöndorf it is possible to look only westwards over the Rhine. This Western Europe was seen to rest on the basis of a Franco-German entente (Weidenfeld, 1979, pp. 33–40). His enduring anti-communism meant a very close identification with the policy of the United States and an unwavering hostility towards the Soviet Union. In the field of external relations it was possible for Adenauer to shape a coherent policy out of this bundle of conflicting prejudices; there was at that time no tension between his reliance on the French in the field of European integration, and on the Americans for security. The French were content to follow the American lead in security matters in face of the Soviet threat, and the Americans were the most committed supporters of Western European integration.

Adenauer's foreign policy was a clear-cut option for the West; he believed that Germany's interests were essentially identical with those of the Western powers and that they would be willing to grant Germany a genuine partnership by gradually dismantling the discriminatory status of the occupation regime.

This had to be preceded by an unmistakable German option for the West, for only then would the Western powers trust Germany enough to lift the discriminatory legislation. Adenauer's genius was to see that the emergence of Germany as a political force had to be identified with the pattern of co-operation that was being established in the Western world.

This meant above all a willingness by Germany to make concrete concessions to the French, the main opponents of Germany's rapid return to major importance, in return for France's intangible trust and goodwill; without these no progress could be made.

This policy of concentration on Western European integration, of a clear choice for the West, might have been expected to founder on the fact that over a quarter of West Germany's population were refugees from the East, and had therefore a strong interest in German reunification. Adenauer was able to neutralize the refugees as a possible focus of opposition to his policy by representing Western European integration as part of a process of strengthening the West in order to 'awe the Russians back to their frontiers'. This policy was shrewdly buttressed by the Equalization of Burdens Law of 1951, which compensated refugees financially for lands they had lost in the East.

After 1949, Adenauer was to be the main architect of European integration. He responded favourably to an invitation from the Council of Europe that Germany become an associate member in 1950, though many counselled that the simultaneous entry of the Saar would mean that Germany was legitimizing the permanent detachment of the Saar from Germany.

Adenauer's handling of the Saar issue is a good example of his general policy on European integration. In Adenauer's view, the tension between legitimate French demands for security against the possibility of a too powerful Germany and the traditional 'Germanness' of the Saar could be resolved only by the Europeanization of the Saar.

He was to hold this view even after it had become apparent to most people that the Saarlanders wished to join the Federal Republic. Adenauer's enthusiastic embracing of the ideas of Robert Schuman, put forward in May 1950, was crucial in making the European Coal and Steel Community possible. This plan for the pooling of French and German heavy industry under a common European authority combined all the elements close to Adenauer's heart; indeed it was very similar to proposals made by Adenauer himself. It was a way of giving more freedom of manoeuvre to the German coal and steel industry; it allayed

French anxieties over their security; and it had the full and enthusiastic support of the American government and of its representative in Germany, John McCloy.

Adenauer's greatest disappointment was the failure of the plans for a European Defence Community. These plans would have taken Western Europe far along the road towards a federal state, but were rejected by the French National Assembly in August 1954. In taking Germany into the Common Market and Euratom, Adenauer was faced with opposition, not from the Social Democrats, but from his erstwhile coalition partners, the Free Democrats, and with distinct reservations from his economics minister, Ludwig Erhard.

More important perhaps than his victory over domestic opposition was his insistence on major concessions to the French in the negotiations; he saw that without these concessions the weak French government of Guy Mollet could not lead France into the EEC. Walter Hallstein, who became President of the Commission of the EEC, was the chief German negotiator and Adenauer's closest foreign policy confidant. This period represents the high point of Adenauer's success.

The period of success for Adenauer ended in the 1960s. His foreign policy had been weakened by the attitude of President John F. Kennedy's administration, which made it clear that it intended to press for a detente with the USSR, despite the continued division of Germany. Unity with the West was thus not necessarily seen to be identical with a concern for German reunification.

In this situation de Gaulle acted as a catalyst of the forces of change. If he had limited himself to asserting French interests within the existing framework, he would not have threatened the cohesion of Germany's foreign policy. But he presented a rival programme, a competing vision of a future Europe. His advocacy of *l'Europe des états*, rather than a supranational Europe, and of the eventual solution of the German problem within the framework of an East–West detente, appealed to different groupings in the Federal Republic, though there was no consensus in support of the total package.

On the other hand, his challenge to the United States, his attack on NATO and his animus against the supranational elements of the European Community embarrassed the German government. It threatened to disrupt the links between the bases of Adenauer's foreign policy: between security alignment with the United States and the entente with France, and between the Franco-German rapprochement and the commitment to European integration. Faced with these antinomies, Adenauer was in a much less happy situation than he had been among the certainties of the 1950s.

After an attempt to deny the tension between these competing views, he indicated that while West Germany must continue to depend on the United States for security, Germany's interests in West European integration lay with France and thus with de Gaulle. This implied a lesser commitment to supranationalism and an endorsement, however unwilling, of the French exclusion of Britain – a major blow to the Community idea. This endorsement was symbolized by Adenauer's insistence on signing the Franco-German Treaty, against considerable internal opposition, just after the French veto on British entry in January 1963.

The Gaullists versus Atlanticists In the period between 1963–6 the CDU/CSU was polarised in European policy terms between the 'Gaullists' and the 'Atlanticists'. It was essentially a struggle between the 'ins' and the 'outs'. The 'ins' held the major ministries, the 'outs' - Konrad Adenauer and Franz-Josef Strauss – were respectively in retirement and in disgrace. The 'outs' however were party chairmen: Konrad Adenauer of the CDU and Franz-Josef Strauss of the CSU. They carried on a continual guerrilla campaign against the government, accusing it of placing too much emphasis on the Atlantic relationship, of neglecting France and of turning its back on the commitment to supranationalism. The Atlanticists were headed by three prominent Protestant politicians, the federal chancellor, Ludwig Erhard, who had succeeded Adenauer in 1963, the foreign minister, Gerhard Schröder, and the defence minister, Kai-Uwe von Hassel. Erhard had been lukewarm about the foundation of the EEC and would have preferred a larger free trade area. As Protestants, it is probably fair to say that they had a less strong emotional commitment to the values and countries of the original Community than Catholic members of the CDU. However, their policies were motivated less by any lack of enthusiasm for France than by the need which every West German government has felt of not letting their policies drift into conflict with those of the United States. In any case the force of 'the Gaullist attack' was blunted by its own incoherence. This rested in the contradiction between support for very close links with France and support for supranationalism, given Gaullist attitudes to supranationalism. It was also the case that no West German politician at that time would have risked serious conflict with the United States given West German security dependence on the United States.

The Grand Coalition As a Catholic south German politician, Kurt-Georg Kiesinger, the federal chancellor and party chairman of the CDU in the period of the Grand Coalition, might have been expected to steer the CDU back to the simple verities of Adenauer's European policy. In fact the imperatives of coalition balance with the SPD and even more of balance within the CDU/CSU conspired to frustrate this. His key foreign policy adviser in the Chancellor's Office, Baron von und zu Guttenberg, a 'Gaullist', was balanced by Gerhard Schröder as minister of defence and Karl Carstens, a long time intimate of Schröder who became state secretary in the Chancellor's Office.

1969–1982 Catapulted out of office after the 1969 election despite being the largest party, the CDU gave relatively little attention to European policy. The party effort was focused on East–West relations and opposition to *Ostpolitik*. *Westpolitik* was very much placed on the back burner in the early and mid-seventies.

> With the CDU this area has acquired a more background role in party programmes, somewhat in contrast with its earlier policy emphasis in government, judging by the small sections devoted to European affairs in the revised Berlin programme of 1971, the Hamburg thesis of 1973, the Mannheim Declaration of 1975 and the Basic Policy Programme of 1978. The last of these while urging the completion of Adenauer's 'historic work in European unification', devoted less than two out of 67 pages to European policy and that towards the end. (Pridham, 1980, p. 320)

The advent of Helmut Kohl as chancellor candidate, party chairman and then chancellor brought some revival of the rhetoric of European integration; it is certainly the case that there is a readier audience for these sentiments in the CDU/CSU than in the other West German parties. Kohl's European posture has also been part of his desire to present himself as Adenauer's political heir. This commitment has been more noticeable at the rhetorical and presentational level than at the policy level. The advent of the Kohl government in October 1982 did bring with it a change of presentation, for example immediate visits to Paris and Brussels, but the element of policy continuity with the preceding SPD/FDP government policy was equally striking.

The Christian Social Union

The Christian Social Union has probably been the most 'European' party in the Federal Republic. This is in line with what one would expect given the generally higher level of support among German Catholics for the ideas of European integration. Despite the postwar inflow of refugees into Bavaria, the confessional balance of Bavaria after 1945 remained unchanged and the CSU has remained a largely Catholic party in membership and electoral support (Mintzel, 1972).

In the early years of the Federal Republic the CSU was relatively inactive in pushing its ideas on European integration since these were sufficiently close to those of Konrad Adenauer for it to have confidence in him representing its views. The model that lay behind such pronouncements as it did make was of a federal Europe. The ideas were distinctive in the degree to which they stressed the Christian character of Western Europe and its function as a bulwark against the spread of communism.

The retirement of Adenauer and Strauss's resignation as defence minister in 1963 propelled the CSU into adopting a much more active policy on European integration. Foreign and European policy-making at governmental level was now in the hands of the Protestant triumvirate of Erhard, Schröder and von Hassel who were perceived by Strauss and Adenauer as being too close to the United States, too keen on detente and not sufficiently committed to the realization of the European idea. Confidential protocols of CSU executive meetings in 1964 in the author's possession indicate co-ordination between Strauss and Adenauer.[1]

In the years after 1963 Strauss developed a European strategy (Strauss, 1965). This strategy had a number of components. Of central importance was the assertion of a much more independent and much more equal role for Europe between the superpowers.

> A united Western Europe should be the first step (*Vorstufe*) on the way to the United States of Europe, a United States of Europe which should include the peoples of Central and Eastern Europe. United Europe should adopt the position of an independent power between the United States and the Soviet Union and thus secure the preponderence of free society in the global political powerplay. (cited in Mintzel, 1977, p. 291)

This central role for Europe would be based on a European political federation with its own means of defending itself.

> A United States of Europe with its own nuclear deterrent under supranational control would form the second essential pillar of a Western defence community in alliance with the USA. (Strauss, 1965, p. 9)

The development of a federal Europe to include the peoples of Eastern Europe would make possible the solution of the German question – Strauss referred to this as the Europeanization of the German question.

> Above all it [i.e. a United States of Europe] would provide the one framework which would make possible the reunification of Germany and avoid all its latent dangers. Germany needs Europe more than any other country . . . In contributing to the formation of a European federation, Germany herself would find a new identity. (Strauss, 1965, p. 9)

These various strands are bound together by profound anti-communism and reflect a fear that the United States would sacrifice German interests in an attempt at accommodation with the Soviet Union (USSR). This hostility to the USSR led to Strauss pinning a great deal of hope on the China card, i.e. the belief that continued disagreement with China would constrain the Soviet Union in Eastern Europe and help keep the 'German option' open. This view was encouraged by the Chinese who hoped that the formation of a united Western Europe would act as a bulwark against the Soviet Union.

Strauss's views appear to have commanded overwhelming support in the CSU. His European policy was opposed at only one executive meeting of the CSU. At this meeting on 10 July 1964 the opposition was led by Frau Dr Probst, a long-time adversary of Strauss, and by Herr von Haniel-Niethammer who declared that 'he personally had grave reservations about consummating a quasi-marriage with Gaullist France – his view was identical to that of Chancellor Erhard (CSU Protocol, 10 July 1964, pp. 1–21). In the ensuing vote however only two votes were cast against Strauss. His erstwhile rival and the major foreign policy spokesman of the CSU, Freiherr von und zu Guttenberg, advanced broadly similar views and there are no indications of conflict over European policy at that time. A major weakness of the CSU approach, however, was the fact that it was ultimately unacceptable to France. Although de Gaulle welcomed the emphasis on European independence, the CSU's espousal of supranational institutions and common nuclear defences were anathema to successive French governments.

In the Grand Coalition, as we have seen, the CDU/CSU ministers were fairly evenly balanced along Gaullist/Atlanticist lines. This, combined with day-to-day political exigencies and the fact that Strauss was tied up with his responsibilities as finance minister, meant that the CSU kept a fairly low profile on European issues between 1966–9.

The CSU out of power in Bonn The early years of the Social–Liberal Coalition were dominated by *Ostpolitik*. The CSU therefore concentrated less on advocating a stronger Western Europe and more on opposing *Ostpolitik*. Their policy of strong anti-communism and pro-German unification rhetoric brought tangible domestic political benefits. It helped to establish the CSU as a potential fourth 'conservative' party throughout the Federal Republic though Strauss's attempt to capitalize on this after the 1976 election foundered on resolute CDU opposition. In Bavaria itself these ideas and opposition to *Ostpolitik* helped the CSU to make significant inroads for the first time into the nationally minded electorate of the Protestant corridor of Franconia. In terms of European policy the CSU was relatively muted. On agricultural policy it vigorously opposed the Mansholt Plan and has generally taken a strongly pro-agriculture line close to the German Farmers' Union (Mintzel, 1977, pp. 261–77). It was very critical of the EMS on the grounds that it would encourage the weaker EC states to become too dependent on Community funds. Strauss and the CSU have also been very close to a number of large industrial and technological interests, particularly in the modern sector and the CSU was very active in opposing any plans for co-determination at a European level, as put forward by the SPD-led government.[2] This closeness to agricultural interests and to modern industry is a hallmark of the CSU. In this strategy the disadvantages for modern industry of costly support for agriculture is minimised by the existence of the CAP.

After the collapse of the SPD/FDP government the CSU was able at least potentially to increase its influence on European policy through Ignaz Kiechle, agriculture minister after 1983. Kiechle's position created difficulties for the CSU in 1984 because of the agreement of the West German government to cuts in dairy production. The difficulties that this created for the CSU ensured that Kiechle took the lead in supporting a West German veto on cuts in cereal prices in 1985 (*Der Spiegel*, no. 20, 1985, pp.21–2).

The FDP

German liberalism has traditionally been divided. From 1949 the Free Democratic Party (FDP) was badly split. The successors to the National Liberals, especially in northern Germany, tended to coalesce around Franz Blücher, Adenauer's first vice-chancellor, while the progressive group identified themselves with Theodor Heuss the first President of the Federal Republic.

In the first years of the Federal Republic the nationalist faction in the FDP made most of the running and produced its own very nationalistic 'German Programme' in 1952. Its nationalism was, however, very largely restricted to rhetoric since, as junior partner in the Adenauer coalition, it basically had to accept the foreign policy line laid down by Adenauer. The FDP therefore supported entry to the Coal and Steel Community. It was, however, much more sensitive than its coalition partners, the CDU/CSU, on the subject of the Saar and the party as a whole opposed the various plans for 'Europeanization' of the Saar.

The party's policy became more decidedly opposed to Adenauer's foreign policy after it withdrew from the governing coalition in February 1956. The new party leader, Thomas Dehler, was a man of deep nationalist convictions and under his leadership the FDP was the only major West German party to oppose the establishment of the EEC. Its opposition was based on three main sets of objections the most general of which was to stress the priority of German reunification over West European integration. During the later stages of the negotiations the FDP was particularly worried by the prospect that the Common Market would actually deepen the division of Germany by creating a tariff barrier along the zonal boundary. The FDP had very close contacts with German industrial circles and it criticized the economic aspects of the Treaty of Rome as vigorously as it condemned the political aspects. The FDP was in favour of a broad free trade area rather than an integrated Common Market, and was particularly opposed to a Common External Tariff. It therefore advocated trade liberalization on the OEEC pattern. The FDP's criticisms of the economic provisions of the treaty were really indirect criticisms of French policy and the FDP was much more outspoken in its objections to French policies than a CDU/CSU led by Konrad Adenauer could ever be.

This opposition of the Free Democratic Party to the ratification of the Treaty of Rome has often been dismissed as political opportunism. The party had supported the Coal and Steel Community and the Defence Community when it was in office and now, out of office, opposed the Common Market and Euratom. In an election year like 1957, opposition to the Common Market was a means of distinguishing the FDP from the two major parties, the CDU and SPD, who supported membership. But the FDP's changed attitude was more than purely tactical, it was also a reflection of profound changes within the party itself, changes which had led to the break with the government coalition. As early as March 1955, Dehler said that he had always thought the EEC to be unviable. The election of Dehler as leader was thus in itself a sign that the FDP would refuse to accept a purely Western oriented foreign policy.

Once the chief advantage to be gained from close alliance with the West – formal political sovereignty – had been achieved, as it was in 1955, and once the danger of a Soviet attack or a communist coup anywhere in Western Europe began to seem remote, it was not surprising that some Germans at least should have wanted to revive Germany's role as a Central European power.

As for the FDP's objections to the economic provisions of the treaty, they can be classed as a mixture of classical liberal doctrines, electoral propaganda and a reflection of the views of the weaker parts of the business community.

But although the FDP's anxieties reflected fears felt by many other groups and parties, the nationalist tone the party adopted did not bring it electoral success and its total support fell from 9.0 per cent of the electorate in 1953 to 6.4 per cent in 1957. These broad lines of policy on Europe were to remain largely unaltered when the FDP joined the coalition with the CDU/CSU in 1961.

In the period of the Grand Coalition of CDU/CSU/SPD from 1966–9 the FDP was really too small to have much impact on policy. These years were, however, very important for the FDP since they saw the victory of the more progressive elements in the party – a victory consolidated by the election of Walter Scheel as FDP chairman in January 1968.

Scheel had always been a supporter of European integration and under his leadership the nationalist appeal of the party was reduced to a minor theme. It never entirely disappeared however. One of the FDP's most prominent spokesmen on Europe, Josef Ertl, the agriculture minister from 1969 until 1983, had until his elevation to ministerial office in 1969 been very much identified with various extreme nationalist groups, including those who advocated freedom for the South Tyrol.

The FDP has filled the post of foreign minister since 1969. Walter Scheel was foreign minister from 1969–74 and Hans-

Dietrich Genscher has held the post in all succeeding governments. The Foreign Office is conventionally regarded as the most desirable post in a West German cabinet after the chancellorship itself and normally carries with it the designation deputy chancellor. Possession of the Foreign Ministry, the Economics Ministry (after 1972) and the Agriculture Ministry meant that the FDP was bound to adopt a higher profile on questions of European integration than had been the case up until 1969. The ministers concerned, however (see Chapters 2 and 3) tended to reflect departmental, rather than party, priorities in their statements and actions. This was especiallv the case in the field of European integration given, as one senior FDP functionary told us, the absence of '*Grundsatzkonflikt*' (fundamental conflict) on European issues. It is significant that the FDP stressed the general reputation of its ministers rather than their success in achieving distinctively Liberal goals in attempting to mobilize the electorate in national and European elections.

The FDP made some attempt to differentiate itself from the other parties at a programmatic level. In its electoral programme for the 1980 federal election there was some attempt to give the electoral pronouncements on Europe a distinctively Liberal dimension. The FDP argued for the universal adoption of proportional representation by the EC for the second direct election in 1984. It argued that the right to vote in the European election should depend on place of domicile rather than country of origin. It advocated the right of the individual to bring cases to the European Court. Among other measures for individual protection was a proposal to improve data protection throughout the EC. In a final blow in the direction of Liberal principles a number of measures to encourage competition were suggested.

The Genscher initiative on European Union The most important European initiative associated with the FDP in recent years has been the Genscher initiative on European Union. There is some difficulty however in deciding to what extent it was a party political initiative. The basic problem is to decide whether Genscher was responding to governmental or party cues. The Foreign Ministry is charged with advancing the general progress of integration and thus has a clear interest in the aims of the initiative. Those in the FDP who were interested in European policy (a small 'ingroup' according to Herr Jeutter, the FDP official responsible for European matters) had three strong reasons for pressing such an initiative. They were concerned to preserve a pro-European climate in the Federal Republic, a climate which was in danger of being undermined through continual conflict over distributional/budgetary issues and fisheries policy, for example. They were therefore keen to back an initiative for which there was still a high level of positive support. It would also have the advantage of distinguishing the FDP from the SPD's European policy since Hans Matthöfer (finance minister) and Manfred Lahnstein (state secretary in the Finance Ministry), both leading figures in the SPD, were perceived as being too aggressive in defending West German interests on budgetary questions. There was also pressure from the Liberal Group at the European Parliament since the FDP was the member party best placed in national governmental terms to launch such an initiative.

An analysis of the genesis of the Genscher initiative further illustrates the difficulty in coming to any conclusion as regards the relative impact of party or government. The first draft of the plan originated within the *Auswärtiges Amt.* It lay dormant for some time and was then presented in public for the first time to the FDP *Dreikönigstreffen* on 6 January 1981. The question remains as to whether this venue was chosen for convenience – it is an important conference well attended by the media – or whether it was in response to pressure from within the FDP, a pressure without which it would have continued to lie dormant in the *Auswärtiges Amt.*

The Genscher initiative was later pursued jointly with the Italian Foreign Office and, for that reason, became known as the Genscher-Colombo (European Act) initiative. This became the basis for the Solemn Declaration on European Union, agreed in June 1983 at the Stuttgart European Council (see Chapter 3).

The Social Democratic Party

The postwar policy of the SPD on European integration has passed through a number of phases. In the early years of the Federal Republic the SPD opposed various attempts at European integration (Hrbek, 1973; Paterson, 1974a).

The force of SPD opposition gradually weakened between 1952 and 1955 (Paterson, 1974a, pp. 115–41). Schumacher, the first postwar leader, a fervent nationalist and a man of an unbending and inflexible disposition, died in 1952. The SPD attachment to socialist goals began to weaken in the face of the economic success of the Federal Republic and public identification of socialist terminology with the much disliked East Germany (GDR). The return of the Saar to Germany looked more and more likely while reunification receded into the distance as a practical option. The separation of defence from the agenda of European integration after the collapse of the plans for a European Defence Community removed a major SPD objection to supporting integration. These various factors were skilfully played on by Jean Monnet who persuaded the SPD leadership to join the Action Committee for the United States of Europe in 1955. He was also aided in securing SPD support for the idea of a Common Market and Euratom by the support of the West German trade unions and the SPD enthusiasm for Euratom.

SPD support for European integration was particularly marked in the early 1960s. There were two main reasons for this. First, the *Deutschlandplan* for a confederation of the two Germanies, on which the SPD staked so much, was reduced to ruins by the development of the Berlin crisis of 1958–61. Secondly, leading members of the *Bundestagsfraktion* (the parliamentary party), especially Herbert Wehner, were attracted by the prospect of coalition with the CDU/CSU and a pro-European policy was likely to help in this. This calculation proved difficult to translate into practice. The problem was that, as Adenauer grew steadily more suspicious of the policy of the United States after the death of Dulles in 1959, he came ever nearer to de Gaulle. This accommodation between de Gaulle and Adenauer scarcely affected Adenauer's view of the correct alliance policy to be followed by the Federal Republic, but it did affect Adenauer's perception of European integration and as the Gaullist challenge to the European institutions mounted, Adenauer often appeared on the point of undoing some of his earlier achievements in pursuit of Franco-German friendship. In this situation the SPD paradoxically found itself criticizing de Gaulle in the name of the values it had formerly attacked in Adenauer, those of European integration and unswerving devotion to American policy.

The SPD's concern to strengthen the democratic element in the European institutions, already a major theme in the years when they were opposed to West German participation, increased in importance once they accepted the principle of membership. The demand for increased rights for the European Parliament was mentioned in the 1961 election campaign and then more strongly in a European Manifesto produced for the 1965 election.

In power in the Grand Coalition of 1966–9, the SPD devoted relatively little time to the development of plans for the reform of the EEC institutions. There were probably three main reasons for this. First, there was the feeling of relief that France had returned to the EC after the 1965 walkout and a desire to let sleeping dogs lie. Secondly, it has also always been the case that opposition parties have been more productive than governments in the production of these plans. Thirdly, SPD foreign policy in government was made much more clearly by Brandt, who had other priorities.

The waning of the party's interest in the Brussels institutions since it became part of the government in 1966 provoked relatively little internal controversy. The only public dispute on the issue in the party occurred in October 1971, over the question of direct elections for the European Parliament. The decision of the SPD parliamentary party to drop its former policy, by which West Germany would proceed unilaterally to direct elections in favour of one which involved waiting until a common European Community approach had been worked out on 'grounds of fairness to the new members', provoked the resignation of Klaus Peter Schulz.

The SPD and European integration under Brandt As foreign minister of the Grand Coalition, Brandt was mainly concerned with *Ostpolitik*. At a more general level, he was preoccupied with the modalities of the interaction of the problems of peace and 'the German Question'. The problem as he saw it was to find 'an orientation which places the German Question in its European context and for this we need a concept which contains the basis of a European Peace Order' (Brandt, 1968, p. 85).

The precise contours of the 'European Peace Order' were indistinct and were delineated differently at different times. It was always clear, however, that this 'European Peace Order' was not regarded by Brandt as an alternative to the EEC but assumed that West Germany would remain within the framework of the EEC.

> We are surely in agreement that our community should not be a new bloc but an exemplary system, which should serve as an important part of a balanced European Peace system. It is in this sense that the Federal Republic of Germany seeks understanding towards the East with the co-operation of her Western allies. (Brandt, 1969, p. 87)

The notion of a European peace system with its pan-European focus, was almost bound to be in tension with the development of a too strongly supranational EEC. In practice, however, the tension usually remained implicit since Brandt's earlier support for European integration, while it was modified by these ideas (in essence those of Egon Bahr), was not completely displaced by them. Moreover, support in the SPD for further European integration remained high, particularly in the *Bundestagsfraktion*. In his first term as chancellor, European integration was definitely accorded less priority than *Ostpolitik*. The Hague summit of 1969 represents only a partial exception, since it is clear from Brandt's speech to the summit conference that he was more interested in the enlargement of the Community (with its attendant advantages for *Ostpolitik*) than in its inner development (Brandt, 1969, pp. 47–54).

By the time of the formation of the second Brandt/Scheel government, the major treaties with the East had been concluded (though the negotiations with Czechoslovakia remained to be completed), and it looked unlikely that any further dramatic progress would be achieved in that area. In this situation Brandt concentrated much more than hitherto on Western European integration. In his second governmental declaration on 18 January 1973, Brandt stated that European Union was to be the foremost goal of the Federal Government (*Das Parlament*, 27 January 1973). While the declaration made some reference to political union, it was merely in terms of greater intergovernmental co-operation. The main emphasis in Brandt's declaration was laid on economic union. The conception of this was a loose one, involving much more consultation and co-ordination than at present prevails between the various governments but stopping far short of the federal model. This emphasis on economic union was associated with the rising influence of Helmut Schmidt, then finance minister, and his belief that some financial discipline would have to be imposed on West Germany's fellow members.

The final objectives of Brandt's European policy remained vague and ambiguous since he never really made clear how the tensions between *Ost*- and *Westpolitik*, between a 'closer union' and the continued existence of national governments, between enlargement and 'deepening' of the Community were to be resolved. Moreover, Brandt's style of describing the European future in very evocative terms, while not in practice being really able to make financial sacrifices for the attainment of these goals, helped to weaken the attraction of the European idea both in the SPD and in the West German public opinion in general (see Chapter 5).

The Schmidt period The direction of SPD European policy changed during Helmut Schmidt's incumbency of the chancellorship (1974–82). There was a much greater emphasis on counting the cost and encouraging budgetary stability. In this context he made some specific suggestions, for example that one of the commissioners be appointed a sort of European finance minister (that is with a budgetary portfolio) and that a European court of auditors be created. In a study prepared for the SPD *Präsidium* shortly before he became chancellor, Schmidt rejected any major West German financial sacrifice such as making West German currency resources available on an EC-wide basis, or higher West German contributions to the EC Budget, in the hope that it would impel other governments to move forward (*Die Zeit*, 17 May 1974).

The main thrust of SPD pronouncements was far less favourable to supranational solutions than it had been since at least 1960. Both Chancellor Schmidt and successive finance ministers, Hans Apel and Hans Matthöfer, were very critical of the EC Commission and they repeatedly made it clear that they regarded intergovernmental consultation and co-operation as the way towards European integration. The most European member of the SPD ministerial team, Katherina Focke, was dropped after the federal election of October 1976.

There was one other major departure from previous SPD policies during the period of the Schmidt chancellorship. Generally speaking the SPD had in its postwar history been much cooler in its attitudes towards France than the CDU/CSU. In the Schumacher period the posture had been one of suspicion and hostility. At a later period the SPD's belated espousal of supranationalism rendered them very critical of Gaullist attitudes and policies. Paradoxically Schmidt, a lifelong Anglophile, who had been the only SPD member to vote against the EEC Treaty because of Britain's exclusion, became very much identified with a European policy of working in tandem with the French. This policy represented an attempt to create a 'zone of stability' in the EC. This could only be done with the French, given British difficulties (Schmidt, 'Time to forget the British Problem', *The Times*, 3 January 1983). The French indeed undertook considerable risks in bringing their domestic arrangements, particularly in the area of the management of the economy, into harmony with the '*Modell Deutschland*' (Story, 1981).

The most distinctive social democratic element in the party's European policy was its emphasis on the social dimension of the Community. From 1970 onwards leading spokesmen of the SPD argued the case for 'turning the Community inside ten years to the most socially progressive area of the world'. At the European summit in Paris in 1972 Willy Brandt had called for a 'social union' of the Community on the grounds that a common social policy would make it easier for many citizens to identify with the EC. In making such a demand Brandt was reviving an SPD perspective on Europe which had played a major role in the 1950s. The detailed suggestions were for a co-ordinated labour market policy, improvement of working conditions, an effective participation by working people in their firms, the conclusion of European wage agreements, a Community social budget, an effective regional policy, reform of adult and professional education and EC regulations for the protection of the environment. These points were extended in the European Policy Programme of the SPD in 1975. This programme stressed the importance of co-determination for the democratization of industry. There were a number of very specific proposals which included the standardization of policies on job security, the necessity of reporting in advance any proposal that was likely to damage the environment, equal participation for employees in the fruits of economic growth and a much closer inspection of subsidies.

In general, however, SPD proposals for Europe while the party was in power were relatively infrequent and statements on Europe had a ritual obligatory quality.

The Greens

Dissatisfaction with the SPD-led government of Helmut Schmidt by some on the left of the SPD and the growth of concern with environmental/quality of life issues led to the gradual formation of the party which came to be known as 'the Greens' (*die Grünen*) in the late 1970s and it took part in the first direct election of 1979. In 1983 it secured representation in the Bundestag and in 1984 in the European election the Greens scored quite highly with 8.2 per cent of the vote.

The broad consensus between the West German parties on political and economic issues does not include the Greens. This is also true in relation to European integration. The Greens' anti-bureaucratic, anti-growth, pro-environmental, participatory ethos leads them to take a much more critical view of the EC than the other parties represented in the Bundestag. The fullest statement of the views of the Greens on Europe is given in their declaration for the European election of 1984 agreed at their March 1984 conference in Karlsruhe.

Their views initially diverged fundamentally from the other parties in relation to the Common Agricultural Policy. Unlike the SPD, which is the only other party to express a critical view of the CAP, the Greens criticized the CAP not only, or even primarily, on the grounds of its cost to consumers, but on the encouragement it gave to the intensive use of fertilizers and pesticides and for its encouragement of large-scale capital intensive farming at the expense of the small farmer.

> The CAP has contributed to the ruin of small and medium sized farms and to the poisoning of the soil, water and foodstuffs. (Karlsruhe Declaration on European Elections, 1984)

The Greens have been most active in the field of agricultural policy since Karlsruhe ('*Grüne Agrarpolitik*', 1985). They have concentrated on measures to protect medium and smaller holdings. Their basic argument has been that prices should reflect the labour input, in other words they are in favour of the maintenance of high prices which protect the relatively inefficient farmer. Their rhetoric against proposed dairy quota cuts in 1984 was very similar to the CSU's (Leonhardt, 1984, pp. 199–200). In that sense they have joined the West German consensus.

Unlike the other parties who are at least at the declaratory level in favour of the expansion of the powers of the European Parliament and Community institutions, in general the Greens are explicitly against any extension of the powers of EC institutions. The Greens are the only party to reject the present Community structure.

> The Greens are part of a comprehensive movement which calls into question the existing structure and goals of the European Community. (Karlsruhe Declaration, 1984)

The alternative preferred by the Greens is devolution to the regions.

> Think globally; act locally! The alternative to the European Community of bureaucrats, bombs and buttermountains is a peaceful Europe of the regions. (Karlsruhe Declaration, 1984)

The strong support that the Greens enjoy among the educated young therefore indicate some weakening in the consensus of support for European integration in the Federal Republic. However, although the main thrust of the Greens' policy on the EC is critical, it is often very difficult to work out what their policy is as their programmes sometimes reflect rather than conceal differences between those Greens who are mildly critical of the EC and those who are fundamentally opposed (Leonhardt, 1984, pp. 195–6).

European policy-making within the parties

In the preceding section we looked at the historical development of the policies of the individual parties on European integration. The general explanation for the consensus on this policy area was contained in the chapter on public opinion (Chapter 5). Throughout this present chapter we attempt to explain some continuing differences within the broad framework of consensus and the emergence of a party, the Greens, which lies outside this consensus. This next section, therefore, examines the manner in which European policy is handled by the political parties.[3]

The CDU/CSU

Although the CDU/CSU have a joint *Bundestagsfraktion*, they are in other respects separate parties and this division is one reason for the greater involvement of extra-parliamentary bodies in the making of European policy in the CDU-CSU as compared with the other major parties represented at federal level. There are two further reasons. In the period between 1969 and 1982, the CDU/CSU were in opposition at federal level and this meant that the party itself rather than the party in government had to concern itself with developing medium- to long-term policies. This necessarily meant some shift to extra-parliamentary bodies since the *Bundestagsfraktion* is primarily concerned, particularly in opposition, with short term reactive policies and tactics. The CDU/CSU has also always prided itself on being a '*Volkspartei*' incorporating a large number of different interests. While the CDU/CSU was in government these interests could be accommodated at governmental level; in opposition more of their input was channelled through the extra-parliamentary party.

The CDU – the federal party headquarters (Bundesgeschäftsstelle) One of the most striking features in the development of the CDU in the 1960s was the continuous strengthening of the federal headquarters (Paterson, 1985a, pp. 60–80). Until then the party had been much less centrally organized and much less well-staffed than that of the SPD, reflecting Adenauer's fears that a too well equipped party headquarters would constrain the party leader.

The *Bundesgeschäftsstelle* has a division with responsibility for European and inter-German policy. The division most involved in European policy is the Economic and Social Policy division. This division has subsections which are very heavily engaged in the making of European policy. They include economic and financial policy; energy and structural policy; trade cycle policy; and agricultural policy. Of these, the section dealing with agriculture has the greatest involvement with EC affairs.

These sub-divisions service a number of parallel specialist committees and the head of the sub-division in party headquarters is normally the secretary of the relevant specialist committee *Bundesfachausschuss*. Each *Bundesfachausschuss* is the main policy-making body in the executive on its own area although ultimate approval must come from the executive as a whole.

These specialist committees, unlike the practice in the other parties, are tied into a complex network of opinion-forming bodies since they are each underpinned by thirteen regional committees (*Landesfachausschüsse*). The *Landesfachausschüsse* are in turn tied to local *Kreisfachausschüsse*. At the federal level the agricultural specialist committee is the committee which is most often concerned with EC issues. It is much larger than the other specialist committees. It includes CDU or CSU ministers of agriculture from the *Länder* and a large number of parliamentarians from the Bundestag or from *Länder* parliaments. The *Bundesfachausschuss* for agriculture meets on two or three occasions a year and EC items, if not specifically mentioned in the agenda, arise in relation to those matters.

The executive committee of the CDU very occasionally deals with EC issues. This tends to happen either when a very significant European issue arises such as the establishment of the European Monetary System or in connection with the planning and organization of European elections. The federal executive committee of the CDU holds official talks with the German Farmers' Union about every eighteen months and prior to every federal election. In the past CDU/CSU ministers of agriculture have regularly attended executive meetings of the German Farmers' Union.

Auxiliary organizations As a '*Volkspartei*' the CDU contains a large range of organized interests. In relation to the making of European policy the most important, alongside agriculture, are the *Wirtschaftsrat* (business interests) and the *Mittlestandsvereinigungen* (small business). Dr Philipp von Bismarck, a prominent CDU MEP, is also chairman of the *Wirtschaftsrat* and Dr van Aerssen, until 1983 the only dual mandated member, was also a prominent member.

Informal organizational channels The key place of agriculture in CDU calculations (see pp. 155–61) has meant a proliferation of extra-parliamentary policy-making networks. CDU and CSU (*Länder*) agriculture ministers meet in their party capacity prior to the meetings of the Bundesrat Agriculture Committee. The head of the agricultural division in the party headquarters and therefore ex-officio secretary of the agricultural *Bundesfachausschuss*, holds monthly consultations with the general secretary of the German Farmers' Union. These routine scheduled meetings are a particular feature of the agriculture sector. In other areas contacts are taken up with relevant interests as and when important issues arise.

The Christian Social Union

The Christian Social Union operates in more or less permanent alliance with the CDU at federal level and in Bavaria as the governing party and articulator of Bavaria's special interests. The organization of the CSU's European policy reflects this duality. The CSU group of MPs has a separate organization, in addition to participation in CDU/CSU *Bundestagsfraktion* groups. The CSU *Landesgruppe* has six study groups, the second of which coincides with the CDU working group on agricultural and economic policy. There is no need for subgroups since only CSU MPs are members.

In Munich European policy is sometimes discussed by the party executive. It was most often discussed during the so-called Gaullist-Atlanticist clash but it was also discussed by the full party executive at the time of the Mansholt Plan and before the direct elections (Mintzel, 1977, pp. 261–7 and 272–98).

There appears to be a division of labour in the CSU in which the party chairman, Franz-Josef Strauss, is given a completely free hand on questions of general integration policy. In individual sectors, particularly agriculture, there is a dense network of specialists in the party headquarters who service parallel committees as in the CDU. Their job is to articulate particular Bavarian interests and feed them into the policy-making process.

The Bundestagsfraktion The CDU/CSU *Bundestagsfraktion* is organized into working groups in a manner which is broadly similar to that of the SPD. Until 1980 there were six broad working groups underpinned by numerous study groups. Since 1980 there have been fifteen working groups and six specialist discussion groups later adjusted to seventeen and five respectively. In relation to European policy-making, the Agriculture Working Group plays a key role. It shadows the Bundestag Agriculture Committee and includes all CDU/CSU MPs who belong to the Bundestag committee. It liaises with the German Farmers' Union and could justifiably be said to be captured by and to speak for the agricultural interest. In the period 1976–80 regular discussions took place between the key CDU/CSU figures on the committree and the DBV. The CDU/CSU representatives were Herr Kiechle (CSU), chairman of the committee, Herr D. Schröder (CDU), deputy chairman, Dr Ritz (CDU), agricultural spokesman for the CDU/CSU *Fraktion*, and Herr Susset, a spokesman of the CDU/CSU in the Bundestag Agriculture Committee, all of whom, except for Ritz, were farmers. Ritz was not a farmer himself but could be regarded as having a vested interest in agriculture as a lecturer on agriculture.

The Free Democratic Party

The making of European policy is a relatively simple process in the Free Democratic Party. There are two main reasons for the simplicity of procedures. First, the small size and resource base of the FDP necessarily entails a much more streamlined set of decision-making organs than in the larger parties. In particular, the small membership of the FDP and its weak power base in nearly all *Länder* means that the extra-parliamentary party is only marginally represented on decision-making organs, and, in the case of European policy, plays almost no role. Secondly, the continuous involvement of the FDP in government since 1969, and its incumbency of the most important ministerial posts in relation to European policy-making (though not agriculture after the government reshuffle in 1983), has meant that the party has tended to rely more on governmental than its own resources.

Within the FDP, European policy is managed within the *Bundestagsfraktion*. The *Fraktion* had six working groups and European matters were handled by working group six (*Europa*). Like other working groups, this was managed by a section head on the *Fraktion*'s staff who also ran the European Office. All

Community business, regardless of whether it be integration policy or specific legislation, was dealt with by the European Office and working group six. It was comparatively rare for EC initiatives to be discussed in conjunction with other parliamentary groups and only occurred on major initiatives.

Two significant changes occurred in the period 1983–4. With the reduced size of the FDP group in 1983 (reduced from 54 to 34) the European working group was dissolved. European issues are now discussed in the working group on foreign and security policy. The second development was the failure of the FDP to exceed the 5 per cent barrier in the 1984 European elections. This brought to an end the involvement of FDP MEPs in the parliamentary group's work in Bonn. Relations with the MEPs had been very close since they were frequently in Bonn. Martin Bangemann, then leader of the liberal MEPs, now economics minister, was in Bonn on a weekly basis as a member of the FDP *Präsidium*.

The FDP arrangements prior to 1983 seemed to work comparatively smoothly. A senior FDP official told us that recommendations of the (then) FDP working group on Europe were automatically accepted by the *Fraktion*. This phenomenon of the expert working group's recommendation being accepted by the whole *Fraktion*, more or less on the nod, is common to all the parliamentary parties with the exception of the Greens. It is perhaps even more marked in the FDP, however, since the demand for committee places does not exceed the supply. This means that all the experts in a particular policy area who wish to be on a particular committee can be. No one has to make do with a second or third choice. Each committee thus tends to encompass the whole field of expertise that the *Fraktion* has in a particular area and therefore the rest of the *Fraktion* is generally in no position to question its judgement.

The SPD

The making of European policy in the SPD is divided between the party executive and the *Bundestagsfraktion* though, of course, there is a great deal of overlap between these two bodies. The party executive is only intermittently active in the making of European policy. It concerns itself with relations with other socialist parties and this can have implications for European policy. Relations with the Spanish and Portuguese parties, for instance, had clear implications for enlargement. It was also responsible for the preparation of the SPD's electoral programme for the European elections and for the management of the SPD's electoral strategy in these elections. It has a European policy subcommittee which is only spasmodically active and may be upstaged by *ad hoc* bodies such as that chaired by Hans Apel in 1980, to suggest reforms to the CAP.

The broad support given by the parties to European integration, its relative lack of saliency as a political issue, and the lack of interest of party members means that there is very little pressure on the party executive to concern itself on a continuing basis with European policy. Indeed, the fact that the party chairman, Willy Brandt, is particularly interested in foreign policy probably means that the SPD executive has taken a greater interest than it would under any other party chairman. The lack of involvement of the contemporary party executive contrasts with the period before 1955 when the SPD was opposed to European integration, then an issue of high political saliency, that was often discussed by the party executive and its committee.

The inner cabinet of the party executive, the *Präsidium*, which meets on a weekly basis, rarely takes a position on European matters since they are normally neither matters of great urgency nor of great saliency. The *Präsidium* is concerned with co-ordinating the party's strategy in the domestic political game and as European issues rarely constitute the focus of party political competition, the *Präsidium* rarely considers this. The major exception to this rule occurred in 1974 when Helmut Schmidt prepared the major paper already referred to for the *Präsidium* (see p. 139).

The Bundestagsfraktion The *Bundestagsfraktion* is, as in other parties, the most important focus of SPD involvement in European policy. As in the other *Fraktionen* work is organized through working groups; each of the six groups is chaired by one of the six vice-chairmen of the parliamentary party. The way in which European issues are dealt with parallels the division of policy responsibilities at the federal level of government. Integration and high political issues are dealt with by the '*Aussen- und Sicherheitspolitik*' working group of the *Fraktion*, while the more routine EC issues and also major specialist policy developments are dealt with by the study groups which together form the economic policy working group. The foreign affairs and security policy working group of the SPD *Fraktion* acts as a sort of co-ordinating point for *Europapolitik*.[4] During the FDP/SPD coalition this institution had very close ties to the successive SPD politicians (Apel, von Dohnanyi and Corterier) who were junior ministers responsible for European policy in the Foreign Office.

The study groups are almost exclusively concerned with scrutiny of EC legislation. The two exceptions to this are the preparation of the annual plenary sessions and the drafting of interpellations tabled in the name of the *Fraktion* on EC matters. Neither of these two activities occupies a great deal of time. The annual plenary session has a ritualistic character and interpellations on European policy are relatively infrequent.

In relation to European policy the study groups are primarily concerned with the scrutiny of legislation. They are part therefore of an essentially reactive process. All EC legislative proposals received by the Bundestag are considered initially by the relevant *Fraktion* study group and evaluated. In the period before the first direct election of June 1979 MEPs were among the less frequent participants due to commitments in the European Parliament. As MEPs are now directly elected they are freed from many of the domestic burdens that weighed so heavily on their delegated predecessors and are thus able to participate more frequently in the work of the study groups.

Relations between MEPs and their parties

The establishment of a directly elected European Parliament raised problems of co-ordination with national parties. After the federal election of 1980 only Willy Brandt (SPD) and Dr van Aerssen (CDU) held dual mandates. Brandt resigned from the European Parliament in 1983 and van Aerssen ceased to be a member of the Bundestag after the March 1983 election. All the parties therefore had to develop special mechanisms for co-ordination. The FDP established the (now defunct) European Committee to co-ordinate the work of FDP deputies in both parliaments. In the SPD a co-ordination office, located in the *Fraktion* and run by Helga Köhnen links MPs and MEPs. SPD MEPs meet about ten times a year in Bonn. In the CDU/CSU three MEPs are normally in the *Fraktionsvorstand* in Bonn. The CDU/CSU *Bundestagsfraktion* has a European Office for co-ordinating the work of the CDU and CSU representatives in the two parliaments. The MPs and MEPs meet annually for a round table discussion. There is also a complex set of arrangements enabling MEPs to bring policy matters to the attention of the parliamentary groups. In general these arrangements seemed to have worked reasonably well.

The MEPs of all the main parties that we have interviewed complained of difficulties in dealing with their parties below the federal level. In none of the parties are there links between the

MEPs and the *Landtagsfraktionen*. MEPs of all parties (not including Greens who were unrepresented until 1984) reported that there was no anti-EC mood in their party but that party members had little real interest in the EC and that party officials were uninterested in the mobilization of support for Europe.[5]

In the period 1979–83 criticism of the CDU/CSU members of the European Parliament hardly existed though they themselves complained about not being taken seriously by the party at home. In our interviews with party members we encountered a great deal of dissatisfaction with the four FDP members who were invariably referred to as the '*Viererbande*' (Gang of Four). However, this criticism had no impact on their failure to be re-elected at the 1984 elections to the EP; that was the result of the FDP's general predicament at that time (Bulmer and Paterson, 1986).

Most criticism was levelled at the performance of the SPD members. This reflects a basically hostile conservative press whose 'European' correspondents as '*verdiente Europäer*' are unlikely to be SPD supporters, and the fact that the SPD itself, like the British Labour Party, is much more critical of the performance of its representatives at all levels. However, beyond these grounds there have been a number of mini-scandals. The resignation of trade union MEPs Karl Hauenschild (*IG Chemie*) and Eugen Loderer (*IG Metall*) six months after the 1979 direct election, exposed the SPD to the charge (not entirely unfounded) that the candidature of these trade union leaders had been a cynical electoral ploy. Throughout the period 1979–82 there was a lot of criticism of the performance of Willy Brandt as MEP, which focused on his failure to appear often enough in Strasbourg. He appeared on eighteen days in total. To some extent this criticism was exaggerated, but Brandt's multiple office holding certainly raised problems. The fall of the Schmidt government meant that the whole burden of representing the SPD fell on Willy Brandt and he announced in October 1982 that he would only continue for a short time; he resigned in early 1983.

West German representation in the European Parliament was significantly modified by the result of the 1984 European election. The FDP no longer has any MEPs since its vote fell under the 5 per cent barrier to representation. This is likely to weaken significantly the input into FDP European policy and make it more dependent than ever on governmental resources. The Greens polled 8.2 per cent and secured seven seats. Particular problems of co-ordination are likely to arise since the Green

MEPs are committed to rotation, i.e. resigning their seats and making way for alternates halfway through the five-year term. To add to this difficulty the MPs they will have to deal with in Bonn will be largely inexperienced since almost the whole of the present *Fraktion* 'rotated' and made way for successors in March/April 1985.

Despite these problems some arrangements have been made. The *Fraktion* employs five people, dealing with European issues, of whom two are more or less exclusively concerned with co-ordination between Bonn and Strasbourg. Green MEPs can take part in all *Fraktion* meetings as they have a philosophy of 'open' meetings. The very loose form of co-ordination developed by the Greens leaves their members in the EP's Rainbow Group with maximum discretion but at the price of possible divergences.

This section has indicated some interesting differences in the policy-making patterns of the parties. For the Christian Democratic parties agriculture has taken a central place in the policy-making structures, indicating its place in the 'politics of support' of the CDU/CSU. The distinctive features of European policy-making in the FDP were its domination by relatively few people and – until 1984 – the much greater role of the MEPs as compared with other parties. The replacement of Genscher by Bangemann as party chairman guarantees the continued interest in European policy on the part of the leadership, the latter having been the leader of the FDP MEPs until 1984. As in other areas, policy-making by the Greens does not follow the pattern of 'domination by experts', that characterizes the other parties.

In all the parties the saliency of European policy was low but was lower in the SPD and the Greens than in the FDP. It was highest in the CDU/CSU but even then was low compared to other policy areas. It is this lack of saliency, rather than an absence of structures, which helps explain the relative lack of impact of the parties on European policy.

The impact of the parties

In the first section of this chapter, we looked at the development of party policies on European integration. The general picture that emerged was of a trend towards convergence in the 1950s followed by the appearance of some nuanced differences within the framework of a broad consensus on the desirability of

European integration and finally the emergence of the Greens. In the second section we attempted to evaluate the significance of European policy to the parties by looking at the way the parties handled the making of European policy. We now wish to look at the impact of the political parties on the making of European policy.

The European level

The West German political parties have firmly established their presence at the European level of activity. The established parties are members of transnational party organizations. The Greens, however, are the exception although they play a leading role in the EP's Rainbow Group, established after the 1984 election. The SPD is a member of the Confederation of Socialist Parties, established in 1974. The FDP is a leading member of the European Liberals and Democrats. Martin Bangemann, the present FDP chairman, played a key role in the transnational party's foundation, which took place in 1976. The CDU and CSU are both members of the European People's Party, also created in 1976. They are also members of a much looser and more conservative grouping known as the European Democratic Union.

Although all the West German parties play leading and influential roles in their respective transnational parties, these parties themselves are singularly ineffective. The transnational parties which played a visible role in the campaign for the first directly elected European Parliament were reduced to an almost negligible role in the second European election of June 1984 (Paterson, 1985b, p. 7). Outside their role in the first European election they have largely been ineffective.

Any influence that the West German parties exert at a European level is indirect. The least indirect form of influence is through the presence of their representatives in the various political groups of the European Parliament. Although relatively direct, this influence is minimal given the very weak powers of the European Parliament. In the case of the representatives of political parties who are in power in Bonn, the degree to which they represent purely party positions in the European Parliament is constrained by quite strong pressures to represent the policy of the Federal Government.[6] It will be interesting to see how effective the Greens will be in the new Rainbow Group since they will be much less constrained by governmental and bureaucratic pressures.

The influence of political parties on the Commission is very indirect. The two German commissioners normally have a partisan colouring. One of the commissioners has always been seen as being recruited through the SPD/trade union axis and the other commissioner is always either from the CDU/CSU or the FDP. The opportunity that this gives for party leverage on individual European policy decisions is in practice slight. Once appointed they are formally independent and will normally be renominated provided they have not seriously been at odds with the incumbent West German government. If European policy were more visible and controversial, there might be a stronger pressure for party leverage on commissioners. The lack of real interest helps to explain a phenomenon that has been much commented on, namely the reluctance of influential West German politicians to agree to act as commissioners. The last really influential figures from the Federal Republic who served as commissioners were Walter Hallstein, whose term ended in 1966, and Ralf Dahrendorf who served from 1970–4. Karl-Heinz Narjes is an arguable exception but his total identification with the EEC has inhibited his chances of becoming really influential in the CDU/CSU.

The two most important decision-making bodies of the Community are the Council of Ministers and the European Council. Here any party influence is indirect, via the Federal Government which participates in both organs.

The national level

At the national level a number of further factors serve to constrain the impact of the political parties on European policy. These factors can be further subdivided into those which are particularly marked in the area of European policy and those which serve to constrain the impact of political parties on public policy generally in West Germany. In the chapter on public opinion we looked at the reasons for the emergence of a general consensus on the desirability of European integration by the end of the 1950s. Since then European policy has possessed a very muted partisan colouring. This has hardly been changed by the emergence of the Greens since, between European elections, they devote very little attention to it. Party policies, as we saw in the opening section of this chapter, are not identical even if none of the established parties openly questions the desirability of the goal. On matters of policy however these differences between the parties have little impact. All the parties, with the exception of the Greens, share a very large number of points of agreement. Points of disagreement are largely a matter of nuance, for example the SPD emphasis on social policy. On long-term policy the most striking difference is between the CSU and the other parties. The cosmic nature of the CSU's long-term goals and aspirations and the absence of the external preconditions that could give them a reality mean that they have no perceptible impact on the content of the European policy of the Federal Republic.

The lack of party impact brought about by the party political consensus on Europe is increased by the relative lack of interest of party members in this area. SPD ordinary party members have very little interest in the Community. The interest of FDP members is greater but still slight. Ordinary CDU and CSU members seem to be more interested but the EC's general lack of saliency as a political issue means that the party professionals have little interest in strengthening the interests of party members in European matters. A very senior CDU official described to us the minority (about 25 per cent) in the CDU, who were interested in Europe, as 'Euro-Freaks'. This lack of interest means that European policy-making and even discussion about policy remains a very specialist matter, settled and discussed in a very narrow section of the political elite. Pressure from the parties on governments in this area is thus correspondingly weak.

A final explanation for the lack of impact of the parties in this policy sector in the last two decades is suggested by the composition of the governments involved. In the Grand Coalition, the relevant ministries were divided between the CDU/CSU and the SPD. Within the CDU/CSU there was a further cleavage between Gaullists and Atlanticists. The basic convention of the Grand Coalition was that policy should only be pursued with any vigour in areas of agreement; areas of contention were simply bracketed out ('*ausgeklammert*'). This convention thus operated to minimize the impact of party politics on European policy.

Governmental composition since 1969 has also contributed to a lack of party impact on European policy. In the five SPD/FDP governments of 1969–82 most of the key posts in relation to European policy were held by the FDP. The FDP provided the foreign minister and the minister of agriculture throughout this period; it also provided the minister of economics for much of the time. Both chancellors were from the SPD but they only intermittently played a leading role in the making of European policy in the last two decades (see Chapters 2 and 3). Since 1973 there has been a minister of state at the Foreign Office with special responsibility for European policy. He was always from the SPD until the coalition collapse of 1982. Since then both incumbents have been from the CDU.

The possession of the key ministries by the FDP in this period serves to constrain party impact on European policy in two important respects. The first respect relates to the relative autonomy of the FDP party leadership from the party in the country. This general freedom of leadership is the precondition for the survival of the FDP since, without it, the party would not have the necessary flexibility to bring about the timely changes of policy and coalition partners at federal and *Land* level that have ensured its survival. In the particular sector of European policy this general feature is faithfully replicated, since as we noted in the second section of this chapter, extra-parliamentary involvement in the making of FDP European policy is minimal and *Fraktion* involvement is restricted to a tight little group of European experts.

The key role of the FDP in this area has led to a further restriction on partisan involvement. It is conventional in West Germany for political parties to exercise extensive patronage functions and, once a ministerial post goes to a particular party, then it is normal particularly for the upper reaches of that ministry to be fairly extensively colonized by public officials who are supporters of that party. This convention does not apply in the case of ministries headed by the FDP due to its size, thus incumbency of the key posts has clearly meant a very minor role for 'political' officials as compared with some other sectors.

In the second of the CDU/CSU/FDP goverments, that of 1983, the FDP lost the incumbency of the Agriculture Ministry. In the case of the new CSU minister, Ignaz Kiechle, it is very hard to decide whether his policy is being affected by the DBV or the CSU since their positions are so similar. A more detailed look at the impact of political parties on the formulation of agricultural policy is given in the case study.

General factors These factors specific to the European policy area interact with and are reinforced by a number of general structural factors which act to inhibit the impact of political parties on public policy in the Federal Republic. General factors particularly relevant to this area include the prevalence of coalition governments and normally the necessity to secure a majority both in the Bundestag and the Bundesrat, bodies with varying party composition. Both these features are held to have moved the system towards 'the politics of centrality' and to an evening out of partisan differences and therefore of the impact of parties.

A marked feature of West German government, the relative freedom of the Federal Bank from partisan pressures, is important in the area of European policy (see Chapters 2 and 3). A final typical feature which tends to shut out political parties is the general policy-making style in Bonn which stresses expertise and in which the federal ministries and bureaucracy in Bonn interact with 'cooperative, trustworthy " professional" organisations which acquire privileged institutionalised status' (Dyson, 1982a, p. 19).

Thus far we have attempted to explain the lack of impact of the parties in the course of the last two decades. The established parties have been part of a general consensus and so it is by definition difficult to disentangle the precise impact of the parties from other institutions and factors. The success of the Greens in securing representation in both the Bundestag and the European Parliament raises interesting questions about their impact. In general they have had relatively little effect in central areas like agriculture. In both parliaments they are more or less isolated, being beyond the consensus and with minimal representation on key committees. Their views on European policy in these areas have been relatively ineffective. On environmental issues by contrast they have been surprisingly influential in moving the Federal Government towards supporting European initiatives on preventing acid rain (emission control of car exhausts), and on lead-free petrol. This is because in this area the Greens' views, which were initially outside the prevailing consensus, have become more and more popular and thus present a potential electoral threat to the government and established parties (Turner, 1986).

Case study: the FDP and the agricultural dimension of European policy

It has been argued in this chapter that the impact of the political parties on European policy, although difficult to separate out, is comparatively slight. This is in marked contrast to Britain where the influence of party considerations has had a very marked impact, particularly when the Labour party has been in power. This general view of the nature of European policy-making in the Federal Republic is accepted by nearly all observers. There is, however, one area of dispute. A number of observers, particularly Anglo-American scholars, have argued that party political considerations have been important or even dominant in the formulation of German agricultural policy (Averyt, 1977;

Andrlik, 1981; Hu, 1981; Neville-Rolfe, 1984). It is further argued by these authors, that in the period 1969–82 the pro-agricultural nature of German European policy was due to the presence of the FDP in government and their 'blackmail' of the senior coalition partner, the SPD. In order to evaluate this view of the determinants of agricultural policy in the Federal Republic it is perhaps useful if we begin by looking at the reaction of German agriculture to the formation of the Common Market and the Common Agricultural Policy.

The initial response of German agriculture to the negotiations for the establishment of the EEC was to display fear and suspicion. The Central Committee of German Agriculture stated at the time of the publication of the EEC draft treaty that 'the project of a European Common Market faces the agriculture of the Federal Republic with very serious problems' (cited in Mahant, 1969, p. 358). Of German agriculture's many objections to, and conditions for, the establishment of the EEC, two predominated. The first of these was opposition to any plans to extend the Common Market in agriculture beyond the European territories of the Six, either in the form of a free trade area or by the association of the French and Belgian overseas territories. The second principal condition for acceptance of the EEC by the spokesmen for German agriculture was consultation during the negotiations and representation in the EC institutions.

Neither of these conditions was fulfilled or was even likely to be fulfilled and yet German agriculture accepted the EEC. There were two main reasons for this. The commitment of Adenauer to the establishment of the EEC was a very strong one and one which was unlikely to be affected by tactical considerations like the potential electoral alienation of the farmers. Moreover the farmers had nowhere to turn since, although the FDP was opposed to the EEC, it was too small to be an appropriate vehicle to block the acceptance of the EEC; and the major opposition party, the SPD, had by that time made it clear that it was committed to support of the EEC and it would not have been likely to change in order to accommodate the farmers who in any case had always been identified with the CDU/CSU and to a much lesser extent the FDP. The second major reason was that during the negotiations the DBV established links with other farmers' organizations throughout the Six and it became clear that it would probably be able to block any developments which were inimical to its interests.

If the farmers proved to be too weak to prevent the establishment of the EEC, they nevertheless continued to exert a great deal of influence on the formulation of policy in their particular sector. How is this possible in an overwhelmingly industrial society? A major part of the answer is to be found in the extraordinary strength and cohesion of the *Deutscher Bauernverband*. It has approximately 750,000 members and represents over 90 per cent of those engaged full-time in agriculture. This is the highest ratio of membership of any interest group in the Federal Republic. Unlike the situation in the Weimar Republic and unlike a number of other continental countries, there are no significant regional or religious cleavages.

This amazingly cohesive group is also helped by a very beneficent mass and elite opinion. As indicated in the chapter on public opinion, West Germans do not rate agricultural surpluses highly as a major problem. The beneficent view of farmers has a number of roots. These include the long term effects of 'the *Blut and Bodenmystik*' of the Third Reich, fear of rural radicalism engendered by the collapse of Weimar, the close relations between urban and rual dwellers fostered by the food shortages of the early postwar period, the fact that one quarter of the population of West Germany have fled from the overwhelmingly agricultural areas of Eastern Germany and the feeling present in the early years of the Federal Republic that the loss of these agricultural lands in the East would necessarily mean subsidizing agriculture in the Federal Republic in order to make good the deficit, for the indefinite future. This deficit had produced extreme hunger in the years after the war and the subsidization of the farming interest was part of the founding compact of the Federal Republic given formal expression in the Lübke Plan of 1953 and the Agricultural Act of 1955.

The high levels of cohesion and of public and elite acceptance of the DBV ideology that farmers perform a vital service to the economy and to the maintenance of the countryside are clearly major political resources for the DBV and the agricultural interest in the Federal Republic. The DBV seeks to use these favourable background conditions in a number of ways. First and most important it cultivates a close relationship with the Ministry of Agriculture. It has been notably successful in this area and the ministry is often spoken of as an example of 'clientelism' or agency capture. It also directs its attention to the Bundestag. Its attention here is directed to control of the Bundestag Agriculture Committee. In the Agriculture Committee for the legislative period 1980–2, 16 of the 26 members were directly engaged in agriculture and the viewpoint of this committee is normally very close to the DBV. Our argument here is that the Bundestag is thus unlikely to act as a countervailing power to the Ministry of Agriculture since it delegates powers to the Agriculture Committee which is securely dominated by the agriculture interest.

The DBV has also been notably successful in getting its supporters into key positions in the CDU/CSU and the FDP. The present minister of agriculture, Ignaz Kiechle (CSU), has for long been a prominent member of the DBV and, but for the requirements of coalition balance, the job would have gone to von Heeremann the DBV president who had been Kohl's choice in the past. Relations with the SPD have never been so close and very few full-time farmers vote SPD.

In the introduction to this section we mentioned two hypotheses. First, that the impact of party political considerations had been important or even dominant in the formulation of German agricultural policy and, secondly, that in the period 1969–82 the FDP was able successfully to 'blackmail' its coalition partner, the SPD, in the agricultural interest. We now examine the first of these hypotheses.

The influence of the political parties on agriculture In CDU-led coalitions farming interests could be expected to have a high priority given the electoral preference of the farming interest for the CDU and even greater importance of the agricultural interest to the CSU (Mintzel, 1972; 1977). However, when farming interests came into direct conflict with European integration in the negotiations for the establishment of the EEC, the farmers' interest lost. This same pattern was repeated during the negotiations for the establishment of the Common Agricultural Policy. German cereal prices were out of line with other countries and the French government presented an alternative which forced Chancellor Erhard to choose between support of German farm interests and European integration. After consultation with the DBV, the Federal Government proposed a drop in cereal prices from DM475/ton to DM440/ton plus adjustment payments to German farmers of DM840m. in 1965 and DM1,100m. in 1966. In subsequent negotiations the Federal Government had to agree to compromise proposals put forward by Commissioner Mansholt for a price of DM425/ton and a steep reduction in compensating amounts. However, they immediately passed an *EWG-Anpassungsgesetz* (adjustment plan) which made very handsome adjustment payments to German farmers. This same procedure was adopted in 1984 when the German government agreed to restrictions on the production of dairy products and then unilaterally paid German farmers handsome compensation amounts. In the controversy concerning the lowering of cereal prices in 1985 Ignaz Kiechle came under very clear pressure from the CSU (*Der Spiegel*, no. 20, 1985, pp. 21–2). In this case the Federal Government supported a German veto on the sinking of cereal price levels and this cut across its broad strategy of integration which was due to be advanced at the Milan summit.

Our argument here is that on agricultural policy the CDU/CSU and FDP tend to reflect the views of the agricultural interest for the reasons outlined. However this is not to say that they have a great impact since routine policy largely arises out of the interaction between the Agriculture Ministry and the DBV. When German policy on agriculture is defeated by its partners in the EC, the CDU/CSU and the FDP can be relied upon to produce a majority to pass compensatory legislation. The parties act here as an insurance for the agricultural interest. Presumably, the reason this procedure was not followed in 1985 was because of the amount of turbulence caused by the 1984 dairy agreement and its effect on the campaign and results of the 1984 election to the EP. This had mobilized the farmers to the extent that they would not be satisfied with a 'compensatory' solution and the CDU/CSU had real fears about how this might work out electorally.

The FDP as 'blackmail' party The coming to power in 1969 of an SPD-led coalition with the FDP which lasted until 1982 did not bring about any significant change in German agricultural policy. This might have been expected since the CDU/CSU, the closest political ally of the DBV, was now in opposition and the SPD had minimal electoral support among farmers. Many scholars, particularly those writing outside Germany, have stressed the role of the FDP and its minister of agriculture, Josef Ertl, in defending farming interests and blackmailing the SPD against the economic interests of its own members into supporting a too strongly pro-agricultural line on European policy.

Such an analysis is too simplistic and even misleading. As already noted, there is a general consensus in the Federal Republic in favour of supporting agriculture and agricultural surpluses are not seen as a burden in the way they are in Britain. It is significant here that the *EWG-Anpassungsgesetz*, already mentioned, was passed *unanimously*. The SPD was thus under no significant pressure from its supporters to curb the spending on agriculture. Moreover, later as a partner in government it was motivated by the fact that it could be argued that EC agricultural spending was in Germany's interest since the Federal Republic was a beneficiary under the CAP. Thus, despite Helmut Schmidt's occasional expressions of desire to reform the CAP and the similar findings of the Hans Apel party commission of 1980, any steam that there was behind the policy in the SPD ran up against formidable countervailing pressure.

The argument that German policy represented a response to the FDP's electoral dilemma ignores a number of factors. Policy emerges out of the interaction between the DBV and the Agriculture Ministry. There is a further convention in the Federal Republic of ministerial autonomy which means that, in default of overriding general reasons, departmental policy is normally accepted. This would imply that the policy of the Agriculture Ministry would have been adopted whoever held the portfolio, unless there had been very strong opposition from the SPD ministers in the Cabinet and particularly from the chancellor. Our information is that the Chancellor's Office abandoned its attempt to make some progress along the lines of the Apel report after the Ministry of Agriculture had sent a number of stonewalling replies. If reform of the CAP had been central to Schmidt he would then have raised the matter further with the minister or in Cabinet.

Finally, the argument that the FDP was so electorally dependent on the farm vote or even felt itself to be so, is somewhat overstated. The FDP was, and remained, overwhelmingly urban. This is not to deny that they had a strong interest in making themselves '*wählbar*', eligible for farmers' votes, but the typical FDP voter remained in the words of a senior official an '*Angestellter*' (white collar worker) rather than a '*Bauer*' (farmer). The same senior official claimed the pro-agricultural line of the European policy of the FRG had much more to do with the relations between the DBV and the ministry and the operating conventions of German government (the principle of ministerial autonomy) than with the influence of the FDP.

These factors are illuminated in an interesting case study published earlier by Simon Bulmer. In a case study of the introduction of the European Monetary System Bulmer focused on the disagreement between the French and German governments about the abolition of Monetary Compensation Amounts (Bulmer, 1983c, pp. 581–2). At issue here was the French wish to include the abolition of Monetary Compensatory Amounts (MCAs) as part of a package deal with the introduction of the EMS. MCAs, which the French saw as giving German farmers an unfair advantage, are variable devices which maintain common agricultural prices in the face of exchange rate fluctuations. The dispute, which was about agricultural rather than monetary policy, was eventually only resolved in March 1979, two months after the EMS should have come into operation.

This chain of events has been interpreted as Chancellor Schmidt being forced by FDP minister Ertl not to undermine farm incomes through a commitment to abolish MCAs. The argument is usually recounted along with figures showing the importance to the FDP of the farm vote. However, this assumed that there was a difference in the parties' positions on the matter. The SPD parliamentary party adopted a position that MCAs should not be abolished until the final stages of the EMS. A very similar viewpoint was adopted in the FDP parliamentary party where some MPs viewed the problem as a product of inadequate consultation by those initiating the EMS. The CDU/CSU, while engaging in some critical attacks on the plans for EMS and on the linkage with MCAs, found its tactics somewhat misplaced as further details emerged. This was because it became clear that the Federal Government was united in the view that 'the introduction of the European Monetary System cannot result in German agriculture bearing cuts in income' (Helmut Schmidt, cited in *FAZ*, 13 January 1979). While Ertl undoubtedly threatened to resign on occasion if his pro-agricultural position was challenged in the coalition, the electoral capital he made for the FDP was very limited indeed.

In the final analysis, therefore, the question of abolishing MCAs became an issue of national interest, conducted at the EC level along intergovernmental lines. This dimension, which dictates that no government shall neglect the interest of its citizens in favour of those in another member state, ultimately eclipsed any party system analysis.

The electoral dimension

In this final section we look at the electoral dimension of European policy. During the early years of the Federal Republic arguments about European policy were at the centre of electoral confrontation. This was especially true of the 1953 election, by which time the SPD had abandoned much of the economic content of its opposition to the CDU/CSU-led government. Europe continued to play some role in the 1957 election where the FDP was the only party to oppose the establishment of the EEC (Paterson, 1974a, pp. 92–100).

In the last two decades European integration has very rarely surfaced as a significant electoral theme. All the parties include references to Europe in their programmes but it is regarded, except by the Greens, as uncontentious. Where differences do persist they are usually contingent on some difference at the level of domestic policy, as with the SPD and social policy. The attention of both the parties and the electorate is focused on the domestic dimension.

The two European elections 1979 and 1984

The advent of direct elections to the European Parliament in 1979 might have been expected to increase the saliency of Europe as a party political issue. This proved not to be the case in 1979. Only very few first-class candidates stood for election and where they did, as in the case of Willy Brandt, they clearly gave their duties in the European Parliament a low priority. The parties were unable to generate any public debate on the EC, partly because of scepticism among party activists and public alike about the value of electing members to a weak European Parliament. There was a very low level of interest in all parties (Menke, 1985, pp. 67–84). Moreover, despite some involvement of transnational parties, the parties submerged their campaigns in the domestic context of the impending 1980 federal election. In the event, turnout was very low by West German standards, being 25 percentage points down on the 1976 federal election figure.

The trends already apparent in 1979 appeared even more clearly in 1984 (Bulmer and Paterson, 1986). There was little public interest in the campaign and meetings were very sparsely attended. It proved even more difficult to mobilize party activists, particularly in the FDP and the SPD, than in 1979. The turnout was even lower than in 1979 (56.8 per cent).

The European election was also more clearly than in 1979 a second-order election (*Nebenwahl*) absorbed into the national electoral cycle. The dominant themes of the campaign were domestic ones and the organization of the election was totally in the hands of the national party organizers with the transnational parties playing next to no role. The elections were clearly viewed by the party managers as a means of subsidizing their primary political goal, namely the pursuit of national political power. The only European issue that arose in the election was that of milk quotas and this was taken care of by a unilateral subsidy to German dairy farmers.

Conclusion

This chapter suggests several conclusions about the role of political parties in the formulation of European policies in the Federal Republic. First, European issues do not now provide a major locus of party political conflict. Foreign policy issues have more consistently provided such a locus in the Federal Republic than in the United Kingdom, a situation reversed in European policy (Paterson, 1981, pp. 227–35). This conflict was often of a purely symbolic kind and ceased in regard to Europe once the Communities were firmly established. Secondly, this party political consensus interacts with the domination of party policy-making in this area by the behavioural patterns of the Federal Government and the Bundestag. These are heavily oriented towards an expert bureaucratic consensus and produce a profound lack of interest among both party members and the public at large. This leads to the third main conclusion, that this is an area in which parties have had a very limited impact on policy.

Two caveats have to be entered against these broad conclusions. The emergence of the Greens now means that there is a party which is represented in parliamentary institutions but which falls outside the established consensus on European integration. In practice, however, this makes relatively little difference since questions of European integration do not appear to be high on their list of priorities. In brief, the established parties are in favour of Europe in a low key manner; the Greens counterpoint this by being against the existing Community but without any sustained interest.

More importantly, a second caveat has to be entered on party impact. Despite Chancellor Kohl's claim to share Adenauer's overriding commitment to European integration in the question of cereal prices, he allowed sectoral pressure funnelled through party channels to overrule general European policy goals. If this pattern were to be repeated, we might have to revise our views on party political impact, at least in the area of agriculture.

Notes

Two recent publications of relevance to this chapter, but not available when it was written, are: Ertl, 1985 and Jeutter, 1986.

1 See especially the meeting of 10 July 1964, Confidential Protocol (cited henceforth as CSU Protocol, 1964), pp. 3–4.
2 On links between CSU strategy and particular interests, see Eisner, 1975.

3 This section draws on material contained in Bulmer, 1983c and Bulmer, 1987, Ch. 4.

4 Following the establishment of the Europa-Kommission (see Ch. 7) the SPD also established a working group to service this body.

5 During the week 13–18 September 1981 we carried out the following interviews: K. Hänsch, SPD MEP (14 September); K. Wettig, SPD MEP (15 September); E. Lange, SPD MEP (16 September); G. Schmid, SPD MEP (16 September); H. Langes, CDU MEP (16 September); J. van Aerssen, CDU MEP (16 September).

6 They receive briefings and papers from the *Auswärtiges Amt* (Foreign Office). Moreover, they are aware that any stance which appeared to harm a significant German interest would be electorally damaging and opposition to the Federal Government can easily be presented in that light.

7 *The Legislative Dimension*

This chapter focuses on the way in which EC legislation is handled by the West German political and legal system. In looking at the relationship between a member state and the EC, it is not sufficient to establish the processes, actors and interests which interact to produce a particular state's policy towards the EC. It is vital also in grasping the precise role of European policy in the system to look at the way the system deals with the question of applying decisions reached at the European level in the national setting.

We look first at the role of the Bundestag and Bundesrat, and focus in particular on the extent to which the legislature is able to participate in the framing of European policy – both in the sense of attempting to influence the stance of the Federal Government at the Council of Ministers in relation to a decision and of passing such legislative acts as may be necessary to give effect in domestic law to a decision of the Council of Ministers. We then look at the process of implementation and assess the degree of readiness to give effect to Community decisions; in a short case study we draw attention to the way in which EC decisions can affect the options available domestically.

In the final section the attitude of German courts to the relationship between domestic and Community law is examined. The attitude of the courts is a vital indicator of the degree to which 'the openness' of the West German system, referred to in Chapter 1, has been preserved.

The role of the legislature

One striking contrast to Britain has been the relative absence of controversy and debate about the question of parliamentary sovereignty. There are a number of reasons for this. First, West German opinion was in general much more favourable to the establishment of the Community (see Chapter 5). Secondly, the loss of sovereignty was much less clear cut in the Federal Republic. At the time of entry into the ECSC, the Federal Republic itself was not a fully sovereign actor and the process of integration was seen as being as much about the acquisition of sovereignty as about losing it. Formal sovereignty remained divided between the FRG and the allied powers. This was especially marked in foreign affairs, so the absence of one centre of sovereignty meant that the Federal Republic could not withhold it. Thirdly, Germany has a much weaker parliamentary tradition than Britain and was therefore less concerned about any departures from it. Fourthly, the Basic Law in Article 24 actually foresaw the possible transfer of sovereign rights to international institutions. This reflected a consensus in favour of transfer which predated the establishment of the Federal Republic. The argument in the early 1950s was not on the principle of transfer but on the issue as to whether the ECSC and EDC in the form envisaged were desirable recipients of the transferred sovereignty or not.

Adhesion to the Community clearly involved a loss of powers for the legislature – a loss more easily measured in the Federal Republic than in Britain because the powers of the institutions are specifically enumerated in the Basic Law. The Federal Republic has a dual legislature. The Bundestag is elected on direct universal suffrage. The second chamber, the Bundesrat, is a delegated body which represents the interests of the *Länder* governments. The loss of powers by the Bundesrat is inextricably linked with that suffered by the *Länder*. Membership of the EC has a necessarily centralizing effect on the institutions of member states and this has helped to tilt the policy-making balance towards the *Bund*. This applies particularly to the formulation of policy but the *Länder* remain central actors with regard to implementation. Precise details of this tension will be covered in Chapter 8.

The European Coal and Steel Community envisaged a strong role for the High Authority and the Council of Ministers was only inserted at a fairly advanced stage of the negotiations. The role of governments and, by extension, of national legislatures, was seen as being fairly minimal. In fact, the ECSC became much less supranational in practice than in theory but that only really became apparent in the coal crisis of 1958–9. The original conception of the ECSC and the greater strength of federalism in the early 1950s meant that Bundesrat and Bundestag procedures to deal with the ECSC were minimal.

The establishment of the EEC raised questions of a different order. The EEC was consciously envisaged as a *Rahmenvertrag* (framework treaty). It was clear from the start that there would have to be a great deal of secondary legislation to give effect to the purposes agreed in the treaty. The institutions were conceived differently with the key legislative role accorded to the Council of

Ministers though it was hoped that over time the balance would tilt towards the Commission. These factors were bound to mean the continuous involvement of governments and to a lesser extent of legislatures.

In three policy areas, namely trade, tariffs and agriculture, where integration is furthest advanced, the power of national parliaments, including the Bundestag, to enact new domestic legislation has been almost totally eroded. In other policy areas the Bundestag is either subject to certain constraints on its freedom of action contingent on EC membership or its general powers remain intact subject to constraints in certain delineated circumstances (Schüttemeyer, 1978). The Bundestag is thus more constrained on economic and monetary policy than on competition policy where it can, but rarely does, take initiatives that would challenge the supremacy of EC law.

The Article 2 procedure

> The Federal Government shall keep the Bundestag and the Bundesrat continually informed of developments in the Council of the European Economic Community and in the Council of the European Atomic Energy Community. Insofar as a decision of a Council requires the making of a German law or has immediate force of law in the Federal Republic of Germany, notification should be made prior to the Council making its decision. (Article 2, Act of Ratification of the Rome Treaties)

Article 2 commits the Federal Government to informing the Bundestag and Bundesrat. The key roles in this process are played by the Permanent Representation in Brussels and the Economics Ministry's European Division. When a Commission proposal is about to be sent to the Council of Ministers, a copy is routed by the Council Secretariat to the Permanent Representation and thence to the European Division of the Economics Ministry. The division there lets the Bundestag and Bundesrat know informally and formal notice with an attached (standardized) letter from the federal chancellor follows a week later. The terms of Article 2 are interpreted liberally by the Federal Government and the two chambers are informed even when the particular item neither requires the making of a German law nor has the immediate force of law in the Federal Republic.

As well as supplying information on specific developments (Article 2, para. 2) the Federal Government is obliged to supply information on general EC developments. It has submitted written reports twice yearly since 1967.

The Article 2 procedure contains a number of inbuilt and probably inevitable weaknesses. The first obvious weakness is that the legislature is only seized of the Commission proposal at the time of publication, i.e. at a very late stage, by which time the opportunity for influence is fairly minimal. A second major problem also involves timing. It is extremely difficult to decide whether a Commission proposal will be considered almost immediately by the Council of Ministers or whether it will be greatly modified in COREPER sessions. If it were to be modified greatly, a Bundesrat/Bundestag report would risk being seen as completely irrelevant. The procedures have been amended to allow the relevant Bundestag committee to return to a particular proposal and obtain updated information from the Federal Government. The crucial point is that the legislature is totally dependent on the Federal Government for getting its timing right. This is not always possible. Schweitzer cites the example of the Bundestag adopting three committee reports, stating that they had no objections to twenty-four items of EC legislation (Schweitzer, 1978, p. 46). In fact they had all been previously adopted by the Council of Ministers.

Procedures for scrutiny

The Bundestag The scrutiny function of the Bundestag is undertaken through the committee system. Between 1965 and 1967 proposals were referred to appropriate committees by the Council of Elders for Integration. It proved to be difficult to convene because of its composition, which included delegates to the European Assembly, and was thus fairly quickly abandoned.

The present system still relies on reference to relevant committees and there was until recently no special committee with exclusive responsibility for EC matters. Referral to the relevant committee is made, as is the case in other policy areas, by the Bundestag president. Where responsibility is shared between several committees, one committee is regarded as being in charge (*der federführende Auschuss*) and has the task of combining the reports of the various committees into one report.

The committee reports are normally adopted without debate by the plenum of the Bundestag. There are a number of explanations for this. Both party and Bundestag committees tend to be dominated by experts. This is especially true of the Agricultural Committee where, normally over three quarters of the members are from an agricultural background. The concentration of expertise and interest (in the committees) means that it is both rare and difficult for someone outside the relevant committee or committees to counter a (committee) report. The committees also shadow federal ministries and there is extensive consultation with officials of the relevant ministries who can, and do, attend committee sessions. Intra-party conflict is minimal partly because the structure and composition of committees acts to dampen party conflict but, perhaps more importantly because, apart from the Greens, there is no basic conflict on Europe anyway. The result is that

> the European policy of the Federal Republic of Germany, with very few exceptions, is either raised above party dispute or displays a large degree of interparty agreement, not least because the government in office collaborates with parliamentarians of all party groups. (Schweitzer, 1978, p. 48)

Table 7.1 *The referral of EC proposals to committees in the Seventh Bundestag, 1972–6*

	In charge (federführend)	*Joint reporting* (mitberatend)
Foreign Affairs	2	1
Home Affairs	—	—
Legal Affairs	12	2
Finance	73	17
Budget	7	64
Economics	500	50
Food, Agriculture and Forestry	362	25
Employment and Social Affairs	40	26
Youth, Family and Health	39	26
Transport, Posts and Telecommunications	50	2
Construction and Urban Planning	—	1
Inter-German Relations	—	3

Note: These figures only relate to referrals; they do not imply that reports were drafted in each case. Nor do they include cases where committees have asked the committee-in-charge for permission to present an opinion (because the EC proposals were not referred to them).

Source: Bulmer, 1987, p. 231. Figures supplied by the committees for a survey by the Bundestag research department.

The key committees for EC proposals are Food, Agriculture and Forestry, Economics, Transport, Employment and Social Affairs, and Health (see Table 7.1). The Budgetary Committee plays a significant back up role monitoring the financial implications of specific EC proposals.

In 1978 all the committees adopted a procedure originally introduced in the Agriculture Committee so that proposals can be accepted without discussion (*Kenntnisnahme*) unless there is a specific request for discussion by a committee member. In effect the sifting process thus takes place outside the parliamentary committees in the committees of the parliamentary parties. Interest groups play a crucial role in alerting committee members to the significance or otherwise of a Community proposal and it is extremely unlikely that a specific request to subject a proposal to scrutiny will be made if an MP has not been alerted by an interest group.

There had been some dissatisfaction with the lack of discussion of EC matters by the plenum of the Bundestag. Under the modification introduced in 1978, each party group has an *Obmann* (foreman) who can request committee consideration of a proposal and automatic discussion by the plenum. The evidence is that it has made very little difference to the plenum.

The Bundestag committees generally consider proposals after the relevant Bundesrat committees. This allows them to have the last word, but at the risk of being too late to have any influence on decisions in the Council of Ministers.

The key conclusion of an analysis of the scrutiny function is that it represents an exaggerated version of factors and processes which are typical of the Bundestag in general. The work of all committees places a marked emphasis on expertise and downplays party conflict. Interest groups are also very active in relation to domestic policy. What is distinctive about this area is the way in which the almost complete absence of public interest and party conflict leads to even more marked domination by experts and interests. These factors can also mean that the committees can be manipulated by the Federal Government. They can, as we have seen, be starved of information but they can also be persuaded, as Simon Bulmer has demonstrated in an earlier study, to produce reports calculated to aid the stance of the Federal Government in a question at issue in the Council of Ministers (Bulmer, 1987, pp. 232–3).

The direct election of MEPs in 1979 led to demands for institutionalized links to replace those that sprang from dual membership. In June 1983 the Bundestag unanimously approved a resolution establishing a *Europa-Kommission*. This body is composed of 22 members, of whom 11 are from the Bundestag and 11 from the European Parliament (Pöhle, 1984, pp. 352–9). It is charged with discussing questions of integration policy and institutions, the 'high politics' of the EC rather than questions of detail. It is likely to be a part of the dignified branch of government rather than the efficient – a view strengthened by the choice of Carl-Otto Lenz, a politician best known for occupying honorific positions rather than for his great political weight, as the first chairman.

More importantly for day-to-day policy, it was also resolved unanimously, on the same occasion, that Bundestag committees should make frequent use of MEPs as experts when EC matters were being discussed. The *Europa-Kommission* itself (and this is one of its weaknesses) is not seen as having an effect on the normal Bundestag committees. 'Die Zuständigkeit der Fachausschüsse des Deutschen Bundestages bleibt unberührt' (Pöhle, 1984, p. 356). 'The responsibility of the specialist committees of the Bundestag remains untouched'.

The Bundesrat The scrutiny procedure inside the Bundesrat is also carried out under the basis of Article 2 but there are some major differences reflecting this chamber's different role in the political system. EC matters are examined by committees but, unlike the Bundestag, there is no overt interest group representation or involvement. The Bundesrat also has a Committee for European Community Affairs. This body is less concerned with actual scrutiny than with combining the specialist committees' reports and reconciling any divergences between the collective view of the Bundesrat and individual states. There is a functional specialization among the states, whereby individual *Länder* take charge of handling reports for the two main committees of EC Affairs and Agriculture. In all cases there is a second state to give assistance and to reassure other members that the leading state is not pursuing its self-interest too ruthlessly.

The general principle of Bundesrat procedure is to ask the *Land* with responsibility for a particular area whether the proposal should be subjected to committee scrutiny. In general, about half the EC proposals received are scrutinized. The criteria invoked are twofold: the importance of the proposal and whether any recommendations can be submitted usefully in the light of the expected timing of the discussion by the Council of Ministers.

The Bundesrat consideration of EC matters is carried out largely by senior officials of the *Länder* governments with ministers attending only occasionally. Generally speaking, the EC Affairs Committee adopts a fairly broad gauge positive approach reminiscent of the Foreign Office, while individual committees take a narrower view. Party politics rarely plays an overt role.

After scrutiny by individual committees, their reports are transformed into a single draft resolution for adoption by the plenum. Plenary debates on European matters are very rare.

The scrutiny function is efficiently carried out by the Bundesrat as one would expect given the expertise of committee members. Although not overtly connected with specific interests, unlike many members of the Bundestag committees, the difference in practice in some areas, such as agriculture, is not great because, although they are officials, their contact with interest groups is close. The procedures of the Bundesrat in this area act to reduce party political conflict and public interest because of their domination by experts.

The use of conventional Bundestag channels

Debates on European matters have been infrequent since the question of entry was settled. There is an annual debate but this does not always take place as federal governments have shown no marked inhibitions about postponing it. Occasionally, use has been made of the '*aktuelle Stunde*', an hour-long adjournment debate on a topic of burning interest. It is however only very rarely that Europe is such a topic and party managers are reluctant to use up these opportunities on a topic with such low saliency.

Use is made both of written questions (*kleine Anfragen*) and written questions followed by a short debate (*grosse Anfragen*) but they have largely been replaced by oral questions. Question time does not occupy a very central role in the Bundestag and a minister does not accord a high priority to his performance in countering them. The actual answers are often made by parliamentary state secretaries. In the case of the EC they often seem to be posed less to expose ministerial weakness than to make sure some domestic interest is not sacrificed in negotiations.

The differences established between the procedures of the Bundestag and Bundesrat reflect the nature of their composition. The Bundestag contains the representatives of the political parties. The Bundesrat is composed of ministers in the *Länder* governments and their civil service alternates. The procedures of the Bundestag reflect a party political setting though in practice, due to lack of party political conflict, interests dominate. The procedures of the Bundesrat are concerned to take account not only of regional interests but also of the fact that *Länder* governments are centrally involved in the process of implementation (see Chapter 8).

The role of the Bundestag and the Bundesrat in the area of European policy is a slightly exaggerated version of their role in other sectors. Their major function is that of controlling the executive, and this is complicated and modified by the fact that the Bundesrat is itself part of the West German executive. They are generally perceived to perform the technical control function of monitoring the possible impact of EC proposals on the West German system very well though the procedures they adopt tend to provide open access to organized interests and reinforce the impression that European policy is very much a closed specialist area.

The law-making function is essentially reactive. It is almost never a question of the legislature initiating legislation but rather with the giving of legislative form to Community acts, a process which we illustrate in the case study.

The educative function of the legislature in relation to Europe is a minimal one. The specialized nature of the procedures and the lack of party political conflict over basic goals ensures that the general public is hardly aware of parliamentary activity in this area.

The implementation of EC policy

The formulation and legitimation of legislation is extremely complex in a multi-layered political system like the EC. The difficulties do not end with the publication of directives and regulations however. A regulation is binding in relation both to aims and methods; a directive is binding in terms of results to be achieved but leaves to the national authorities the choice of form and methods. Whatever form they take, Community legislative acts have to be implemented. Implementation has to be carried out through national and, in the case of the Federal Republic, sub-national agencies. Clearly the manner and effectiveness with which EC legislation is implemented will vary from member state to member state, reflecting differing degrees of administrative competence, attitudes towards the EC and domestic interests.

These differences have been investigated by a group set up by the Research Committee on European Unification of the International Political Science Association. The research on the Federal Republic was carried out under the direction of Professor

Rudof Hrbek and Dr Wolfgang Wessels and the major findings have been reported by Gudrun Schmidt (Schmidt, 1984). Before looking at the major findings of the Hrbek and Wessels study, we give a brief description of the mechanisms of implementation. As in other areas of West German European policy, the most striking feature is the lack of co-ordination. There is no central office or institution responsible for implementing EC laws. There is rather the normal method of assigning each act to a *'federführendes Ministerium'* (ministry in charge). Any control is at most procedural. Reports are asked for but no standard mechanism or criteria exist for evaluating their contents. Expenditures are controlled through the Court of Auditors (*Bundesrechnungshof*). These are only procedural controls however. They do not investigate the effectiveness of the funds used in relation to specified goals.

The most important conclusion of Hrbek and Wessels was that the Federal Republic compared very favourably with other EC member states in relation to the ease and effectiveness of implementation of Community legislation. This very positive view was largely based on interviews with German civil servants and their explanations, not surprisingly, were related to the norms and practices of German civil servants. They argued that one explanation was to be found in the federal system of West Germany. Civil servants are accustomed to working with different levels of governments in the context of West German federalism. They have therefore no inhibitions about implementing a law which has originated at a different level. Unlike the French, they do not perceive this as a threat to sovereignty. German civil servants, in common with other German elites, saw themselves as being pro-integration. This pro-EC feeling leads to a bad conscience in cases like the 6th VAT directive where difficulties have arisen and they have found themselves unable to comply. The pro-EC feeling is an alternative and stronger explanation for their lack of inhibition about sovereignty and willingness to implement Community legislation.

There were three further major explanations advanced in the study. Civil servants were seen as being characterized by a general openness towards partners (governmental or social) as well as a general orientation towards consensus and avoidance of conflicts, a habit of mind which is easily transferred to the implementation of Community legislation. More questionably, they argue that implementation is eased by the negotiating procedure of West Germany. (The conventional view would be that this is characterized by duplication and lack of co-ordination, making implementation difficult.) They present the procedure as being characterized by extensive consultation at the negotiation stage with the agencies, including the *Länder*, which are likely to be involved in implementation. They also argue that the German attention to technical details avoids problems at the implementation stage. The final explanation involved anticipated reactions. German civil servants are aware that business interests, especially importers, will monitor any failures in the legal transfer and management of Community acts in their sector. The argument here is that German economic interests are more likely to seek legal redress against the bureaucracy than economic interests in neighbouring states like France.

The view presented by Hrbek and Wessels is a preliminary one. It is interesting in that academic attention has been normally focused on the formulation stage and here the Federal Republic has been compared unfavourably with France and Britain. Hrbek and Wessels' study is only a preliminary one and the views it presents are perhaps too rosy. The procedure of relying on the self-evaluation of the bureaucracies is open to question. They may also have exaggerated the pro-EC control exerted by economic interests. It is possible to imagine areas where the balance of economic interests is overwhelmingly protective and they are likely to be in league with, rather than opposed to, the bureaucracies. One final point is the importance of the pro-EC attitudes of the elites. If this slackens very significantly then the difficulties of implementation would increase.

Case study – the German Chemicals Law

The German Chemicals Law of 1980 has been chosen as a case study for a number of reasons.[1] It is in the area of environmental legislation where there is an increasing tendency for new regulations to originate as EC decisions since it is both a key area of interest to the Commission and an area where the Federal Republic is reluctant to press ahead unilaterally out of fear of damaging its industrial competitiveness. It is also an example of where the Federal Government implemented an EC directive though the need for regulation was strongly contested by the relevant sectoral interest.

The Chemicals Act of 1980 is concerned with attempting to ensure that new chemical products brought on to the market are safe. The chemical industry, which is one of the best organized and most economically powerful sectors in the Federal Republic, has always been strenuously opposed to public regulation. It has always been its view that environmental matters were best left to the industry. There had been no domestic pressure to implement the original EC directive on chemicals of 27 June 1967 (Richtlinie 67/548/EWG). The climate began to change in the 1970s. This change was initially largely external. A number of leading Western industrial countries introduced chemicals laws in the early 1970s, e.g. Sweden 1973, Japan, 1974 and Canada, 1974. Significantly, pressure originated with the proposal by the French government in May 1975 for EC-wide regulations on chemicals and the environment. This was taken up by the Commission which proceeded to work on a revision of the EC directive of 1967.

The initial response of the *Verband der Chemischen Industrie* (VCI), the interest group of the German chemical industry, was to try and persuade CEFIC, the peak group of the European chemicals industry, to dissuade the Commission from proceeding on the formulation of a revised directive (Zimmermann, 1981, p. 162).

However, in this instance, the VCI failed to persuade CEFIC to adopt its view and CEFIC supported the idea of EC-wide regulation though it was weakened by lack of VCI support. The VCI was more successful with the Federal Government which transmitted to the Commission the opposition of the Federal Government to state regulation of the bringing of new chemical products on to the market (VCI, 1976, p. 20).

The Commission was not deterred by the opposition of the Federal Government and published a draft directive on 8 September 1976 (*Amtsblatt der EG*, Nr C260/4, 5 November 1976).[2] The Commission proposal envisaged that new products should be tested by the firms who would then notify public bodies of the results. They would then decide whether it was safe to bring them on the market. There were no major exceptions and no minimum quantities below which testing and notification were unnecessary.

The VCI has extremely close relations with the Economics Ministry which are managed through the responsible 'desk', the *Chemie Referat*. The chemical industry sees the Economics Ministry as its *Anwalt* (attorney) in government. As we have already noted, the Economics Ministry has the primary day-to-day responsibility for European policy and in this situation the Economics Ministry, after 'close consultation' with the VCI, produced a counter-proposal at an EC conference in Paris on hazardous substances.

The Economics Ministry and the VCI were embarrassed by

union disclosures that the letterhead on this proposal was neither that of the VCI nor the Economics Ministry, but that of Farbwerke Hoechst – Frankfurt.[3] The counter-proposal suggested a weakening of the Commission draft. It rejected a general notification procedure for new products and envisaged instead a threshold procedure. There was no mention of existing chemicals (*Altstoffe*) and procedures were to be relaxed in relation to exports to the Third World.

The final directive approved by the EC Council of Ministers on 19 June 1979 indicated that the VCI and the Economics Ministry had been relatively successful in their attempts to get West German views accepted. There was now to be a notification and testing procedure for new products on this threshold basis. There was to be a 45-day delay between notification and bringing on to the market. The directive did not apply to '*Altstoffe*' (existing chemicals).

Implementation The position taken by the VCI, and still more the position of the Federal Government, might lead one to expect that the latter would not implement the directive. In fact by 1981, the official expiry date, the Federal Republic was one of only four member states to have implemented the directive. The others were France, Denmark and Ireland. There are two main reasons for this. A general explanation in line with the study by Hrbek and Wessels would relate this to the general readiness of the Federal Republic as '*Musterknabe*' to implement legislation. A second, and in our view much more powerful explanation in this case, was that, although the German chemical industry had been opposed to the proposal, it had succeeded in making significant modifications. It was also aware of more far-reaching chemicals laws (Norway, USA 1976); and it felt that environmental pressure, which was starting to make itself felt by the end of the 1970s in the Federal Republic, might move a future Federal Government to introduce a much more far-reaching law. In such a situation prudence dictated sticking with the implementation of the EC directive which it had influenced and ensuring that no German secondary legislation went beyond this.

That there was a danger of the German legislation going beyond the EC directive was clear to the VCI. The Interior Ministry, the ministry with responsibility for environmental questions, had started to draft a law after the Commission proposal of September 1976. The draft proposal produced by Environment Section U119 of the Interior Ministry on 27

December 1977 envisaged a much stricter control of the production of new chemicals than the EC directive.

The major victory of the VCI was to get the Economics Ministry to intercede with Chancellor Schmidt and the ministry in charge (*das federführende Ministerium*) for the overseeing of the secondary legislation was changed on 12 September 1979 from Interior to Youth, Family and Health; a ministry which at that time possessed few environmental experts and which did not have the same access to the views of the – by now very active – environmental groups, as did the Interior Ministry.

The legislative stage The draft bill was produced on the basis not of the controversial 1977 Interior Ministry draft, but of the 1979 EC directive. The VCI had an appreciable impact on this draft bill.

In August 1979, i.e. only two months after the Council of Ministers' decision, the draft bill went to the Bundesrat. At this stage the VCI and the BDI intensively lobbied *Länder* governments through their regional offices. The Bundesrat made one hundred and four observations on the draft, of which the Federal Government immediately accepted fifty-six. The Federal Government also agreed at this point to change the ministry in charge from Interior to Youth, Family and Health.

The draft bill was then considered by the Bundestag. The committee in charge was Youth, Family and Health and the draft was also sent to the Economics Committee and the Budgetary Committee.

These committees established a sub-committee under the chairmanship of Dr Hasinger, the directly elected CDU deputy for Leverkusen, the company town of Bayer chemicals. The parliamentary phase was dominated by the chemical interest and party political differences played no appreciable role though one SPD deputy did vote against the agreed draft at the final reading in the Bundestag plenum on 25 June 1980. The revised version was agreed to by the Bundesrat on 4 July 1980 and it became law on 25 September 1980.

The final version was not perceived as threatening by the industry. The pre-marketing notification is forty-five days. It does not include substances which are produced in quantities of less than one ton per year. Long-term effects have to be tested only when a substance is produced in quantities of more than 100 tons per year. There is no provision for control of '*Altstoffe*'. The law is enforced by 'a closed circle of professionals'. It is significant here that a leading commentary on the chemicals law is jointly authored by a VCI official and an employee of the *Bundesumweltamt* which is partially responsible for enforcing the law.

This case study illustrates the key role of the Bundesrat in the implementation process. The Bundesrat had a major impact on the proposed legislation while the Bundestag had a negligible impact in this case. It also highlights the formidable capacity of a leading industrial interest group to have an impact on a proposed directive both at European level and at domestic level. Particularly noteworthy at the domestic level is the way in which responsibility for implementation was switched to a ministry that was perceived as more industry-friendly. In the light of these factors, implementation proceeded smoothly since it was now seen both by the Economics Ministry and the industry as the least worst solution.

The relationship between EC law and German domestic law

As mentioned earlier in the chapter, there is no centralized system in the Federal Republic to monitor the implementation of EC law. In relation to financial matters some control is exercised by the *Bundesrechnungshof* but the major control is that exercised by the courts. There is a whole range of courts in the Federal Republic, providing for judicial review of legislative action and legal control of administrative acts. The process of judicial review culminates in the Federal Constitutional Court in Karlsruhe and administrative acts are controlled by a dense network of *Verwaltungsgerichte* (administrative courts).

It is open to any individual to appeal to the courts if he feels that the executive has interfered with his rights by adopting or failing to adopt an item of EC legislation. The existence of this widespread access to legal redress and the readiness of West German individuals and firms to engage in litigation does act as a significant incentive to public officials in the Federal Republic to implement EC legislation. This widespread availability of legal redress against state action or lack of action has meant that the question of the applicability of Community law has quite often been introduced. In these situations the courts normally seek a preliminary ruling from the European Court of Justice (ECJ) – a procedure (*Vorlageverfahren*) set out in Article 177 of the Rome Treaty. Of the 1078 preliminary rulings dealt with by the ECJ in the period from its establishment to 1982, 405 came from the Federal Republic, a much higher number than from any other member state. In 1979 for example, 33 out of 106 requests for preliminary rulings originated in German courts. Two were from the Federal Constitutional Court, one was from the Federal Administrative Court, nine from the Federal Finance Court (an indication of business pressures), five from the Social Court and sixteen from non-federal courts.

The applicability of Community law raises the general question of the relationship between EC and German domestic law (Ress, 1984). The dominant theme in the jurisprudence of the European Court of Justice has been that this relationship and the whole question of the applicability of EC law is one that should ultimately be decided not by national courts but by the European Court of Justice itself. Initially this view was strongly echoed in the jurisprudence of the Federal Constitutional Court, the *Bundesverfassungsgerichtshof*. The *Bundesverfassungsgerichtshof* ruled in 1971 on the basis of Article 24, para. 1 of the Basic Law that sovereign acts of the inter-state institution (in the case ruled on, a judgement of the ECJ) should be 'recognized' by the original exclusive sovereign body – in this case the Federal Republic. In a further decision of 9 June 1971 it ruled (on the basis of a preliminary ruling by the ECJ on 16 June 1966) that there were no constitutional objections to the *Bundesfinanzhof* according primacy to Article 95 of the Rome Treaty *vis à vis* existing German tax law. They based this ruling on the argument that the ratification of the EEC Treaty in conjunction with Article 24 of the Basic Law had created a new autonomous European legal order, which penetrated the German legal order and which should be applied by German courts.

The *Bundesverfassungsgerichtshof* concluded:

> On the basis of this legal position, the German courts have been obliged since the establishment of the Common Market to apply these legal ordinances, which, although part of an autonomous 'ausserstaatliche Hoheitsgewalt', on the basis of the interpretation of the European Court of Justice have direct effect inside the state and overlay and supersede existing national law; only in this way can the subjective rights created by the Common Market be given to its citizens. (cited in Ress, 1984, p. 45)

However, the bold assertion of the superiority of Community law has been somewhat played down in more recent rulings by the *Bundesverfassungsgericht* (BVG). In the so-called 'Solange Beschluss' of 1977 the court took the view that it was inappropriate to talk of the superiority of EC law, *until* it incorporated a set of fundamental human rights passed by a legislature. Until then the priority should be for the representatives of both systems to bring about a convergence of the legal orders. The spirit was one of interdependence rather than hierarchy.

This 'Solange Beschluss', which had attempted to tone down the initial enthusiastic endorsement of the primacy of EC law by the *Bundesverfassungsgericht*, was very much criticized however and, in more recent decisions, the BVG has taken a line more in conformity with the 1977 decisions (Ress, 1984, pp. 46–7).

The interrelated questions of the control of the implementation of Community acts and the supremacy of EC law was raised in a very acute manner by a decision of the *Bundesfinanzhof* on 16 July 1981 (Ress, 1984, pp. 56–9). In a whole series of decisions beginning with the so-called Leberpfennig Judgement of October 1970, the European Court had ruled that not only regulations (*Verordnungen*), but also *Richtlinien* (directives) should be considered as having self-executing force in national systems. Legally directives were to be placed on the same plane as regulations once the period of time allowed for incorporation into national regulations had elapsed. This ruling established the primacy of Community secondary law and was the basis of the requests by German courts for preliminary reviews by the European Court of Justice.

This practice was given a massive shock by the decision of the *Bundesfinanzof*. In order to understand its significance it is necessary to sketch in some background. The case involved the application of a number of provisions of the 6th VAT directive of 1977. The German regulations for implementing this directive came into force in January 1980 rather than as had been foreseen in the directive, in January 1979. The view that would probably have been taken by the ECJ would have been that the directive could be said to have been binding and to supersede pre-existing German tax law from 1 January 1979, i.e. the period foreseen by the original Council decision.

In fact, the *Bundesfinanzhof* refused to refer the case to the ECJ for a preliminary ruling and rejected the direct applicability of EC directives on the basis of a 1978 decision of the French *Conseil d'Etat* (the so-called Cohn–Bendit decision), and of Article 189 of the Rome Treaty.

> The set of legislative instruments available arises out of Article 189 of the EEC Treaty. This distinguishes between regulations and directives. A regulation has immediate validity. It is binding in all its parts and applies directly in each member state. A directive, by contrast, is binding as regards

the goal to be achieved for each member state, but leaves the choice and form of means to national institutions. It therefore follows, beyond any possible doubt, that a directive is binding for signatories to the treaty but also that it cannot displace directly valid law in the member states. To this extent, then, the sole legislative competence of the member states is left untouched. The conventional jurisprudence of the ECJ on the applicability of directives relies only on Community law. There is therefore no case for a preliminary ruling (*Entscheidungen des Bundesfinanzhofs*, vol. 133, 1981, pp. 471 ff).

This ruling of the *Bundesfinanzhof* remains an exception, albeit a very important one. The Federal Administrative Court has confirmed the self-executing force of directives. Two other German courts, the Finance Court of Münster (27 November 1980) and the Finance Court of Hamburg (4 September 1981) asked the ECJ for a preliminary ruling on the same question as the *Bundesfinanzholf*. In both cases the ECJ reiterated its view of the unimpeded effect of directives. The Finance Court of Lower Saxony in its decision on this matter ruled on 3 March 1983 in favour of the interpretation of the ECJ and against that of the *Bundesfinanzhof*.

Nevertheless, both the 'Solange decision' of BVG in 1977 and the VAT decision of the *Bundesfinanzhof* indicate that the early assumptions that pro-integration sentiments would lead German judges always to accept the superiority of Community law have to have a question-mark put against them. These decisions have a treble significance. They indicate that pro-integration sentiment among a key elite (German judges) is arguably weaker than in the past. They signify that at least in legal terms 'the openness' of the system is not quite as universally accepted as before. Lastly, as the VAT decision by the *Bundesfinanzhof* indicates, implementation would be inhibited if the courts were generally to take a less friendly line on the supremacy of Community law.

Conclusion

The Bundestag and Bundesrat clearly play a subordinate role in both the formulation and implementation of European policy. This subordinate role is particularly marked in relation to formulation of policy. In relation to implementation, the fact that civil servants are largely located in the *Länder* and that it is the *Länder* who will actually implement policy gives the Bundesrat an important role, as illustrated by the chemicals law case study (also see Chapter 8).

The lack of party political conflict and the orientation of the legislature towards committees both strengthens the role of experts and provides, as we again saw in the case study, very high access, even an initiative role, to economic interests.

The readiness of West German governments to implement EC decisions remains very high. Indeed one could argue that it is primarily in this sense that the Federal Government remains the *Musterknabe* of the EC. Federal governments can be just as obstructive as other EC governments in not going along with an emerging consensus in favour of a common policy if it appears to conflict with specific German interests and values. They can, as seen in the steel case study (Chapter 3), continue to press objections even when they themselves think they are on weak legal ground.

Once a decision has been arrived at, West German governments are, comparatively, ready to implement the decision. This readiness clearly relates to the general support by West German elites of the idea of European integration and the necessity felt by post-Hitler Germans of making these arrangements work. German civil servants pride themselves on being much less guilty of chicanery than the bureaucracies of some other member states and make distinctions between '*die Germanen*' (principally the FRG) who play it straight on detailed implementation, and '*die Romanen*' (principally Greece, Italy and France) whose bureaucracies often frustrate the goals of Community policy at the stage of detailed implementation. These views reflect both the legal culture of West German public servants and the fact that, with the strongest economy, West Germany has a stronger interest than other member states in seeing that EC rules, especially in relation to competition policy, are observed.

The attitude of the courts towards the relationship between EC and domestic law is of vital importance as the continuous controversy in Britain over the relative claims of the supremacy of EC law and parliamentary sovereignty has shown (Collins, 1984, pp. 21–9). The prevalence of legal values in the political administrative culture of the Federal Republic means that its importance is even greater there. If the view of the *Bundesfinanzhof* in the VAT case that directives did not have a self-executing force after the expiry of the time limit for implementation, had been accepted by other German courts, then it would have had clear and obvious negative effects on the continued readiness of West German governments and public officials to implement EC decisions.

Notes

The first part of this chapter draws on information in Bulmer, 1987, Ch. 5.

1 A number of analyses of the 1980 Chemicals Act have now been published but only the Berlin Diploma of Monika Zimmermann, (Zimmermann, 1981, pp. 155–83) takes full account of the EC dimension and we are indebted to it for some of the detail in this case study.

2 A major factor in the persistence of the Commission was the passing of the US Control of Toxic Substances Act (1976). This act was misread in Western Europe. The European reading was that it provided for case by case testing and establishment of information requirements, both of which could be used to keep out European products. This naturally increased the pressures for harmonization and further strengthened the Commission's hand since negotiations with the US could only succeed on the basis of a unified European legal basis.

3 This is not the only example of imperfect co-ordination on the part of the West Germans at that time. Interviews in the Commission in April 1986 referred to instances where representatives of German industry were agreeing to expert reports in the OECD Business Committee on the proposed directive which they subsequently opposed in Brussels.

8 *The* Länder, *West Berlin and the European Community*

The most important structural feature of West German politics is the federal system of government. Its intention and result is to disperse power rather than to have it all concentrated in one centre of government. For some, a federal system is regarded as the goal of the European Community, although this objective seems to become increasingly distant at the present. Paradoxically, there is a slight incompatibility between German federalism and EC membership. Membership of the EC has led to power becoming centralized in Bonn on policy matters discussed at the European level. Thus as European integration has widened in scope, many policy areas – for which the *Länder* hold responsibilities under the German constitution – are now discussed in the Council of Ministers. In this body it is the Bonn government which represents German interests. In consequence, not only has European integration failed to establish federal union at a Community level, but it has also affected the federal balance within West Germany.

A survey of the EC's impact upon the German *Länder* (and West Berlin), with a view to examining this problem area, must comprise several aspects. First, the fundamental question of how the *Länder* are affected by the EC must be answered. This will set an agenda of issues which may be covered thematically at a later stage. Secondly, it is necessary to establish which channels the *Länder* employ in order to put across their views. Attention may then be turned to the EC policy issues which regularly affect *Länder* interests. A central problem here is that, under Article 73 of the Basic Law, exclusive responsibility for foreign policy – including integration policy (as defined earlier) – is claimed by the Federal Government. The problem is that integration necessarily involves activities in areas of *Länder* responsibility, such as agricultural structural policy, environmental issues and regional policy.

Not surprisingly, the *Länder* have been dissatisfied with the

Federal Government's wish to be the sole channel of views in EC negotiations on these policy areas. The various and, primarily, informal means by which the *Länder* have sought to counter losses of power will be assessed in order to establish the EC's impact on federalism.

The special position of West Berlin is examined in a final section. Successive Berlin politicians have displayed a keen interest in securing the status of the city's western sectors through establishing a close integration into the EC. The motives embrace a mixture of political, economic and security benefits which West Berliners believe to be attainable from such a relationship. For its part, the Bonn government has also sponsored the city's interests in European integration. However, West Berlin's involvement in the EC has not been without difficulty due to the intricacies of the Four-Power Agreement.

The *Länder*

The European Community and co-operative federalism

In this overview of the *Länder* and West Berlin in the EC two particular lines will be followed. First, the EC's impact will be examined in political terms rather than in the constitutional-legal manner which has dominated German analysis. Following the tradition of the *Rechtsstaat* (and of their professional training), German analysts have seen the problems in terms of the constitutional principles raised. Thus Birke (1972) has examined the impact of the EC treaties on the legal competencies of the *Länder*. Oetting (1973) has investigated the constitutional aspects of the federal states' attempts to secure Bundesrat involvement in EC policy-making. Secondly, none of the contributions to the theme of *Länder*–EC relations – whether from the German constitutional-legal approach or from a public administration perspective – has used the overall context of the Federal Government's European policy as a framework within which to view sub-national government's viewpoints. In this study, by contrast, the overall context is of considerable importance, both in connection with the policy-making procedures and with the policy content of the *Länder*.

The importance of the overall context derives from the layering of policy-making. There is essentially a three-tier system of government, involving the EC, the Federal Government and the *Länder* governments. The intermediate tier is of greatest importance because of the Federal Government's position as a 'controller' (Cox and Jacobson, 1984, p. 12). We have already noted that the Federal Government's centrality to European integration gives it a powerful voice in policy-making. Although it does not have a *right* of veto, the Federal Government does have sufficient 'clout' to veto EC proposals in the Council of Ministers (Henig, 1980, p. 27). At the same time, because the Federal Government is able constitutionally to ignore any advice/requests from the *Länder*, it can impose policy on subnational government.

The different nature of the Federal Government's position regarding the *Länder* on the one hand, and the EC on the other, derives from the different negotiating climates. Policy-making in the European Community has experienced more favourable conditions for agreement and integration, such as the 'fair weather' conditions of economic growth during the 1960s. *Bund-Länder* policy-making is characterized by different conditions, however. Co-operative federalism is a negotiating climate to which the EC aspires; in Germany it is reality. Thus, with very occasional exceptions, the Bundesrat does not become embroiled in the inter-state wrangling of its European counterpart, the Council of Ministers.

This distinction is worth making because it highlights the fact that an examination of *Länder* EC policy and policy channels in the overall German context must take account of the atmosphere of which they are one part. 'Co-operative federalism' best summarizes these circumstances. Scheuner has characterized this concept as 'where detailed tasks require a uniform and agreed co-operation of all the participants: the Federal Government, the *Länder* and the local authorities' (quoted in Kunze, 1968, p. 1). Characteristic of these detailed tasks are the newer, technical policy areas. Typically, they have come on to the political agenda after the share-out of responsibilities codified in the 1949 Basic Law and thus became residual powers for the *Länder* under Article 70, paragraph 1. The 1969 finance reform measures were brought about to enable the *Länder* to fund these new responsibilities. The Troeger Commission, which prepared the ground for these measures introduced the principle of co-operative federalism to Germany.

The purpose of detailing this *Bund-Länder* policy climate is to indicate that these newer, technical policy areas under *Länder* responsibility are conducted in a de-politicized manner. This represents a contrast with the sporadic *Bund-Länder* conflict on sensitive domestic political issues, such as budgetary, fiscal or counter-cyclical policy. On these subjects, *party* political conflict sometimes occurred between the Bundesrat and the Federal

Government. This has scarcely occurred on the newer policy areas into which the European Community has sought to widen integration, thereby disturbing the delicate balance of power between *Bund* and *Länder*.

Open political conflict between the *Länder* and the Federal Government over an issue of European policy is almost inconceivable. Co-operative federalism and the permissive consensus which exists between the political parties over European integration militate against such conflict and the *Länder* governments are committed to European integration. In sum, therefore, the behaviour of the *Länder* regarding EC affairs has been characterized by the consensual framework of *bundesfreundliches Verhalten*.

The European Community's impact on the Länder

The Federal Republic's commitment to join the European Coal and Steel Community inevitably involved some loss of autonomy on the part of the *Länder*. However, the loss of sovereignty was not an issue when the Treaty of Paris came into operation in 1952. This was because the FRG was still *regaining* powers from the allies. ECSC membership – with the allies' encouragement – represented a means whereby control of certain industries could be regained. In addition, Germany was prepared to make real sacrifices in pursuit of international acceptance. This was supported constitutionally by Article 24 of the Basic Law, which permits the transfer of sovereign powers to international organizations. These factors, along with a positive commitment to European integration on the part of *Länder* politicians, meant that sovereignty was not a disputed issue of the type familiar to observers of the United Kingdom's very reserved espousal of Europeanism. This positive attitude of *Länder* politicians has continued to overrule constitutional objections to new EC legislation up to the present day.

Under the circumstances of ECSC membership, North-Rhine Westphalia was at first the state almost exclusively affected. This was because the Saar only became sovereign West German territory in 1957 (Hanrieder and Auton, 1980, p. 122). All the German states are now affected, however, and by many different EC policies.

It is difficult to discuss the nature of the EC's impact in general terms because there are numerous factors at work. First, EC membership has affected *Länder* activity in the legislative, executive and judicial sectors. Secondly, the extent of such impact is dependent upon the (wildly fluctuating) extent of integration in the particular EC policy area. Thirdly, the specific effect on the powers of the *Länder* depends on the degree to which the states held power in the first place. Similarly, each state has a different balance of economic and social interests which determine the saliency of EC legislation. Hence agricultural structural policy is of no interest to Hamburg or Bremen.

The most significant impact on the legislative powers of the *Länder* is to be expected where they have exclusive authority. However, there are few such areas: police matters, education (up to higher level) and issues of local government. In other policy areas the *Länder* governments and the Federal Government may have concurrent legislative powers; the *Länder* may be required to legislate within a federal framework law (*Rahmengesetz*); there are the special circumstances of 'joint tasks' legislation (Article 91a, Basic Law); or the *Länder* may have no power whatsoever (foreign affairs, defence etc.: Article 73, Basic Law).

There are six main policy areas in which *Länder* legislative powers are affected by the EC.

Educational and vocational training Several articles of the EEC Treaty place constraints on this policy area where the *Länder* have exclusive authority. The EEC Treaty's commitment – under its Article 57 – to the mutual recognition of educational qualifications acts as a general constraint on *Länder* autonomy. The Community's various activities in vocational training involve further constraints (Hull and Rhodes, 1977, p. 15). An area of potentially much greater impact is the issue of educational provision for the children of intra-EC migrant workers (Hull and Rhodes, 1977, p. 11).

Occupational law Again the concern is to facilitate the free movement of labour: by harmonizing occupational law. An EC programme of 1961 'called for harmonization in the liberal professions (including, for example, journalism and teaching), responsibility for which, in terms of occupational law, lies predominantly with the States' (Hull and Rhodes, 1977, p. 15).

Environmental protection The EC has increasingly sought to take environmental policy initiatives. Ranging from the prevention of the pollution of waterways, such as the Rhine, to the protection of migrant songbirds, such proposals have had a mixed reception in the *Länder*. The tenuous justification in the Treaty of Rome for intervention in environmental affairs has caused this attitude.

Articles 100 and 235 could be bent to justify almost any new EC legislative interest. For this reason Article 235 is known as the *Gummiklausel* in the FRG (Everling, 1976).

Transport policy Potential EC encroachments relate to two parts of transport policy: the standards to which roads are made up as part of the EC's wish to harmonize the weights and dimensions of heavy goods vehicles; and the fees charged for port and harbour facilities. Such legislation may equally relate to local authorities.

Regional policy First, EC membership had the effect of further peripheralizing some *Länder* due to their location away from the Rhine–Rhône-centred common market of the Six. Schelswig–Holstein was affected in this way and drew up a programme to mitigate the effects (Birke, 1972, pp. 57–8). Secondly, the EC's attempt to prevent unfair competition through state aids has restricted *Länder* autonomy in regional policy. Thirdly, active EC regional and agricultural structural policies have had further impact on existing joint task policies in the FRG.

Harmonization Articles 99 to 102 of the EEC Treaty have varying impacts: Article 99 on financial and fiscal harmonization; Articles 100–102 on administrative harmonization. The harmonization of taxation could affect such *Länder* revenue sources as their share of VAT, beer tax, motor vehicle tax etc.

Overall, the exact loss of legislative power depends on the form of EC legislation. Community 'regulations' have direct binding effect; 'directives' by contrast are only binding as to the results to be achieved (Article 189, EEC Treaty). The latter may permit the *Länder* to retain discretion (e.g. on agricultural structural policy), although this is not guaranteed (Jaspert, 1982, p. 17).

The loss of powers is equally significant in the executive sector. Administrative practices may not discriminate between EC nationalities, for instance in *Länder* (and local government) tenders for contracts (Hull and Rhodes, 1977, pp. 29–35). More significantly, due to the EC's lack of executive agencies of its own, most European legislation is administered as if national law. This means that the *Länder* administer large parts of EC legislation: of broader significance than the six areas referred to above. EC 'regulations' do not allow the *Länder* to implement legislation as they see fit, contrary to the principles of German legislation (Article 38, Basic Law). Hence the *Länder* lose further autonomy and the pre-existing trend towards 'administrative federalism' is reinforced, whereby they increasingly become the executive agencies of the Federal Government (Smith, 1980, pp. 212–5).

A further issue relates to financing the implementation of EC legislation. Not surprisingly, the *Länder* are averse to *both* losing executive autonomy *and* having to endure additional expenditure. This whole issue has been disputed between the *Länder* and federal governments and was investigated by the Bundestag's *Enquête-Kommission 'Verfassungsreform'* (Morawitz, 1981, p. 14–16).

The final impact of the EC has been on the judicial competence of the *Länder*. Here *Länder* courts have lost certain powers in matters which have become subject to Community law (Hull and Rhodes, 1977, pp. 19–20; Birke, 1972, pp. 28–31).

Länder *involvement in EC policy-making*

In the face of the EC's encroachment upon their autonomy, the *Länder* governments have sought vigorously to secure their right to be heard by the Federal Government. However, there has been an aversion on the Federal Government's part to make any formal or constitutionally binding agreement which might give the *Länder* a foothold. In consequence, a whole series of predominantly informal and bureaucratic procedures has been built up with no logical pattern. Indeed, the procedures add to the already sectorized policy-making inside the Federal Government. The channels through which the *Länder* put their views divide into direct contacts with the European Commission and, secondly, by enlisting the Federal Government's assistance as an intermediary at the European level. The latter includes several possible courses of action: using the Bundesrat; including EC affairs in *Bund-Länder* committees dealing with domestic policy; a new *Bund-Länder* procedure for EC affairs instituted in 1980. Also there is the *Länder* Observer.

Direct contacts with the European Commission

There are several contacts of a direct nature between the *Länder* and the Commission. They are all informal because the Federal Government is not prepared to compromise its exclusive constitutional responsibility for foreign affairs (Article 32, Basic Law). *Länder* ministers and other politicians have made information visits to Brussels in numerous guises but they are required to inform the Bonn Foreign Office of their itinerary (Morawitz, 1981, pp. 95–7). Birke has noted some instances where EC decisions may have been influenced by *Länder* politicians (1973, pp. 58–60). For example, Hamburg was specifically excluded from EC legislation on customs zones following the mayor's talks with the Commission explaining the potential impact on the city's freeport status. Such visits are usually for the purpose of exchanging information, however. Significantly, the Federal Government took a negative view of the Bavarian government's wish in 1979 to open a representation in Brussels and the plan was dropped (Morawitz, 1981, p. 35). A similar response was elicited from the Federal Government in another case, which involved wine bottles. This followed Bavarian Prime Minister Strauss's direct intervention with the EC Commission, which was threatening the continued use by Franconian wine-growers of the distinctive, flask-shaped 'Bocksbeutel'. Recently, some *Länder* have set up economic promotion offices in Brussels (*Financial Times*, 8 May, 1986).

Visits by the Commission to *Länder* governments have also taken place. They have been of a fact-finding nature and have concerned, for instance, wine-growing and – more recently – regional policy (Schmitz-Wenzel, 1969, p. 152). Direct contacts between the Commission and *Länder* governments must remain limited, however, in order not to tax the flexibility which the Federal Government has allowed. Since almost all contacts between the *Länder* and the Federal Government are informal any withdrawal of co-operation by Bonn would hurt the *Länder* most, although this would imply a breakdown of co-operative federalism.

Utilization of the Bundesrat

The Bundesrat's position in the German political system is to represent the interest of *Länder* governments in federal policy-making (Ziller, 1979). It is logical, therefore, that the *Länder* sought to establish their consultation by the Federal Government through this institution in the first instance. Initial efforts in this direction at the time of accession to the ECSC were obstructed, however (Hull and Rhodes, 1977, p. 37; Oetting, 1973, pp. 22–6). During the debates on the ratification of the Treaties of Rome the Bundesrat again expressed concern about loss of *Länder* autonomy. On this occasion the Bundesrat was successful because it won the right to be informed (together with the Bundestag) of legislation proposed by the EC. This right was embodied in Article 2 of the 1957 Act of Ratification of the Treaties of Rome, outlined in Chapter 7.

As noted, the Bundesrat brings together the collective technical and administrative expertise of the *Länder* governments with a view to close co-operation with the Federal Government. The exact manner of how this takes place varies according to the operating procedures of individual committees (Bulmer, 1987, pp. 263–4). But in all cases *Länder* civil servants and their federal counterparts are able to exchange views on EC proposals. Hence the caution of Article 2 has translated into co-operative federalism in the spirit of Article 53, Basic Law. Essentially, this has occurred for two reasons. First, the states have undertaken a continual search for channels for presenting their views to the European Community; the European Parliament is the latest of these (Jaspert, 1982, pp. 29–32). Secondly, the Bundesrat's scrutiny machinery has been oiled by other agents, notably the *Länder* Observer and working groups of government officials.

Federal committees and EC policy-making

Co-operative federalism has brought with it a plethora of specialist committees of varying political-administrative status. Kunze estimated that there were some four hundred such bodies, with the Conference of *Länder* Prime Ministers at the apex of their somewhat haphazard organization (1968, pp. 135–44). Of particular note are three working groups of *Länder* 'European officials': for agriculture, transport and economics. However, other committees may discuss EC issues, such as the *Bund-Länder* planning committees for the joint tasks of regional policy and agricultural structures.

The complex interactions of such federal committees – including their relationship to the Bundesrat – cannot be unravelled here (Bulmer, 1987, pp. 257–63). The committees' importance lies in the fact they are frequently composed of the same officials who appear in Bundesrat committees. Since the Federal Government has integrated most EC policy into domestic policy-making channels, the *Länder* are sucked into a similar pattern of behaviour. This also applies where the *Länder* are responsible for administering EC policy. The federal committees thus form an important facet of *Länder* links with EC policy but their meetings are irregular.

The 1980 Bund-Länder *procedure*

After some tentative discussions dating from 1975, an agreement was reached in 1979 between Chancellor Schmidt and the Conference of *Länder* Prime Ministers on a new procedure for informing the states over EC issues. Again the detailed operation of this procedure is unnecessary here and is extensively documented by Morawitz (1981).

Although of greater significance than earlier attempted agreements, the new procedure is limited to where the EC affects the essential interests of the *Länder* or their exclusive responsibilities (*Kompetenzen*). In cases of the latter, the Federal Government would promptly inform the *Länder* of EC proposals with the promise to represent their views in the Council of Ministers. The *Länder* view – to be reached unanimously – would only be deviated from if overriding foreign or integration policy goals necessitated this. Furthermore, in cases affecting exclusive powers of the *Länder*, the latter may ask to send two delegates to consultative bodies of the Commission, COREPER or working groups. This procedure came into effect in September 1980 on an experimental basis, having been embodied in governmental procedures (§85a *Gemeinsame Geschäftsordnung II der Bundesregierung*).

The main impact of this procedure has arguably been to further complicate an already fragmented system. This is largely because the procedure does not replace any of the existing alternative channels. Although the Bundesrat may not now be used in matters of exclusive *Länder* competence, it *may* in matters of essential interest, if the *Länder* so wish, thus creating a double-tracked system.

In other cases the procedure merely codifies existing behaviour. For example, there had been *Länder* representatives on EC committees discussing regional policy, wine-growing and agricultural structures for some time (Oberthür, 1978). The *Länder* Observer's position is given broader recognition than before. However the Federal Government's interpretation of the new procedure was considered to be very rigid – indeed, perhaps questionable – by the *Länder*. In 1981 the *Länder* governments were seeking a meeting with the Federal Government with a view to obtaining a more liberal interpretation of their 'essential interests'. By summer 1983 the achievements were miniscule although the procedure's experimental phase had been extended. One example of the problems concerned the 1980 British budgetary settlement which resulted in increased German contributions to the EC Budget. Inside Germany this was to be financed by increasing certain taxes which are levied jointly by the federal and *Länder* governments (see Chapter 3). Nevertheless the Federal Government did not consider the essential interests of the *Länder* to have been affected.

The Länder *Observer*

The post of *Länder* Observer (*Beobachter der Länder bei den Europäischen Gemeinschaften*) was established after agreement between the *Länder* and federal governments in 1959. The Observer's importance is not as an expert scrutineer but as an agent expediting the presentation of *Länder* opinions to the Federal Government through the various channels outlined above. Additionally, he is permitted to attend sessions of the EC Council of Ministers, where he can observe that the *Länder* view – expressed through whatever domestic policy-making channel – is put across at the EC level. His accreditation to the German delegation is only as an observer but this does permit him to obtain non-public EC documents. His detective work in sifting through these may enable him to give advance notice to the *Länder* governments of legislation likely to affect them.

About a third of his time is spent at EC institutions with the remainder being spent in Bonn. His functions when in the FRG include reporting as an *ex officio* participant in the Bundesrat's EC Affairs Committee, writing reports to his employers, the *Länder* governments, and distributing EC documents to them, thereby short-circuiting the more lengthy Bundesrat referral procedures (Oberthür, 1978). This is important since the correct timing of the presentation of *Länder* views to the Federal Government is crucial to their success.

Under the 1980 procedure some changes have occurred, giving further functions to the Observer, although the nature of his role is essentially unchanged. His role is essentially that of a 'sorting office', receiving information from the Bonn government and dispatching it to the appropriate *Länder* policy-making agency (Morawitz, 1981). The increased workload of the Observer under the 1980 procedure led to the appointment of an assistant.

Recurrent EC issues of concern to the Länder *governments*

The importance of *Länder* opinions is directly related to sub-national government's expertise in the policy area concerned. In turn, this expertise is a function of *Länder* importance in domestic legislation (its formulation and its implementation). An example may be used to illustrate what is meant here. If a CDU/CSU-dominated Bundesrat were to dispute the opinions of an SPD/FDP federal coalition on EC co-determination policy – as occurred in fact – the Bonn government would disregard the Bundesrat's advice. Why? First, the *Länder* do not have any significant domestic authority in this policy area. Secondly, to the extent that party politics is important, the Federal Government will consider itself alone to have a 'national' democratic mandate. If the same occurred in agricultural structural policy, however, a different outcome would transpire. First, the *Länder* have a large stake of domestic policy responsibility (Blaschke, 1977). Indeed, the Bundesrat could obstruct domestic enabling legislation (of an EC directive), thereby causing Bonn considerable embarrassment. Secondly, domestic agricultural structural policy is dependent upon a framework of co-operative federalism for its successful implementation. The Federal Government could not risk losing this.

For this reason, it is where the *Länder* have lost autonomy under EC membership that their views are of greatest relevance. Hence it is in those policy areas already identified that *Länder* views are likely to have a major influence on the Federal Government's position in the Council of Ministers.

As was mentioned earlier, the EC's objectives regarding the free movement of labour have represented a challenge to the states' responsibility for education and some occupational law. Many of the EC's objectives have been turned into practice. However, a particularly thorny issue which has repeatedly caused concern to the *Länder* has been the question of educational provision for immigrant labour. Since any EC measures would only concern labour from other member states, the main group involved was originally Italian labour (some 600,000 workers in 1976), although with Greek accession a further 400,000 were involved (Hull and Rhodes, 1977, p. 11). EC law is such that discrimination is open to challenge in the courts. However, the *Länder* have ensured that no EC legislation is passed making the provision of education mandatory for the children of this immigrant work-force. The Federal Government was obliged to obstruct such legislation in the mid-1970s by stating in the Council of Ministers that the EC proposal could not be accepted 'for domestic reasons'. The *Länder* Observer pointed out in an interview that his presence at the relevant Council sessions was to check that the Federal Government did not deviate from its promised position as part of a package deal.

The transport policy area and the general question of harmonization share a common feature. This is that the impact is by no means restricted to the *Länder* but also affects local authorities. EC legislation on highway construction and non-discriminatory public contract tendering are, in consequence, not purely a *Länder* problem. Moreover, given the generally high standard of German roads and the fact that tendering still revolves around the cheapest bid, the main (i.e. non-administrative) costs of this legislation are not borne by governmental agencies.

Agricultural structural policy and regional policy may be taken together because they are both joint tasks and function in a similar way. In addition, the EC legislation in these areas has been similar in that it has not necessitated major changes to existing domestic policy. In both cases, however, the EC Commission's *original* proposals caused considerable opposition in the FRG, although not for any reasons specifically associated with the *Länder* (Bulmer, 1987, pp. 334–75; below, Chapter 9). The European Regional Development Fund merely put a small additional sum of money from the EC at the disposal of the federal and state governments, with the latter deciding on the projects to be aided. The impact of this was primarily in terms of some extra administrative work. The picture is fairly similar for agricultural structural policy, although the *Länder* governments initially feared considerable losses of autonomy. This essentially leaves the impact of the EC's control over state aids. Here the effect is more of principle than actuality because the West German social market economy does not espouse interventionist policies of the type restricted by the EC. The limited intervention that has occurred, e.g. by *Länder* and federal governments in areas affected by the steel crisis, has tended to fall within policy areas where the EC itself is being interventionist. Thus the meshing together of *Länder* and EC policies has fallen more into administrative details than major policy conflicts.

Finally, there are the environmental policy questions which have increasingly come on to the EC agenda with an impact on *Länder* functions. Directives setting standards for bathing water, pollution of waterways through to conservationist measures regarding migrant birds have had rather a significant impact. The Federal Government generally has negligible expertise and is obliged to consult the *Länder* extensively, as exemplified by the songbirds case (Bulmer, 1987, pp. 279–86). Not untypically, German legislation was sufficiently strict in this case that the EC's proposed standards were already being met largely. However, the Commission was likely to impose considerable work on the *Länder*, for example by requiring twice-yearly reports on the directive's implementation. One can imagine with the plethora of environmental proposals being made by the EC that the cumulative effect on *Länder* administration is significant. Since the only benefit Germans saw as accruing from the songbird legislation was the outlawing of the Italian and French sport of shooting transnational (German?) songbirds, such as skylarks and ortolan buntings, the general view was that the costs should fall on the 'culprit' nations. Nevertheless, the environmentalist and Europeanist perspectives of the *Länder* defeated legalistic objections – only to find the Council of Ministers exclude skylarks from the final leglisation in order to obtain an agreement of any sort with the Italian and French governments! The Federal Government has been aware of the costs the *Länder* might incur over EC environmental legislation and invited them to attend various meetings in Brussels, even formalizing their consultation in matters concerning pollution measures for the Rhine (Morawitz, 1981, p. 11).

From the above examination it is clear that the EC's impact on the *Länder* has been repeatedly to involve them in extra administrative costs. Although important legislative rights of the *Länder* have been lost in principle, the actual effect has not been that great because the FRG is environmentally aware, on the one hand, and non-interventionist in economic policy, on the other.

Local authorities and the European Community

Local authorities in all EC member states have been affected by various items of legislation: public tendering and highway standards being two examples already identified. It is worth noting here that the local authorities' national associations operate rather like interest groups in their manner of dealing with the Federal Government. The three organizations involved – *der Deutsche Städtetag*, *der Deutsche Landkreistag* and *der Deutsche Städte- und Gemeindebund* – represent different types of local authorities. They act as interest groups *vis-à-vis* the Federal Government which has recognized them as policy-making partners in its procedures (Hull and Rhodes, 1977, pp. 25–9). In addition the three organizations jointly established a Brussels information office in 1964 which is used for keeping in touch with EC legislative developments (Pünder, 1970, pp. 102–32).

West Berlin, the Federal Republic and the European Community

Although the constitutional-legal status of West Berlin is defined in the 1971 Quadripartite Agreement, the Western powers nevertheless take a different view from the Soviet Union regarding West Berlin's status. The Bonn government – while recognizing that West Berlin is under the four powers' authority – has sought to integrate the Western sectors into the Federal Republic as much as possible. One means by which successive federal governments have sought to do this is through incorporating West Berlin into the European Community. For their part, the authorities of West Berlin have regarded incorporation in the EC as vital to the well-being of the city's economy. With a declining population and a vulnerable economy, action is needed to prevent a situation which would be against the objectives of the city authorities, the Federal Government and the Western allies.

As Morgan and Bray (1982) note in their concise outline of the subject, West Berlin's position in the EC has only begun to create problems since the 1971 agreement. The difficulties essentially stem from 'the fact that the Quadripartite Agreement was silent on the question of West Berlin's links with the European Community' (Morgan and Bray, 1982, p. 86). With the agreement's apparent halt to West Berlin being used for political ceremonies or governmental offices of the FRG, the Bonn government saw the possibility of establishing EC offices there as a substitute measure. This position coincided with Berlin's desire to forge closer links with the EC. What therefore are the links between the FRG, West Berlin and the EC?

First, EC legislation applies in West Berlin (Schumacher, 1980). Typically this is brought about by the inclusion in EC legislation of the formula '*Berlin ist integraler Bestandteil der Europäischen Gemeinschaft*'. If German legislation is required to enact an EC directive this will also be applied in West Berlin, as is the norm in domestic policy. The Western allies examine EC legislation so that the Soviet Union is unable to argue that they have given up their responsibilities (thus setting a precedent for East Germany ruling East Berlin). There are many potential problems under this heading, not least what would happen if a common EC passport is introduced for West Berlin (Morgan and Bray, 1982, p. 88).

Second, the activities of the EC on West Berlin's territory have extended beyond the agriculture commissioner's attendance at Berlin's agricultural fair (*Grüne Woche*). Of greatest significance has been the establishment of the European Centre for Vocational Training. This led to protests by the Soviet Union and East Germany so that the Western allies might be reluctant to risk further tension by allowing new EC bodies to be established. Nevertheless, the West Berlin administration was keen on such a move for political reasons and for prestige.

Third, West Berlin has been affected by EC activity in the same way as was outlined for the ten *Länder* of the FRG. In view of the fact that federal legislation is normally applicable in Berlin, the impact is similar in most areas. In regional policy, the EC permits the special concessions under the *Berlinförderungsgesetz* which is the much more interventionist Berlin counterpart of the joint task regional policy of the FRG. West Berlin receives money from the ERDF as well as from other EC sources, such as the Social Fund.

Fourth, there have been difficulties stemming from the inclusion of West Berlin in agreements between the EC and third countries, especially where Eastern bloc countries are involved (Morgan and Bray, 1982).

Fifth, the sensitive issue of West Berlin directly electing members of the European Parliament has been avoided. The Soviet Union would be very critical of the issues raised in the event of that occurring. Instead three MEPs are *selected* by the House of Representatives in Berlin in the same manner as the Berlin members of the Bundestag are chosen.

These issues require close monitoring by the Federal Government which acts as West Berlin's mouthpiece in the Council of Ministers: a role which is permitted under the Quadripartite Agreement. West Berlin is clearly committed to European integration although it is dependent on other governments to achieve its objectives. It is also worth noting that, in contrast to its attitude towards the *Länder* in maintaining its constitutional right to represent West Germany in foreign affairs, the FRG has assumed this power regarding West Berlin and has expanded it into areas where its authority under the Quadripartite Agreement is uncertain.

Finally, there is a tacit agreement not to discuss issues relating to Berlin in the European Political Co-operation process, not least because the United States would be absent from discussions.

Conclusion

The EC's impact on West Berlin and the *Länder* has been significant. In terms of constitutional principles the effect has been great; in political terms the impact has been less due to their support for European integration. However, developments in 1986 have placed a question mark against even this. The 1986

Single European Act, which gives the EC responsibility for environmental policy and sets out a timetable for completion of the internal market, has cut across *Länder* responsibilities, thereby creating significant problems. We have already outlined the attitude of the *Länder* on environmental policy. They have now complained that the Federal Government has negotiated away their competencies in this policy sector for the sake of European policy. A similar picture applies to aspects of the internal market, including freedom of establishment. The Bavarian CSU government and SPD state governments have joined forces and threatened to obstruct the ratification process by blocking the necessary Bundesrat approval (*Financial Times*, 8 May 1986; *FAZ*, 19 April 1986). They have complained about the lack of consultation during the drafting of the Single European Act.

Hitherto the *Länder* have had reasonable, albeit relatively informal, channels for putting across their views to the Federal Government. Should *Bund-Länder* co-operation break down, the Federal Government's European policy will be further weakened by internal divisions. The expertise and decentralized responsibilities of the *Länder* are central to their involvement in the formulation of German European policy. This situation mirrors their role in the co-operative federalism of domestic policy. As with the major associational interests, so the federal states have important information to offer the Federal Government on EC affairs. Although the opinions of interest groups are valued, given the West German preoccupation with social peace, it is the question of governability that makes the states' co-operation vital. Thus the *Länder* are not a sectional interest but have the same governmental duties (and an electoral mandate) as the Federal Government itself. Until 1986 their views were given careful consideration in Bonn even if no embracing *right* of consultation was granted. It must be assumed that some accommodation will permit this situation to continue, despite the challenge posed by the Single European Act.

9 *The Federal Republic of Germany and the European Regional Fund*

A case study of German interests in the European Community

The European Regional Development Fund (ERDF) was established by the EC Council of Ministers in March 1975. It brought into operation a loose framework which permits the Community to grant financial support to national regional policies. Only a small part of the fund concerns regional action taken directly by Community institutions. In consequence, the objectives for which ERDF aid is granted are diverse, being a function of the policy priorities of the national government receiving support. In many cases EC funding is treated in a cynical manner by national governments, particularly in the prevailing European climate of public expenditure cuts. The ERDF is frequently considered by German governmental officials to have more in common with a marshalling yard, in which sums of money are shunted around for budgetary purposes rather than to give additional assistance in pursuance of regional policy objectives. In 1975 Chancellor Schmidt described the ERDF as merely a mechanism for redistributing finance 'clothed in a pair of bathing trunks with "regional policy" painted on them' (quoted in Carr, 1985, p. 95).

In view of the fund's modesty, many protagonists of the ideal of European integration find it depressing that to arrive even thus far took a considerable length of time. Between the October 1972 Paris Summit communiqué, in which the national governments finally recognized the need for a regional policy at the Community level, and the fund's establishment in March 1975, some thirty months had passed by. Blame for this delay can be apportioned to all member states to varying extents. For those who see Germany as a '*Musterknabe*' – the model country pressing for the ideal of European integration – its behaviour will paradoxically be seen to have contributed to this delay.

Clearly it is outside the remit of this case study to undertake an examination of all the EC member governments' action in the negotiations leading to the fund's establishment. There are already two studies which deal with the establishment of the regional fund from such an overall European perspective (Wallace, H., 1977; Talbot, 1977). The objective here is to examine the German role in the establishment of the ERDF, to analyse the motivations of the Federal Government and to establish how far they match a general framework of 'interests' of governmental European policy as a whole. This means that reference will be made to themes which have been examined in earlier chapters.

The first of these arguments concerns the political and economic importance of the FRG to the establishment of the ERDF. It will be argued that its economic importance is derived from its position as the major net contributor to the EC Budget. Since any regional policy represents the transfer of resources from rich regions to poor ones, the ERDF is based in large measure upon the FRG's economic well-being. In order to balance the Community's dependence on German economic welfare, the Federal Government could legitimately expect a major say in the shaping of the fund. In the extreme it could veto proposals, if they were held to be unacceptable. Its centrality to the financing of the fund would give the German government the negotiating strength to take an obstructionist line.

Among the specific issues which must be examined in this context are the extent to which the Federal Government played upon Germany's political and economic importance to the establishment of the fund. Was its motivation the desire to establish an effective regional policy? Were other issues equally important?

The second of the themes which must be examined concerns the political and economic importance of the ERDF to the FRG. It is difficult to separate the political and economic aspects here since they are closely intertwined. Moreover, it is artificial to examine the regional proposals in isolation from the Community's policies as a whole. Thus, in political terms, the Federal Government would be aware that a regional policy should assist economic convergence, which in turn would create greater cohesion between the member states. Increased political solidarity would create an atmosphere more favourable to policies which could give West Germany greater economic benefits. Examples of economic policies which would have been beneficial in the early 1970s were Economic and Monetary Union or an EC energy policy. The interlinking of policies in this manner was recognized by German negotiators at the Council of Ministers. Equally, however, the German government occasionally gave the appearance that, since a regional policy had no immediate benefits for Germany, it did not warrant a high priority in governmental attention.

A third theme which is to be examined concerns the argument that much of the Federal Government's behaviour at the Council of Ministers can be explained in terms of attitudes which are entrenched in domestic politics. These attitudes may derive from fears common to most political actors and organizations in response, for example, to past economic and political crises. Such shared attitudes and orientations are part of a unifying political culture shared among decision-making elites. Alternatively, the attitudes may be more sectional in nature, reflecting the special interests of particular political organizations. Such interests may be associational ones put across by interest groups. Equally, they may be institutional interests, put across by such bodies as the *Länder* governments, which have identifiable interests to articulate *because of* their governmental functions.

The final theme which is to be illustrated, concerns the fundamental argument that underlies the preceding analysis, namely that German European policy is conducted in a 'sectorized' manner. During the negotiations on the establishment of the ERDF the German government's position, particularly on the size of the fund, changed dramatically on several occasions. This, it will be argued, was one manifestation of the problems which a sectorized, unco-ordinated EC policy-making style can bring about. At the Community level of negotiations other member governments may find the unpredictability of the German policy to be a cause of frustration. The counter-argument to this would postulate that the shifting German position was a product of the volatile international economic climate at the time, due to the oil crisis and its effects. The validity of this argument must be checked as part of the analysis.

The development of a regional policy

The Community's commitment to a regional policy

The impulses towards a European Community regional policy were rather slow in developing. At the time of the EEC's establishment all member states were experiencing economic growth and little thought was given to regional problems. In consequence, there was no specific reference to the policy area in the Treaty of Rome. In the mid-1960s the Commission began to give some attention to regional policy. Initial measures were agreed in 1971 when legislation was introduced to remove unfair state aids in *national* regional policies (negative integration). The question of a positive EC regional policy came about in the context of the 1969 summit meeting at The Hague, where EMU was agreed upon. The achievement of EMU would have involved member governments losing important national economic policy instruments. An EC regional fund would thus be needed. The first enlargement of the EC, also agreed to in 1969, led to the membership of the United Kingdom and Ireland. Both these states had regional problems and became important allies of the only existing proponent of a regional policy, namely Italy.

Britain in particular wanted a regional policy in order to offset the fact that it would gain little financial benefit from other EC policies, especially the CAP. In consequence, the British government was particularly keen in pushing its case at the Paris Summit of October 1972. As has been noted the demands made at the summit received public attention and thus heightened expectations in the potential beneficiary states because of the publicity which summit conferences receive (Wallace, H., 1977, p. 138). The communiqué issued at the summit's conclusion stated:

> The heads of state or of government agreed that a high priority should be given to the aim of correcting, in the Community, the structural and regional imbalances which might affect the realization of economic and monetary union.

A regional fund was to be established by 31 December 1973.

German ministerial attitudes to the EC proposals

Before examining the negotiating position of the Federal Government at the EC Council of Ministers, it is important to take note of the different parts of government that were involved. First, the Foreign Office took responsibility for much of the conduct of policy prior to the fund's establishment. As a new area of EC activity, regional policy was considered to fall within the Foreign Office's responsibility for integration policy. This was underpinned by the fact that the general Council of (Foreign) Ministers was the main location of ministerial negotiations in the Community. The Foreign Office's familiarity with regional policy was thus based on its responsibilities for co-ordinating integration policy in the FRG; expertise on regional policy instruments was located elsewhere.

The main location of regional policy expertise at the federal level is the Economics Ministry. Its section (*Referat*) which deals with domestic regional policy took on the tasks of overseeing the technical aspects of the proposed fund. The Federal Finance ministry was also involved in policy-making because its Subdivision VB has the function of monitoring all EC developments with implications for the Federal Budget. Thus the size of the proposed fund concerned these officials. These ministries, however, only represent those with responsibilities at the federal level. Since domestic regional policy is a 'joint task' (Article 91a, Basic Law), the federal and state levels of government share powers in policy-making. The *Länder* governments were particularly concerned that their powers or autonomy should not be restricted by the ERDF. The ten state governments complete the complex picture of governmental agencies primarily affected by the proposed fund. In fact West Berlin and the Federal Ministry for Inter-German Affairs – defending regions weakened by the postwar division of Germany – were also involved at the margins but will not be examined here. The overall picture of dispersed governmental power indicates that considerable co-ordination would be needed to ensure coherence in the German position in Brussels.

In order to appreciate the significance of this dispersion of executive responsibilities for regional policy, some comments are necessary on the attitudes of the federal ministries involved. Essentially the *Länder* governments were of less importance until the ERDF was set up and their role will be examined below. Moreover, their views were centred on the Bundesrat where scrutiny of the regional policy proposals was being carried out.

As has been noted, the Foreign Office is the ministry most favourably disposed to European integration. This is true of the senior officials as well as of the FDP ministers in the period since 1969. However, the co-ordination of European policy has been the function of a Foreign Office parliamentary state secretary (later termed minister of state) since 1972. During the period of time relevant to negotiations on the ERDF's establishment, the post was held by two SPD politicians: Hans Apel (1972–4) and Hans-Jürgen Wischnewski (1974–6). Both took a much more pragmatic approach to integration than their FDP foreign minister: Scheel and Genscher respectively. Hans Apel, one of Helmut Schmidt's political allies from Hamburg, had spent a period working in the European Parliament. However, neither this nor his earlier pro-integrationist writings prevented him from making outspoken attacks on European institutions, especially the Commission. It was no coincidence that, after becoming chancellor, Schmidt appointed a pragmatist to take over his old post as finance minister, namely Hans Apel. Wischnewski was later appointed to the post of minister of state in the Chancellor's Office, 1976–9, where – as Schmidt's confidant – he was entrusted with various special tasks. In sum, therefore, both junior ministers in the Foreign Office with responsibilities for European integration were masters of *Realpolitik* rather than of Europeanist rhetoric. Thus the Foreign Office's traditional Europeanism was tempered by the responsible ministers whose lines of communications in terms of allegiance were to Helmut Schmidt rather than to the foreign minister, this situation being promoted by their direct participation in the Cabinet.

The Economics Ministry was not significantly involved at this ministerial level in the negotiations leading to the establishment of the ERDF. Its main involvement commenced once the fund had been established. Moreover, the Economics Ministry's traditional role as protector of the principles of market forces – in both domestic and EC contexts – did not apply since regional policy is one of the 'interventionist' dimensions of the social market economy. Checking the EC proposals on regional policy was left to the regional policy *Referat* which examined the proposals on their technical merit. Neither the Economics Ministry nor the Foreign Office wanted Germany to receive aid from the ERDF. However, the former ministry felt it should lobby for the most effective regional policy on behalf of the major contributors to the fund, namely the German taxpayers. In fact, as a result of the bargains struck in the Council of Ministers, the FRG ended up in receipt of 6.4 per cent of the fund's initial allocations. This resulted in the Economics Ministry becoming more involved in the management of the ERDF than it had anticipated.

The Finance Ministry had the function of overseeing the financial aspects of EC policy and, specifically, the impact upon German contributions to the Community Budget. Sub-division VB was responsible for drawing up papers on this impact for the benefit of other ministries. At the political level, the ministers, Helmut Schmidt (1972–May 1974) and Hans Apel (May 1974–February 1978), were responsible for outspoken comments on the Community's finances (*Finanzgebaren*). Their criticisms, although not specifically directed at the regional policy proposals, none the less coloured the ministry's approach to them. Specific comments were kept within governmental circles but this should not conceal the fact that successive EC proposals were examined critically, with the Finance Ministry's brief such that it could even question the merits of having a European regional fund at all. In essence, the Finance Ministry's attitude bolstered the government's resolve to attain an *effective* regional policy. In this ministry, effectiveness was determined by the amount of financial resources involved rather than in the Economics Ministry, where the criteria concerned the policy instruments and types of projects that would be eligible for EC aid. For the Economics Ministry, therefore, the Commission's proposals to make large areas of the Community's surface area eligible for aid were unacceptable because this 'watering-can' approach was incompatible with an effective tackling of the very weak regions. From the Finance Ministry's perspective, the watering-can approach was regarded as an ineffective use of Community funds, to which the FRG was the main contributor. The European Commission's 'success' in securing the opposition of both these ministries was the primary factor behind German obstruction of the proposals. Moreover, as Helen Wallace has noted (1977, p. 150), the Foreign Office was opposed to proposals in which the French would be net beneficiaries of the fund. Equally, however, it would appear that other member states, notably Britain, seemed oblivious to the complex position of the Federal Government, either through inexperience of EC affairs or because the German government had not made its position clear in the Council of Ministers (Wallace, 1977, p. 151–2).

The important opposition of both the Economics Ministry and of the Finance Ministry was linked to positions held in connection with domestic regional policy. This is administered as a 'joint task' (*Gemeinschaftsaufgabe*) of federal and *Länder* governments. The federal level, consisting of the Economics Ministry and the Finance Ministry, votes *en bloc*; the *Länder* governments (normally their economics ministries) vote individually, with Berlin being included in this (*BT-Drucksache* 8/3788, 13 March 1980, pp. 7–8). The role of the Finance Ministry in the joint task is to conduct financial control over the federal part of the fund. In effect it also acts as a lobby *vis-à-vis* the Economics Ministry, by forcing the latter to justify its faith in regional policy. Under the SPD finance minister, Hans Matthöfer (1978–82), there was scepticism from the political level about regional policy's value in general. Matthöfer favoured structural policy measures which were organized by industry rather than by region. He also was a proponent of research and technology policy, an interest which had been enhanced when he was minister responsible for that area from 1974–8. During the period of negotiations on the establishment of an EC regional policy, the Finance Ministry had no vested interests whatsoever in such a policy. Due to the fact that the Foreign Office was in charge of negotiations, the Finance Ministry's caution was directed at that ministry rather than at the Economics Ministry, as in the joint task.

For the Economics Ministry, opposition to the EC proposals revolved around the types of projects that would be eligible for EC support. In contrast to the Finance Ministry, it took a rather more enlightened view of an EC regional policy, recognizing that without one the objective of Economic and Monetary Union would be unattainable.

The Economics Ministry, however, remained critical of several aspects of the proposals. The most significant of these related to the apparent espousal of the watering-can principle (*Giesskannenprinzip*) by the EC Commission, particularly in the Thomson Report (Talbot, 1977, pp. 203–13). A cursory glance at the regions of the FRG that were eligible for assistance from domestic policy would suggest that the watering-can principle applies there, too. This, however, is not the case because policy is based on a series of nodal points (*Schwerpunktorte*). The surrounding area is regarded as a catchment labour market; it does not receive aid, however (Casper, 1979). This subtle difference appeared to be lost on the British government, for example. It also seemed more interested in the quota share-out than in the manner in which national governments would spend their quota. The Economics Ministry, however, wanted aid to be concentrated on Southern Italy, Ireland and parts of the United Kingdom.

At the more technical level of policy the Economics Ministry had two criticisms which it pursued. First, it opposed the system of interest rebates – subsequently adopted – since they were to be administered through the European Investment Bank (EIB). Not only did this involve considerable administrative work, arguably in disproportion to the money involved, but interest rebates were seen in a bad light for two further reasons. Academic research had shown rebates to be ineffective in terms of the goals of regional policy (extra employment) because of the protracted nature of the assistance. Also, since finance ministries prefer cash transfers rather than extended credit from the EIB, it was not likely to be popular for budgetary reasons. In the event, use of the rebates by member states has been miniscule, reinforcing the Economics Ministry's argument.

The second technical issue which the Economics Ministry

disliked in the EC regional policy debate concerned infrastructure measures. The Economics Ministry did not want to see infrastructural investments being undertaken which would have no impact on the labour market. This again related to policy effectiveness since there was a fear that national governments might build a motorway or a new airport without adequate research being conducted into whether a lasting effect would be achieved in terms of job creation. One thinks here of the party political considerations behind the decision to build the Humber Bridge (marginal constituencies in Hull). Clearly, the FRG would not be keen to see 'its' money being spent for electioneering purposes in another EC state.

It is clear from the outline above that the criticisms which the Economics and Finance Ministries were making of the Commission's proposals derived from their respective attitudes towards domestic regional policy. We must now examine how far the Foreign Office incorporated these views into its brief of negotiating the establishment of the ERDF. This can be achieved most effectively by a short chronological outline based upon government press releases and ministerial statements. In this outline attention will be paid especially to links with other policy areas under discussion.

Germany's evolving negotiating position

In the period between the summits at The Hague (1969) and Paris (October 1972) the Federal Government did not actively pursue the establishment of a regional fund, since other items – EMU and enlargement – were more pressing. However, at the 1972 summit Willy Brandt put forward his ambitious nine-point social programme – '*deutsche Initiative für Massnahmen zur Verwirklichung einer europäischen Sozial- und Gesellschaftspolitik*' (*BPA-Bulletin*, 20 October 1972). A regional and structural policy was one of the items on the programme. Its links with the development of EMU were stressed (Müller-Roschach, 1974, p. 172). By this stage, however, the Commission had already soured the atmosphere concerning regional policy by pressing for the interest subsidies option, attracting opposition from Finance and Economics Ministries in the FRG (Sasse *et al.*, 1977, pp. 15–16).

Despite the stated objective of the Paris Summit to establish the fund by the end of 1973, it was not until autumn that discussions even reached the ministerial level in the EC. Already divergence had become evident between the German Cabinet's proposed fund size of UA50m. for each of the first three years and the

Commission's July 1973 proposals for a fund of UA2,250m. of which the FRG alone would contribute UA630 million! (Sasse *et al.*, 1977, p. 16). Although the specialists in the Economics Ministry were already opposed to the 'watering-can principle' in the Commission's plans – about half the EC's territory would be eligible for aid – Hans Apel was still referring to the neglect of social policies, such as regional policy, in the Treaty of Rome in a television interview at the end of September 1973 (*BPA Press Release*, 27 September 1973). The atmosphere changed, however, once the State Secretaries' Committee had met to discuss German attitudes on 9 October 1973. This meeting witnessed an airing of technical criticisms of the Commission proposals and, as Sasse notes (1977, p. 17), no suggestions were made to increase the size of fund acceptable in Germany until 17 December 1973, at the time of the Copenhagen Summit. It is worth noting, therefore, that no clear *political* (i.e. ministerial) statement had been made by this stage to give the FRG's partners any idea that the Commission's proposals were considered too magnanimous. Indeed, in November, Willy Brandt, speaking at the European Parliament in Strasbourg, had made favourable comments about the ERDF's establishment by the end of the year (*BPA-Bulletin*, 15 November 1973).

The December 1973 proposals of UA750 million for a three-year period emerged during the ill-fated Copenhagen Summit, which was overshadowed by the oil crisis. Although the Summit blandly 'committed' the EC to establish the ERDF by the end of the year, the aspiring beneficiaries – Britain, Ireland and Italy – had been surprised by the German government's proposed fund size. At the Council of (Foreign) Ministers, Apel reinforced his government's unwillingness to increase the fund's endowment, resulting in a much-publicized clash with the British foreign secretary, Sir Alec Douglas-Home (Morgan, 1978, p. 50). Interviewed on the German television programme 'Tagesschau', Apel criticized the unrealistic expectations of the three potential beneficiary states, stating: 'We are not the paymasters of the Community' (*BPA Press Release*, 18 December 1973). This statement, which launched a thousand other German government speeches, 'logically' progressed to Apel's statement on radio the following day (referring to Britain's demands) that 'friendship cannot be bought. Nor do I offer my wife money to be faithful' (*BPA Press Release*, 19 December 1973).

On a less popularized level, Apel was now emphasizing the German government's unwillingness to support the watering-can approach; its desire to see the ERDF's establishment made conditional on progress to the second phase of EMU; and links were also being made with the need for a common approach on energy policy following the oil crisis. Moreover Apel's arguments were fortified by Cabinet support on 19 December 1973. Government spokesman Grünewald announced that the Foreign Office was to co-ordinate policy with the chancellor and the finance and economics ministers (*BPA Press Release*, 19 December 1973).

For convincing evidence of the fact that the Federal Government was not giving intelligible signals to its fellow member states, one needs only look to the most accurate assessment of policy from within government circles. This is contained in the information given by the head of the European Division of the Economics Ministry to the 21st (private) sitting of the Bundestag Economics Committee on 5 December 1973 (Parlamentsarchiv, Bonn). Dr Everling gave a clear assessment of the links perceived by the Federal Government with other policy areas (EMU's second stage, energy policy, improving the EC's financial management, strengthening the European Parliament's powers and progress on social policy). With the benefit of hindsight it is straightforward to say that these expectations were too great. However, they undoubtedly represented the platform of the government in its negotiations at the Council of Ministers some two weeks later. The technical arguments criticizing infrastructure measures, interest subsidies and the 'watering-can principle' were also present. Yet the irony remains that it should be in the Economics Ministry's European Division where such transparent views were held, for this branch of the sectorized governmental administration was not particularly involved in EC negotiations on the fund. The regional policy *Referat* – responsible for the technical analysis of proposals – is in a separate division of the ministry. The European Division's main involvement stemmed from chairing, or providing secretarial services to, the interministerial committees at *the specialist level.* This situation thus appears to reinforce the general comment on Germany's EC policy-making that 'the administrative and political levels are not sufficiently in gear with one another when the government position is being defined' (Sasse *et al.*, 1977, p. 19).

After the Cabinet had increased its fund proposal to UA1,250m. in January 1974 negotiations came largely to a halt in the Community due to the British general election and the ensuing minority Labour government. Moreover, the death of President Pompidou and the subsequent election of Giscard d'Estaing, together with Chancellor Brandt's resignation and replacement by Helmut Schmidt had created a new climate in the EC. The main ministers involved in the negotiations on the ERDF had changed and a fresh start was possible. Renewed impetus was provided by the British government's commitment to a re-negotiation of the terms of entry prior to a referendum on continued EC membership. This caused more urgency in negotiations. The Italian and Irish governments indicated their willingness to participate in the 1974 Paris Summit, proposed by President Giscard d'Estaing, only if a prior commitment to the fund had been achieved (Talbot, 1977, p. 248).

Foreign Minister Genscher was making positive statements about reaching a decision on the ERDF in the month preceding the December 1974 summit. Helmut Schmidt seemed to exercise his chancellorial power to strike up better relations with the British government, especially Foreign Secretary James Callaghan, on the subject of the fund. Other bilateral talks preparatory to the summit paved the way towards agreements. The new minister of state in the German Foreign Office, Hans-Jürgen Wischnewski, continued to emphasize links with progress in other policy areas – combating inflation and unemployment along with strengthening the European Parliament's position. Equally, he made an implicit connection between Britain's importance as an export market and taking a conciliatory attitude towards establishing the fund. Effectively, this was done at the Paris Summit, although some technical issues had to be resolved before the eventual conclusion of negotiations in March 1975. The eventual size of the fund was UA1,300m.: over eight times the German Cabinet's proposal in May 1973!

It is interesting to note that the negotiations were conducted more effectively by the Schmidt/Genscher government. Yet this was during the period shortly after the oil crisis when a cautious approach might be expected. Why did this situation come about? First, there were factors external to the German policy-making process. The Commission re-thought its proposals which became less inflammatory for the Germans; there was a dilution of the watering-can principle and Germany's contribution to the fund was reduced. The British government adopted a less blunt approach in its negotiating approach. Secondly, the policy-making framework in the Federal Government was made more straightforward. The relevant ministers became more actively involved once the issue had received considerable publicity at the end of 1973. They were able to break through the sectorized policy framework that had prevailed prior to this clash and thus give internal cohesion to the policy. Schmidt's personal involvement, such as through his talks with Wilson and Callaghan following his address to the Labour Party Conference at the end of November 1974 (encouraging continued British membership), was important. It emphasized the unifying principles of German government organization: the chancellor principle and the cabinet principle rather than the principle of ministerial autonomy (Article 65, Basic Law). Having said that, very few of the policy links were satisfied to Germany's benefit; the watering-can principle was not eradicated and infrastructural aid was incorporated in the ERDF. To the (few?) outsiders who compared German policy objectives with the outcome, a most unsatisfactory picture emerged, even in the light of the uncertainty brought about by the oil crisis. Such a comparison would also be consistent with increasing public disillusionment with the EC, particularly since regional policy did not bring any net benefits to the FRG.

Other policy-making participants

We now turn to a brief examination of other participants in the German policy-making process, although it will be argued that their involvement in the fund's establishment was not important. First, the *Länder* are directly involved in the making of domestic regional policy. Indeed, they are involved in the management of the ERDF. At the time of the negotiations establishing the fund, the *Länder* governments were consulted both through the *Bund-Länder* committees on regional policy and through the Bundesrat. However, to the extent that the Federal Government considered the EC negotiations to be integration policy (under the Foreign Office's leadership), so the *Länder* governments' right to be heard declined due to their lack of constitutional authority on foreign affairs. Discussion of the EC proposals was conducted in the *Bund-Länder* planning committee established under the 'joint task' legislation and in its substructure meeting at the civil servant level. The main reference point for these discussions was the interlinking between the joint task and the proposed ERDF, including the technical criteria for aid which the Commission was proposing. However, since the *Länder* had no formal constitutional authority to comment on the ERDF until it was established, fuller use was made of the Bundesrat where the state governments were able to register their views in a more official manner.

The Bundesrat scrutiny took place in the committees responsible for agriculture, economics and finance; the Committee for

EC Affairs brought the reports together into a coherent document for acceptance by the Bundesrat plenum. In the reports all committees argued in favour of a fund because of its importance to the realization of EMU. The Commission's proposed size of UA2,250m. was criticized as excessive, as were some of the criteria for aid which it put forward. The Bundesrat, unlike the Foreign Office and Economics Ministry, wanted Germany to receive ERDF aid and pressed for the Zonal Border Area (*Zonenrandgebiet*) to be included as an ERDF aid area. This reflected the states' regional interests. Further, the Bundesrat requested that EC aid should be used *additionally* to existing national assistance, an issue which will be referred to later. Finally, the Bundesrat pointed out that the *Länder* have constitutional responsibilities for regional policy and requested representation in EC policy-making bodies such as the Regional Policy Committee (*BR-Drucks* 547/1/73, 1 November 1973). Through their special constitutional position and their expertise, the *Länder* were able to put over a distinctive opinion. In the event the Federal Government granted the *Länder* the place of one deputy member in the German contingent of two full and two deputy members on the EC Regional Policy Committee.

The Bundestag and the political parties may be examined together, particularly since it is the *parliamentary* parties which are concerned with the reactive formulation of opinions to EC proposals. The scrutiny in the Bundestag's Economics Committee was referred to above because of the clear assessment of the Federal Government's position that was given by Dr Everling. What views did MPs present in the committees? Essentially they pressed for a link between the establishment of the ERDF and the attainment of the second phase of EMU, along with progress on an energy policy. The similarity of views to the Federal Government's was also reflected in the desire to see greater discrimination in eligible areas to avoid the watering-can approach. The committee also demanded that the funds be used additionally and this intention was confirmed by representatives of the Economics Ministry. The only distinctive viewpoint was the request that the European Parliament should have some control over the ERDF. The Bundestag has consistently pressed for a strengthening of the European Parliament. At this stage there was no party conflict over the ERDF in the scrutiny committees involved: those for budgetary affairs, agriculture and economics (see committee protocols of meetings in December 1973, Parlamentsarchiv, Bonn).

Outside the committees and after their scrutiny, however,

party conflict built up following Apel's rejection of British demands at the Council of Ministers in mid-December 1973. Apel's statements that the FRG was not prepared to be the EC's paymaster were picked up by the CDU/CSU parliamentary group in connection with conflict over the *Ostpolitik*. Werner Marx, then chairman of the parliamentary party's Working Group on Foreign and European Policy, saw a contradiction between the SPD/FDP government's unwillingness to contribute to the ERDF while granting loan facilities and aid to East European states as part of its *Ostpolitik* (*CDU/CSU-Fraktion press release*, 19 December 1973). In January 1974 the CDU/CSU parliamentary group's spokesman on European policy, Franz Amrehn, reiterated Marx's comments, criticizing Apel's 'coarse' negotiating style and accusing the government of 'treating the friends and alliance partners of the West worse than governments which are repeatedly necessitating (us) additional armament measures' (*CDU/CSU-Fraktion press release*, 18 January 1974). Like the government, the CDU/CSU rejected the watering-can aspects of the ERDF.

The SPD's responses to these claims illustrate the air of unreality that seems to prevail when an EC issue suddenly gains attention. SPD MP Alwin Brück, referring to the Cabinet's increased offer of UA1,250m. – now twice the size of the government's offer criticized by the opposition (!) – reinforced the view that the FRG should not be over-burdened with financing the EC. This, he argued, explained why the government's UA1,250m. proposal had been 'supported' by German citizens (*SPD-Pressedienst*, 21 January 1974). How this support had been indicated was unclear. In other press statements Hans Apel countered CDU/CSU criticism by arguing that the problems over regional policy were due to the EC's policy-making process. In particular, the unanimity rule which CDU Foreign Minister Schröder (and others!) had permitted in 1966 as the solution to the French 'empty chair' crisis was to blame (see Apel's report to the *SPD-Vorstand* in *BPA Press Release*, 18 January 1974).

The contribution of political parties to the Federal Government's negotiations on the ERDF's establishment seems minimal. In the committees the parties were in considerable agreement over the size and policy methods which the fund should have. The conflict in the public arena was largely rhetorical, seeking to exploit the government's isolation in negotiations in Brussels.

Finally, some brief comments are in order regarding the role of interest groups in the government's formulation of policy. Their contribution was small, probably because of the untypical nature of the issue. Since at no time did it really appear that the 'joint task' domestic policy was under threat, there was unlikely to be any immediate effect on firms seeking regional aid. The result of this was that the central economic interest groups presented views favouring the establishment of a regional fund provided that existing national policy was not threatened and that progress continued on EMU. Thus the general pro-integration position of the central economic organizations prevailed. A typical example of this was provided by the DIHT, representing the regionally-organized chambers of industry and commerce which, under the 1956 *Industrie und Handelskammergesetz*, are legally entrusted with certain tasks, including collecting information for the government on economic regions (Weber, 1977, pp. 100–3). The DIHT's working group on regional policy has taken close interest in the ERDF and this continues in the form of regular reports. Regional chambers have taken EC Commission officials on secondment in the Zonal Border Area in order to show its special regional problems.

Implementing the regional policy

The German government and the additionality question

The Federal Government, the *Länder* and interest groups have continued to be involved in presenting views on the ERDF since it came into operation. An issue on which this involvement has occurred with particular vigour is the question of additionality. The EC Commission had intended ERDF aid to be supplementary to existing national aid. National governments, however, have seen fit to disregard this intention and, by various means, have either presented the budgetary details of their national regional policy in such a way that the avoidance of additionality cannot be seen (the Federal Government). Alternatively, they have indicated that ERDF aid is theirs and it is thus their affair how the money is spent (United Kingdom). This gives a new interpretation to the concept of the EC's 'own resources.' If the FRG represents a model Europeanist member state, one could expect additionality to be pursued. Although Helen Wallace (1977, p. 156) states that in 1975 the German economics minister undertook to use ERDF aid additionally, this has remained a pious hope which, once again due to the sectorized nature of governmental policy-making, was obstructed by the Finance

Ministry. Again we may see how different ministerial attitudes prevail – in this case on a substantive policy issue – and again the preoccupation with financial control assumes paramountcy. The metamorphosis of the Federal Government's commitment to additionality into its behaviour of budgetary pragmatism calls into question the genuineness of the original intentions. This policy contradiction, it would appear, has never been reconciled at the *political* level, since the amount of ERDF aid which the FRG receives is not very great.

Essentially the difference of views is between, on the one hand, the Foreign Office, the Ministry for Inter-German Affairs and the Economics Ministry and, on the other hand, the Finance Ministry. The three ministries favour the use of ERDF money additionally. The Foreign Office regards additionality in the FRG as setting a *communautaire* example; the Ministry for Inter-German Affairs recognizes that any additional aid to the Zonal Border Area would be beneficial to its concerns; the Economics Ministry argues that the objectives of the ERDF are undermined if aid is not employed additionally. The Finance Ministry which, in the negotiations on the establishment of the ERDF had bolstered the arguments for an *effective* regional policy, presents an official line that additionality *is* respected, while unofficially acknowledging that additionality does not exist 'as such'. The official and unofficial views are reconciled by a judicious manipulation of the figures. The Finance Ministry is able to carry this off by virtue of its centrality in the budgetary process at the federal level.

The Finance Ministry is obliged to present the figures in such a manner that additionality appears to obtain in order to comply with domestic legislation. The ninth plan of the regional policy joint task states that 'the (European) regional fund aid is additional to national expenditure on regional policy' (BT-Drucksache 8/3788, 13 March 1980, p. 10). Why is this provision circumvented? German receipts of ERDF aid have, according to Finance Ministry officials, been important in two respects. First, they have moderated cuts in federal expenditure on regional policy as compared with other domestic policies. Secondly, the EC aid has been a background factor enabling other federal programmes to go ahead, such as those countering redundancies by Volkswagen in the mid-1970s and the shedding of manpower in the steel industry. Finance Ministry officials emphasized that 'pure' additionality would not be implemented until the main recipients – Britain, Ireland and Italy – did so.

It is interesting to note that officials in the Economics Ministry saw the Finance Ministry's obstructionism as stemming from two arguments. First, reference was made to the ministry's opposition to the 'financial demagoguery' of the Commission and of the European Parliament. Secondly, the Finance Ministry's general scepticism about the effectiveness of *domestic* regional policy was quoted.

Bearing in mind that the Federal Government only takes responsibility for half domestic regional policy expenditure, it is worth noting that the Finance Ministry's actions have consequent repercussions in the *Länder*. Most of the *Länder* have employed a loose type of additionality, putting EC aid towards special regional programmes. However, since each state's finance ministry holds the purse strings, the exact budgetary behaviour varies. In Hesse the Economics Ministry has had to demonstrate that the EC aid is indispensable for it to fulful its regional policy targets. It failed to prove this in 1979 and the money was shared out between all ministries, thus totally ignoring the principle of additionality.

Conclusions

What conclusions can be reached from this examination of German behaviour over the ERDF's establishment and functioning?

First it is clear, both from the broader issues associated with the ERDF's establishment and from the technical matters of policy implementation, that Germany's policy style was (and is) sectorized. Attitudes differed markedly between ministries, which in itself is nothing especially noteworthy. However, the attitudes were not reconciled before being put across in the European Community's institutions. It necessitated a virtual crisis in negotiations at the Council of Ministers (in December 1973) in order to obtain Cabinet intervention in favour of policy coherence. In the additionality question the decisions reconciling different viewpoints were taken by permanent secretaries. Neither the ministers nor the Cabinet were involved at the vital stage in the decision regarding the non-implementation of additionality. The Finance Ministry permanent secretary was able to oblige his Economics Ministry counterpart to concede additionality. This was achieved because the latter ministry is dependent on the former's financial resources in order to conduct *domestic* regional policy. In this instance, an agreed position was necessary in order that the federal ministries could present a united front in the joint task policy commitees.

The costs of this sectorization were transferred to the potential beneficiary states. The United Kingdom, in particular, was affected by the failure to establish a regional policy in 1973. The UK must, however, share some of the blame for the negotiating crisis due to its misjudgement of the 'bottom line' in the German negotiating position. In view of the fact that the German position changed dramatically, this is scarcely surprising.

Because of its initially quite unrealistic proposals for the ERDF's size, the German government was obliged to improvize its negotiating position. This was done in two ways: by changing the issues on which it wanted progress in return for approval of the ERDF; and by increasing its fund size proposals. The ability to move from a fund proposal of UA150 million to UA1,250m. in the space of December 1973/January 1974 was quite spectacular.

A second conclusion concerns the Finance Ministry's centrality as a policy-making participant. It had a major role in the establishment of the ERDF by bolstering the other ministries' efforts to achieve an *effective* fund. However, it then rendered the fund *ineffective* in the FRG by reneging on the principle of additionality. Seen from a Community perspective these two positions are contradictory; from the Finance Ministry's viewpoint they are quite compatible. Consistency stems from the Finance Ministry's mission of controlling public expenditure, whether in the federal or the Community budget.

The Finance Ministry is particularly able to pursue such a position with regard to new policies. As far as the financial control of existing EC policies is concerned, this attitude is not pursued to such an extent. Thus the Finance Ministry has been relatively weak in trying to restrain CAP expenditure because it has not wished to interfere in another ministry's domain. This is yet another product of sectorization. Once ERDF payments have been made to the Federal Republic, the Finance Ministry asserts its powers to allocate expenditure as it sees fit. The Finance Ministry's consistency in maintaining a tight rein over expenditure derives from the fear of inflation and, more recently, the specific problems of public expenditure during the recession. A further factor is that the Finance Ministry is not convinced of the value of regional policies, whether in a domestic or an EC framework. Against this background and conscious of the need to trim expenditure generally, the Federal Government reduced its contribution to the joint task domestic policy by 20 per cent in 1981 (Littlechild, 1982).

A political actor or organization is only able to influence policy if in possession of the necessary political commitment. By virtue of its budgetary responsibilities the Finance Ministry has the influence to make its views count, both in the formulation of German European policy and, hence, in the policy agreed by the European Community itself. However, this presupposes that the Finance Ministry's objectives equate with those of the Federal Government as a whole. For organizational reasons the Finance Ministry's policy towards the EC will be uni-dimensional, i.e. measured in terms of tangible expense. Yet the fact remains that if the Finance Ministry pursues an active European policy (i.e. restricting expenditure) while other ministries pursue essentially reactive ones, budgetary limitations will form a central part of German policy, beyond collective or Cabinet policy. If the Federal Government were able to harness its budgetary concerns to a *coherent* European policy, a clearer position would emerge for the benefit of other member states. This case study shows that a breakdown of talks was necessary to stimulate a collective approach to policy, however. A policy of financial restraint then lost all credibility as the German proposed fund size increased almost tenfold in a period of two months – and during the turbulence following the oil crisis!

Carl Lankowski's argument that the government's behaviour over the establishment of the ERDF was part of a German accumulation strategy, implemented by a planned capitalist crisis orchestrated at the EC level, is somewhat difficult to sustain in the light of the evidence outlined above (Lankowski, 1982a). First, his argument is that this accumulation strategy 'was no accidental occurrence but, rather, the result of deliberate policy co-ordination at the highest levels of the West German government' (p. 109). This view gives an unjustifiably flattering diagnosis of governmental co-ordination. Secondly, his view would be more tenable if the fund size had not been increased in December 1973/January 1974; or if any of the policy linkages had borne fruit; or if the technical policy demands had been adopted by the EC. In the absence of all these, the regional fund negotiations do not suggest that a German 'accumulation strategy' was being imposed in the Community by this means.

A third conclusion concerns the ERDF's importance to the Federal Republic. This was – and remains – miniscule in terms of direct financial benefits. The government was also unable to secure benefits in other policy areas in support for concessions made over the fund's size. Neither the second stage of EMU nor a common energy policy – the two links advocated – were achieved.

A final conclusion relates to explaining the government's European policy in terms of domestic politics. The main difference from domestic policy concerned the non-technical involvement of the Foreign Office. With this exception most of the positions could easily be seen to relate to stances adopted on domestic policy, whether by the federal economics or finance ministries, by *Länder* governments or by parliamentarians in economic problem areas. Indeed, the whole basis of sectorization was the division of responsibilities for domestic policy.

As a tailpiece it is worth noting that in 1981 the Commission proposed (somewhat belatedly) to restrict aid to only the really poor regions of the EC (Klein, 1981; Armstrong, 1985, pp. 330–1). This of course was one of the German government's original objectives. The 1981 proposal would have made the FRG ineligible for ERDF aid. At the same time, however, the Commission proposals aimed to increase the non-quota part of the fund that would not be subject to national control in the same way. This proposed move received some support in the Foreign Office but little, if any, in the Finance Ministry. In the event none of these changes was implemented when the fund was renewed for 1981. From 1984 the ERDF was reformed. There is now no distinction between quota and non-quota components. Instead each member state has an 'indicative range' within which aid will normally be granted, with the EC having more decision-making discretion than before (Armstrong, 1985). For the FRG this range was set at 3.76–4.81 per cent of the ERDF, a figure which has since been amended slightly with the Iberian enlargement.

10 *Special Relationships, Germany and Europe*

In the preceding chapters we have analyzed the domestic sources of West German European policy. However, as was emphasized in Chapter 1, there is a strong element of interdependence with other states in West Germany's foreign relations. This is reflected in the importance of certain special relationships to an understanding of West German European policy. In this chapter we explain how two of these relationships have an impact on that policy by referring to the Franco-German relationship and to that between East and West Germany.

Although much emphasis has been placed in this study on the influence of domestic factors upon the FRG's European policy, it must be recalled that there are specific reasons for their importance in the German case. These reasons are also of vital importance in explaining the significance of special bilateral relationships in West German European policy. The openness of the FRG's political system is unique in the EC and reflects the origins of the FRG as the successor state and the reaction to the Nazi regime. The Federal Republic and its Basic Law were created in a process of interaction between the Western allies and the emerging democratic elites. The FRG did not shake off occupation status and attain formal sovereignty until 1955. The acceptance of an open international economy and the security protection and continued presence of the Western allies was a precondition of its creation. This openness to external influence was reinforced by the advocacy by the early Adenauer governments of a supranational approach to European integration. This meant that West German policy-making institutions were not created to defend a tightly defined national interest but reflected an openness to European solutions on the part of Adenauer and his key foreign policy adviser and implementor, Walter Hallstein. Openness is characterized by the readiness of West German elite and mass opinion to accept foreign influence as legitimate. To this 'penetrated' political system of the FRG (Hanrieder, 1967) has been added the strong element of interdependence in its trading patterns with West European neighbours, outlined in Chapter 4.

The constraints imposed by the origins of the Federal Republic are the key to understanding its special position. *Sovereignty* was heavily qualified in the economic and military areas; *nationhood* was not encapsulated in the new state, which was officially regarded in West Germany as a transitional structure prior to reunification; and a centralized *state* was anathema to the Western occupying powers which had suffered heavy losses at war with the Nazi state. By contrast with France and the United Kingdom, the FRG has been unable to use sovereignty and the nation state as conceptual reference points. At the domestic level this has resulted in a decentralized political system, with significant results for the formulation and substance of European policy – as outlined in earlier chapters. It has also resulted in certain key bilateral relationships having a significant, although indirect, impact upon European policy.

Relationships with all three former occupying powers may be considered as relevant here. West Germany shares a security dependence on the United States with other members of the Community. Its geographical position, the Berlin dimension and the presence of very large numbers of American forces combine to give it a heightened character. To be sure, there are also some policy areas where an Anglo-German partnership is of importance (Morgan and Bray, 1986). Nevertheless, the most structured bilateral relationship of relevance to European policy is that with France. Franco-German reconciliation is the bedrock of European integration itself and has been formalized since 1963 in a treaty of friendship. As one of Helmut Schmidt's aides is reported to have said, 'America is our most important ally. France is our closest ally' (quoted in Simonian, 1981, p. 217). In the context of European policy, France is *both* the FRG's closest *and* most important ally. This situation continues despite the passage of time since the high-point of Franco-German partnership, namely during the 'reign' of Schmidt and Giscard.

The other interdependency of the FRG is of a rather different nature and stems from the postwar division of Germany. The division both of Germany and of Europe was a key negative stimulus towards integration in Western Europe and towards Franco-German reconciliation itself. Although the treaties which were secured between the Brandt/Scheel government and the chief East European states facilitated some reconciliation between the FRG and its Eastern neighbours, unresolved territorial claims remain. These have played a role in German policy in both the EC and in EPC. In the second part of this chapter the impact of

German-German relations upon the FRG's European policy is examined.

The Franco-German relationship

> For the Federal Republic the relationship with France is a value not an interest. (Philip Windsor)

The key relationship in the Federal Republic's European policy has been that with France. This has been well catalogued in the extensive study undertaken by Simonian (1985). In the early years of the Federal Republic Adenauer's long-standing preference for a close Franco-German relationship was of central importance to the latter's European policy. It was also an inevitable product of the United Kingdom's postwar decision not to participate in the closer forms of integration where sovereignty was conceded. This meant that the Federal Republic's commitment to European integration would necessarily involve a close relationship with France. Further, the relationship was bound to be defined by France, given the FRG's need to gain international acceptance. From the outset the Franco-German relationship was subject to some turbulence. For example, it came under some strain when the limits to French support for European integration were revealed by the French parliament's refusal in 1954 to ratify the European Defence Community (EDC) Treaty. But in broad terms the relationship remained of central importance throughout the 1950s and was the very foundation of the ECSC.

The coming to power of General de Gaulle in 1958 led to contradictory developments in Franco-German relations. The Gaullist creed of national sovereignty and hostility to supranationalism were at odds with the integrationist attitudes and policies of successive German governments. Gaullist hostility to the United States was also fundamentally at odds with the (paramount) security needs and other perceptions of the Federal Government. Despite these tensions, it could be argued that the foundations for a future closer relationship were established during these years.

In the period 1959–63 de Gaulle made relations with the Federal Republic the central component of his European policy. The FRG's need for international acceptance conveniently matched de Gaulle's need for a broader basis upon which to develop his foreign policy goals. The relationship culminated in the 1963 Franco-German Treaty. However, the utility of the relationship was undermined by the hostile reception given to the treaty in the Bundestag (see Chapter 6), resulting in the insertion of an Atlanticist preamble which 'explicitly rejected the French model of transatlantic relations' (Wallace, W., 1986, p. 210). The strengthening of the Franco-German relationship in a formal structure occurred at a time when Atlanticist sentiment was reaching a new high point in the FRG, symbolized by Erhard's replacement of Adenauer as chancellor later in 1963. Despite this divergence of views between the partner states, an extensive machinery for co-operation and consultation was put in place and this has proved to be of great long-term significance.

One of the key impulses motivating French support for the Franco-German relationship has been the fear that the Federal Republic might turn towards the East and create a new security threat from East of the Rhine (Wallace, W., 1986, p. 211). Thus, when the Brandt-Scheel government turned its attention to the *Ostpolitik*, relations remained cool between the new chancellor and de Gaulle's successor as president, M. Pompidou. The new president retained a Gaullist opposition to supranationalism while Brandt was one of its foremost exponents – but at the rhetorical level. There were also substantive differences on key policy issues, notably the divergent attitudes on how to proceed to an Economic and Monetary Union (see Chapter 3). Moreover, there was a marked contrast in personality and style between the two leading politicians. Significantly, it was during this period of West German preoccupation with the *Ostpolitik* that France became convinced that the United Kingdom's membership of the EC was desirable for foreign policy reasons. In consequence, France made some efforts at establishing an Anglo-French relationship, albeit without a formal basis, as a counterbalance to the Franco-German partnership. The significance of Anglo-French relations came to an end when Mr Heath lost office in 1974.

The golden age of the Franco-German relationship came with Schmidt's replacement of Brandt as federal chancellor and the election of Giscard d'Estaing as successor to Pompidou as French president; both events took place in May 1974. There was an important convergence of views between the two political leaders on a range of issues relevant to the EC and EPC. Nevertheless, this agreement did not extend to all policy areas, for agriculture remained a source of tension between Schmidt and Giscard. Even so, their strong personal rapport provided an important dynamic which permeated the machinery of Franco-German co-operation, as already established under the 1963 treaty.

The initial phase of relations between Schmidt and Giscard focused on the procedures of European and international co-operation. Unlike their predecessors, Schmidt and Giscard had held important domestic policy portfolios and gave these as much weight in their new offices as 'traditional' foreign policy, if not more. There were already powerful impulses demanding that political leaders should cut through the jungle of bureaucratized foreign economic relations; Schmidt and Giscard took the lead (Bulmer and Wessels, 1987; Bayne, 1986; Putnam and Bayne, 1984, p. 8). Giscard d'Estaing, like his predecessor, M. Pompidou, called for the holding of regular EC summit meetings, at the Paris Summit in December 1974. Unlike Pompidou, however, Giscard did not envisage these meetings being restricted to diplomacy and EPC matters. Schmidt held similar views and his support was crucial. From this Franco-German procedural initiative, which was agreed to by the nine EC member states as part of a wider institutional package (including approval in principle of direct elections to the EP and the commissioning of the Tindemans Report on European Union), emerged the European Council. This institution proved to be the launchpad for several important Franco-German policy initiatives within the EC. It must not be forgotten that it was also a Franco-German initiative which launched the annual seven-power Western economic summits (Bayne, 1986).

Together the two political leaders stamped their essentially interdependent vision of the international economy upon the proceedings of the European Council. The biannual Franco-German summits, the triannual meetings of the European Council and the annual Western economic summits provided broad, interlocking frameworks for the articulation of mutual interests, especially in the field of monetary relations. The rapport between Schmidt and Giscard was based on a common language (English!) and on shared interests. Neither was an enthusiastic supporter of supranational integration. Giscard often had to play to a Gaullist-oriented electorate, thus precluding integrationist adventures. Nevertheless, he was able to overcome some of the more rigid Gaullist doctrines, for example by breaking down the barriers between EC and EPC activities (Wallace, W., 1983, p. 387). At the same time Schmidt was less equivocal about his distaste for supranational institutions than Brandt. Neither leader envisaged that the European Council should give a high priority to theological debates about European Union. This was reflected in the short shrift given to the Tindemans Report, when it was presented.

Once the procedural framework for Franco-German co-operation within the EC had been laid, attention shifted towards the substance of policy. Thus it was in the period 1977–81 that a Franco-German 'axis' was recognized in the EC (Simonian, 1981; 1985). Convergence of views had been promoted with the appointment in 1976 of Raymond Barre as Giscard's prime minister. Barre's deflationary economic policy, with its strong emphasis upon counter-inflationary measures and on raising the competitiveness of French industry through reliance on market forces, took many of its cues from 'the German model'. A further source of encouragement for Franco-German convergence on international affairs was the performance – as perceived by Schmidt (especially) and Giscard – of Mr Carter as American president. As Simonian puts it, 'both Schmidt and Giscard had been highly critical of Carter's stand on human rights' (1985, p. 270). They saw his stand as a threat to detente in Europe. Schmidt in particular was highly critical of Carter's 'benign neglect' of the dollar which led to large speculative flows of money into the German Mark.

The most spectacular achievement of the Franco-German relationship was the elaboration over the period 1978–9 of the European Monetary System. This was remarkable, although it was a much less ambitious venture than EMU, in that the technical policy disagreements of the early 1970s were so rapidly overcome. As outlined above (in Chapter 3), the EMS initiative was primarily the work of Helmut Schmidt. However, it was carefully hatched following Franco-German incubation. The initiative was first discussed at a bilateral summit in Rambouillet, only a few days before the European Council session of April 1978 in Copenhagen, where it was introduced to the other EC heads of government. Schmidt would have been less willing to pursue the proposal had France not embarked on similar economic policies to those of his own government. Furthermore, the fact that the German presidency of the EC (July–December 1978) was immediately followed by French incumbency gave a full year for the project to bear fruit.[1] These factors, together with the lack of American leadership in monetary relations, were indispensable to the creation of the EMS.

To be sure, the introduction of the EMS was delayed because of a significant misunderstanding between Schmidt and Giscard over the phasing out of Monetary Compensatory Amounts. These devices, aimed at ironing out fluctuations in farm prices due to currency fluctuations, were deemed less necessary once the EMS was in place. Nevertheless, for German farmers MCAs had brought increased incomes, albeit to the annoyance of the French. This demonstrated that the Franco-German relationship had its limits. The introduction of the EMS was delayed for two and a half months as a result.

Other areas where divergences persisted between France and the FRG were industrial policy and international trade. Helen Wallace argues that the Franco-German entente served to play down such differences of view. 'Habits of consultation encouraged tolerance of the other partner's idiosyncracies' (Wallace, H., 1986a, p. 162). This was where the Franco-German treaty began to pay dividends. With appropriate stimuli given by the political leaders, a whole pyramid of bilateral committees at ministerial and civil service levels became more purposeful. For the Federal Republic, with its historically conditioned avoidance of unilateral political leadership in the EC, the Franco-German relationship performed an important 'alibi' function.

In the period since the election of Mitterrand to succeed Giscard in 1981 and the replacement of Schmidt as chancellor by Helmut Kohl in 1982, the relationship has lacked such clear leadership. Disagreements also became more fundamental, especially those relating to the EC's internal and external commercial policy (see Chapter 3). Neverthess, the relationship prevented such divergences from becoming too damaging. Important co-operation remained, albeit at a symbolic level, where Mitterrand and Kohl were able to work together to some effect. In 1984, in the build-up to the European elections, they were able to announce simplified customs facilities between their two countries. In 1985, despite continuing differences on important issues, like President Reagan's Strategic Defence Initiative, the desirability of a new round of GATT negotiations, and the greater importance attached by the French government to EUREKA, Kohl and Mitterrand presented a Franco-German draft treaty for a European Union to the June 1985 Milan session of the European Council. This draft, which was in fact limited to EPC and security policy, bore an uncanny resemblance to a British proposal, but was influential in shaping the EPC treaty contained within the Single European Act, signed in February 1986 (Wessels, 1986).

What, then, has been the broad impact of the Franco-German relationship upon the Federal Republic's European policy in the period since 1969? At a minimal level the relationship has been able to smooth over any major differences of view between the two member states. This damage limitation function is important to the two states most active in the EC, given that the United

Kingdom's interest in European initiatives is limited and that governmental weakness restricts Italy's scope in this regard. The effect of the relationship today is to provide a co-ordination reflex whereby France and the FRG are able to bring about small modifications to each other's European policy. They thereby avoid the fundamental conflicts which soured relations – and integration as a whole – in the mid-1960s. In a sense France can exert influence on the FRG's European policy, provided that domestic interests permit, but this is part of a two-way process. For example, Helen Wallace argues that

> the modifications of French economic policy in 1982 and 1983 reflect an adjustment much encouraged by German pressures, in this instance strengthening the arguments of the more moderate members of the French government. (Wallace, H., 1986b, p. 143)

In the absence of a channel for the articulation of such pressures, namely the Franco-German relationship, one might question whether France would still be a member of the EMS. French withdrawal would certainly have been a blow for the FRG's European policy and for the EC as a whole.

A second effect of the relationship has been that West German initiatives in the EC have been presented overwhelmingly in Franco-German clothing. We have already explained that, for historical reasons, successive German governments have avoided unilateral moves in European policy. The Franco-German relationship not only overcomes this legacy but also provides a basis whereby the governments of the two largest EC economies can mobilize the torpid EC policy process. As Helen Wallace puts it, 'if a Franco-German deal could be stitched together even on issues difficult for one or both, the other participants in the negotiations would generally fall into line' (1986a, p. 162). Thus a Franco-German framework has brought a higher success rate to the initiatives of German European policy.

A third effect of the Franco-German relationship has been to give some reinforcement to the sectorization of the FRG's European policy. We must remember that the extensive bilateral discussions held at various levels between the two governments are essentially conducted on a specialist basis. Each country has a co-ordinator entrusted with maintaining an overview of the relationship but he does not become involved in the substance of bilateral negotiations except on cultural and educational matters (Wallace, H., 1986b, p. 140). In other words there is no agency in Bonn with the task of checking whether views expressed by one federal minister to his French counterpart are compatible with those expressed by another German minister to *his* opposite number. The greater degree of centralization in the French government ensures greater compatibility. Thus, to take the agricultural policy area (examined in detail in Chapter 3), it would be possible for the German and French agriculture ministers to come to a close understanding on the CAP – but against West German interests as a whole. It has been argued that, despite having significantly different interests, the French and German agriculture ministers have formed a marriage of convenience to obtain high agricultural prices (Wallace, H., 1986a, p. 159). The Franco-German relationship in the agricultural sector may also be seen as a powerful obstruction to reform of the CAP: even when it was the official policy of the Federal Government!

In the aftermath of Chirac's appointment as French prime minister in March 1986, following the Socialists' failure to obtain an overall majority in legislative elections, this agricultural collusion seemed especially likely. The appointment of M. Guillaume, a former head of the French farmers' union, as Chirac's agriculture minister was particularly noteworthy. One of Guillaume's first meetings was with his West German counterpart, Herr Kiechle. 'You are a farmer and I am a farmer' was the French minister's greeting to Kiechle (*The Times*, 27 March 1986). Their meeting was aimed at strengthening collaboration between Bonn and Paris over agricultural prices and expenditure. This new partnership will be followed with some interest.

Thus, in sum, the Franco-German relationship has been of great importance to the articulation of West German interests in the EC.

German-German relations and the EC.

The importance of 'the German question' to the FRG's role in the EC has been quite different from that of Franco-German relations. The impact has been to insert an important 'no-go area' in the substance of German European policy. The effect of this is not restricted, as one might expect, to EPC but also affects the whole basis of trade, as set out in the EEC Treaty.

A key component in the relationship of German-German relations to the present study is the fact that the FRG still has unresolved territorial claims. Admittedly the FRG is not alone in this because both the Irish Republic and, less clearly, Greece have similarly unresolved claims on their neighbours. Nevertheless, the cases of Ireland and Greece exhibit a number of important differences from that of the Federal Republic. In the Irish case the dispute is with a fellow EC member, the United Kingdom, and in the Greek case the quarrel is with a potential member (and an associate), namely Turkey. The key difference relates to the potential impact of these disputes upon the EC. Were Irish claims to sovereignty over the whole island granted, or were some adjustments made in the area of tension between Greece and Turkey, there is no reason to suppose that this would change the orientation or weight of these states within the EC. This is emphatically not the case in relation to the FRG. A reunified Germany would not inevitably wish to remain an EC member. Even if it did, a new state of such size and power might fatally unbalance the Community.

For the time being, considerations such as these are clearly hypothetical even though reunification is enshrined in the Basic Law. Even so, the Federal Republic has had to live with the division of Germany and make arrangements accordingly, including in EC agreements. The first interzonal trade agreement, providing for free trade between the two parts of Germany, was signed in Frankfurt-am-Main immediately after the creation of the two German states in October 1949. It represented on the West German side a desire to keep the German question open and to soften the edges of the choice that had been imposed. It was also an important interest for the FRG to try and reduce the isolated status of West Berlin: an interest which has been considered in Chapter 8.

The East German interest in the trade agreement had much more of an economic character. The agreement offered an avenue of access to Western technology. It afforded entry for particular sectors of the East German economy, such as textiles, to an important market. At that time there were also political motives as the GDR wished to present itself as the torch-bearer of German unity.

During the negotiations for the establishment of the EEC, the preservation of interzonal trade was a major West German interest; indeed it was a precondition for participation (Jansen, 1977). The West German negotiators were guided by four considerations:

1 The wish to keep the German question open and not to prejudice future reunification;
2 The wish to preserve a set of arrangements which were already in operation;

3 The desire to take account of the special constitutional position of what was still called in the FRG, 'the Soviet Occupied Zone';
4 The ability to extract a visible concession from France, the dominant participant in the negotiations.

The other partners agreed to a Protocol on Interzonal Trade being added to the Treaty of Rome. In the case of France, this was seen as a *quid pro quo* for the arrangements to accommodate France's ex-colonies. However, all partners recognized that such a protocol was necessary for West German participation. It was the price that had to be paid to ensure the Federal Republic's integretation in the West.

This becomes clear if we look at Article 1 of the protocol. Its territorial application is imprecise and implicitly underwrites the position being taken by the Federal Government at that time of not recognizing the Oder-Neisse line; it refers to German territories outside the area of application of the Basic Law.

In operation the protocol has worked well, although it has given rise to a number of difficulties because of the problem of deciding whether or not the German Democratic Republic (GDR) should be treated by the FRG's EC partners as a 'normal' third country. Typical of these difficulties was a case involving the Netherlands.

The Netherlands had first begun to export agricultural produce to the GDR in 1962 and continued to do so at an increased rate until 1965. The Dutch government then applied for export subsidies from the European Agricultural Guidance and Guarantee Fund (EAGGF). Despite an objection from the Federal Government, this request was approved by the EC Commission. To signify its opposition to the subsidy, the Federal Government deducted from its contribution to EC finances a sum equivalent to the subsidy paid to the Dutch government.[2] It placed the issue on the agenda of a May 1966 meeting of the Council of Ministers.

At this meeting the Federal Government spoke against the subsidy on three counts. First, it argued that the GDR could not be a third country for any EC member state because the protocol declared that the GDR was not a third country for West Germany. It was also argued that it would discriminate against West German agriculture if other countries received subsidies for exporting agricultural produce to the GDR. Thirdly, it insisted that such a subsidy would be tantamount to recognizing the GDR. Faced by these arguments the Council ruled that national subsidies would be permissible in such cases but that there should be no EC subsidies on agricultural exports to the GDR.

This ruling came under some pressure after the conclusion of the Basic Treaty in November 1972. In the wake of the Basic Treaty the GDR was officially recognized by all West Germany's partners in the EC. The Basic Treaty does not however provide for the official recognition of the GDR by the FRG. Each state recognized the other's permanence and inviolability but the Federal Republic stressed that the GDR was not and could not be a foreign country as far as it was concerned.

The Basic Treaty provided for the maintenance of the Interzonal Protocol. In its public pronouncements the Federal Government stressed the *modus vivendi* character of the Basic Treaty in line with its policy of keeping the German question open. The GDR stressed the permanent character of the agreement and presented it as being tantamount to full recognition.

To those outside the Federal Republic the Basic Treaty often did appear to approximate full recognition and the 1966 ruling was increasingly seen as anomalous. The decision was in fact repealed by the Council of Ministers on 14/15 April 1975. The new regulations had two main provisions.

1 With regard to the export of agricultural produce, the GDR should be treated by all members as part of Community territory and agricultural exports would therefore not be eligible for Community subsidies. Any national subsidies should only be given after discussion with the Federal Government.
2 With regard to the import of agricultural products the assumptions were partially reversed. Agricultural imports are to be treated as an internal transaction by the Federal Government but by all other members as if from a conventional third country.

The Federal Republic is concerned to preserve a quasi-monopoly position with regard to trade relations with the GDR. It has persuaded the Commission not to answer any correspondence from the GDR.

Interzonal trade represents approximately 2 per cent of West Germany's external trade (1.6 per cent in 1984) and approximately 10 per cent of East Germany's external trade. The GDR is only the thirteenth most important trading partner of the FRG (1984 figures), a place it shares with Denmark, but the Federal Republic is the GDR's second most important trading partner. The FRG's principal exports to the GDR correspond to its principal exports overall i.e. chemical products, iron and steel products, machine tools. The GDR exports textiles, agricultural products and mineral oils. This trade causes some problems for the Community. These can be classified under three headings.

Semi-finished goods A significant proportion of GDR exports to the FRG, especially in the textiles sector, is in the form of semi-finished goods. It is not possible to control re-export of semi-finished products once they are finished in the FRG.

East European agricultural products It has often been asserted that East European agricultural products are channelled through the GDR in order to gain preferential entry on to the EC market.

When is a product a GDR product? The difficulty here is with the products that may only have a small amount of work done on them in the GDR. In one infamous example Swiss cheese was packed in the GDR using West German machinery. The Federal Government now makes some attempt to control and to test whether goods have been mainly produced in the GDR.

These problems, although irksome to other members of the EC, should not be exaggerated as the FRG does try to ensure that inter-German trade is not abused as a backdoor into the Community.

Until now the Protocol on Interzonal Trade has been seen as part of '*the acquis communautaire*' and has not seriously been questioned either by the Commission or by West Germany's partners. There is some reason to believe that this view will come under increased pressure and accordingly we sketch two alternative scenarios to illustrate possible developments.

One future of the Community, perhaps unlikely but by no means excluded, is of the EC progressing towards even deeper integration and harmonization. In such a future the Protocol on Interzonal Trade might be seen as comparable to the transitional arrangements between the United Kingdom and New Zealand, i.e. essentially short-term arrangements to cover the painful and expensive transition period after a divorce. There is clearly a difference in that divorce between the two Germanies was produced by the pressure of external events and powers, not by the wishes of the two states, and that the Germans themselves regard the rupture as a separation rather than a divorce. Nevertheless, Jansen is surely echoing the views of a great number of people inside and outside the FRG when he asks 'can it not be said with reference to the advanced integration of the EEC and the increasing division of the two German states which has now taken legal form that the protocol constitutes a more and more unacceptable foreign body in the EEC system' (1977, p. 103).

Whatever the origins of the division of Germany, the tension between the aspiration to German unity, represented by the protocol, and the desire for deeper integration remains. In this sense there has always been a latent tension between the support of West German governments for greater integration and harmonization and the maintenance of the Protocol on Interzonal Trade.

Even at present, there is some disquiet in the Commission which is rarely viewed publicly. One concern of the Commission is that this trade takes place unsupervised by any EC institution. The Commission complained in 1973 that it was not even kept informed, and indeed there is no obligation under Article 3 of the Protocol for the Federal Government to provide such information. It means too that Community regulations, for example, on rules of origin or regulations regarding food and health safeguards are not applied to intra-German trade. This occasioned considerable criticism in a number of member countries in the wake of the Chernobyl nuclear accident in 1986. The Commission imposed a ban on agricultural products from Eastern Europe in the wake of the accident. It did not apply however to inter-German trade in agricultural produce. Another consequence is that a not inconsiderable part of German trade escapes direct Community harmonization pressures.

An alternative scenario which is more readily apparent in the present situation is of a Europe which is not progressing towards closer integration. In this intergovernmental Europe, where the Community is the arena for competitive bargaining between national interests, one or more partners might reopen the issue as a way of exerting leverage on the Federal Republic. So far this has been the 'dog that didn't bark' since the interest of the other EC member states in keeping West Germany firmly anchored in the West has been so great that this has not been seen as a card that could safely be played. It is, however, entirely possible to imagine it being played by Community partners as a way of expressing disapproval of the scope and nature of German-German relations if they appeared to become too close.

This section dealing with the impact of the German question on the FRG's European policy has concentrated on the economic dimension. Yet it should not be forgotten that German-German relations have also had an important impact upon EPC. Political co-operation really only commenced at the time when the Federal Government was concluding its treaties with the East. As a result EPC did not have to cope with problems of recognizing the GDR, as exemplified by the Dutch case. Rather, the West Germans were keen that the moves towards normalization, that were achieved through the *Ostpolitik*, should be given a broader basis in Western Europe. This was achieved by EPC and the Conference on Security and Co-operation in Europe. Thus, although the impact of German-German relations has been more visible on EPC, the interzonal trade agreement shows that this was not a new development.

Once some normalization was achieved through the *Ostpolitik*, successive governments have sought to ensure the continuation of (at least) a European detente. This has been a persistent and noticeable feature of West German attitudes towards EPC. The wish to enable EPC to deal with security policy has been one reflection of this and has been aimed at limiting the effects of the cooler superpower relations in the mid-1980s. Security policy was a significant part of Genscher's European initiative which was agreed as the Solemn Declaration on European Union in 1983 during the German presidency.

The impact of German-German relations upon both EC and EPC areas shares a common trade-off between, on the one hand, West German interests and, on the other, those of the other member states. In the former case, West German policy is given broader multilateral legitimation. In the latter instance, the involvement of the EC member states en bloc serves to ensure that the Federal Republic remains committed to Western Europe, thus dampening any fears of a renascent reunited Germany. Hence the objectives of both parties are quite different, but they are mutually supportive in a European framework.

Conclusion

We have sought here to demonstrate that the Franco-German partnership and German-German relations play crucial roles in the FRG's European policy. Both these bilateral relationships involve some 'foreign' or external influence upon the FRG's European policy. This influence is, none the less, far removed from the traditional form of diplomacy. Among the three traditional 'markers' of diplomacy – sovereignty, the national interest and the central role of governments – only the last is fully retained in the two relationships. When this is combined with the fact that much of the substance of the two relationships concerns technical policy areas such as trade, it can be seen that we are indeed dealing with a condition of economic and political interdependence. The effect of this is to cause further diffusion in the mainsprings of European policy by adding to those 'purely' domestic sources outlined in earlier chapters.

Notes

1 The consecutive sequence of the German and French presidencies of the EC institutions was broken in 1981 when Greece became a member state.

2 The 'own resources' system of the EC Budget was not in operation at this time.

11 *Conclusion and Future Prospects*

In the introduction we raised the question of the likelihood of the FRG becoming the political pacemaker of the Community. The barriers to such a development are indeed formidable. The long shadow of the past still means that other members, especially France, would find it very difficult to accept the FRG playing a '*Vorreiterrolle*' (leadership role). This reluctance on the part of France to accept too manifest a German leadership is part of the 'mind set' of West Germans leaders and when they aspire to a leading role, as in the Adenauer and Schmidt periods, it is carried out on the basis of very close co-operation with the French government. The external obstacles to West German leadership are complemented by some deeply engrained attitudes held in West Germany, for instance within political and administrative elites. West German leaders like to adopt a model role ('*Musterknabe*') in pressing for integration (see Chapter 1). This basically reflects the situation in the post-Third Reich era, with the FRG's international acceptance being made dependent on good behaviour. Even if these circumstances have changed with the passage of time, it is very difficult to proceed from the junior role implicit in West German self-perception as '*Musterknabe*' to one of leadership where the FRG plays a dominant role in defining the goals and purposes of the EC.

These historical, attitudinal constraints upon the FRG's role in the EC are matched by the striking limitations imposed by the internal policy-making style. We have looked in detail at the inputs into the European policy-making machinery of the FRG. These included public opinion, political parties, interest groups, the *Länder*, the Bundestag and the Bundesrat. Playing a leadership role in the EC does not appear to be something which is actively wished by the West German parties or by public opinion. Although opinion is generally favourable to European integration, it is seen as much less important than domestic politics. The sensitivity of public opinion to the budgetary issue acts to constrain the Federal Government in the exercise of its most important political resource, its wealth. Public opinion is in any case clearly less important than party and elite opinion. In general they, together with public opinion, have been part of a permissive consensus prepared to go along with policies generated in technically oriented policy communities. Opinion in the legislature has borne the imprint of interest groups. The Greens constitute an exception here although even their views on agriculture have areas of convergence with the established agricultural policy consensus.

The policy-making process is basically driven by the demands of the West German economy articulated through sectoral and peak interest groups. These groups are basically happy with the status quo. Any attempt by West Germany to lead the EC more positively would almost certainly involve higher costs without significantly increasing the economic benefits. The agricultural sector of the economy is less happy but it seems likely that the leadership position on maintaining agriculture price levels will be taken by the French rather than the Germans (see Chapter 10).

The most significant barrier to a leadership role for the FRG is constituted by the nature of the governmental process by which these inputs are converted into policy. This is generally both reactive and fragmented. Its key characteristics, namely sectorization, incrementalism and consensual relationships within discrete policy communities assist the maintenance of a permissive consensus in public opinion towards European integration. They do not however facilitate the playing of a leading role in the EC, given the importance of the competitive bargaining arena provided by the Council of Ministers and the European Council. These obstacles inherent in the pluralistic framework of West German institutions can be overcome by a chancellor who has a strong political base and a mastery of the administrative machine. Under Adenauer, West Germany presented a coherent and active policy because he had a very strong political base and the brilliant staff he collected in the Chancellor's Office enabled him to dominate the nascent ministries. Moreover, his closest European policy adviser, Walter Hallstein, became successively permanent secretary in the Foreign Office and then president of the EC Commission. The only other chancellor under whom the FRG has attempted to play a more active role was Helmut Schmidt. Schmidt had a less strong political base than Adenauer but was a master of administrative and policy detail. The policy environment in which he operated was more difficult than during Adenauer's chancellorship. The loose and unco-ordinated nature of the German policy-making machinery was less of a bar to Adenauer, given that he was pursuing supranational goals as an objective in its own right. In the early Adenauer period the character of the Community as an *arena of co-operation* was of overwhelming importance to the FRG and the 'open' nature of West German policy-making was less of a disadvantage. Under Schmidt, the EC was still an arena of co-operation but the need for international rehabilitation had receded and the Community's character as an arena of political and economic competition had become more apparent. In such an environment the open and fragmented nature of West German policy-making was more of an inhibition to playing a leadership role and it took a leader of Schmidt's unusual gifts and his close relationship with Giscard d'Estaing to overcome these difficulties. When Helmut Kohl became chancellor, he very much identified himself at the rhetorical level with Konrad Adenauer. But in practice he has not been able to emulate Adenauer. The general picture under his chancellorship in both domestic and European policy has been the reassertion of the *Ressortprinzip*. Different ministers have pursued conflicting policies and only rarely does Chancellor Kohl appear able to develop a clear and recognizable governmental policy. He has also been much criticized for his failure to master policy detail and for the weaknesses of his administrative and co-ordinating staff in the Chancellor's Office in comparison with that of his predecessor. Our argument is that these difficulties go deeper than any inadequacies of the present chancellor. The difficulties faced by the Federal Republic in producing a coherent policy and even more in playing a leadership role become much clearer on examining three policy outputs, agriculture, environmental policy and the policy on European Union.

Agriculture

The agricultural sector poses critical problems for the management and coherence of West German European policy. In the Adenauer period the specific demands of the agricultural sector were subordinated to the primacy of the government's general goals on European policy. In succeeding governments the price and support levels agreed proved fairly advantageous to farmers in Germany as elsewhere. The pressure, particularly from the United Kingdom government, to keep price levels down and to make a start on restructuring them began to put the agricultural community in West Germany under some pressure. West German farmers were able to escape the worst effects of this price restraint by the manipulation of Monetary Compensatory Amounts. In 1984, after a great deal of external pressure, the

German Agriculture Ministry had to agree to the phased dismantling of the MCAs. The Federal Government made this conditional on its partners agreeing to national compensatory payments to German farmers of approximately DM 2,000m. In May/June 1985 agriculture minister Ignaz Kiechle vetoed a proposed cereal price cut in the run up to the Milan Summit. This completely cut across the basic stance of the Federal Government on European policy which was to support the moves away from unanimous voting in the Council of Ministers. Dissatisfaction with the dairy quotas and agricultural price levels played a major role in the campaign for the 1984 election to the European Parliament. After then electoral pressures increased. The SPD made something of a comeback in public favour and competition at the electoral level was, for a period, more intense.

Election results in local elections in Schleswig-Holstein in early 1986 were disappointing for the CDU. Party strategists expressed considerable anxiety about the impact of the farm vote in the closely fought *Land* election of Lower Saxony in June 1986. The CSU was, as always, determined to prevent any erosion in its share of the poll in the Bavarian *Land* election of September 1986.

These anxieties have been well exploited by the DBV and they have managed to extract a number of concessions from the Federal Government (Klaus Broichhausen, 'Die umworbenen Bauern verkaufen ihre Stimmen teuer', *FAZ*, 9 April 1986). The Cabinet agreed on Monday 11 May 1986 (*FAZ*, 14 May 1986) to a support package of DM 800m. for farmers. This is made up principally of DM 450m. through reduced contributions to social insurance and (subject to consent of EC) DM 208m. of extra aid to disadvantaged regions, which now make up over half the FRG's agricultural land. The remainder of the DM 800m. relates to a decision in late 1985 to reduce farmers' pension contributions. Significantly most of this aid is referred to as recurrent (*unbefristet*).

The Federal Government has continued to support research on transforming agricultural crops into bio-ethanol. This can be added to petrol for use in automobiles up to a level of some 5 per cent of the content of the fuel. Such a process is technically feasible. It is, however, very expensive and its already doubtful economic rationale has been totally undermined by the drop in the price of oil in 1986. Implementation of this project would now require such a high level of subsidy that it will probably not be proceeded with. The Finance Ministry has however been prevailed upon to sit on its objections until after the Lower Saxony *Land* election of June 1986 (*Der Spiegel*, 9 April 1986).

The pressure from the farmers predetermined the West German negotiating position on the annual agricultural price review which was concluded in Luxembourg on 25 April 1986. The FRG, together with the French government, argued for increases of up to 4 per cent. This was rejected and prices were frozen. However, farmers in weak currency countries like Britain and France, obtained disguised increases in income by the change in the value of the national green currencies in which farm prices are calculated. Small farmers, especially in the Federal Republic, will benefit from a levy on large cereal producers. The difficulty is that even this settlement will, it is calculated, add £1 billion to the EC farm budget (*Sunday Times*, 27 April 1986).

This means that the Community has the choice either of raising the level of EC VAT revenue from its present 1.4 per cent or making cuts elsewhere in the budget. As agriculture already consumes the lion's share of the budget and as the EC is in the midst of an industrial recession unparalleled since the 1930s, this would look like a very compromising alternative.

The finance minister, Gerhard Stoltenberg, has argued that there can be no increase in the 1.4 per cent VAT figure until 1988 and, even then, it should be raised only to 1.6 per cent rather than the 1.8 per cent that many believe to be realistic. Stoltenberg continues to argue that the financial ceiling agreed to at Fontainebleau in 1984 should be adhered to. The narrow margin available to a federal finance minister due to the exigencies of the West German federal revenue raising system (Chapter 3) and the sensitivity of West German public opinion to the size of EC budgets make this a predictable policy. The failure to reconcile and co-ordinate these policies at the Bonn level does however mean that it is very difficult to see what sort of leadership role the FRG could play. The policy of Stoltenberg would suggest the United Kingdom government, and perhaps the Commission, as a natural ally. The demands articulated by Herr Kiechle suggest France and a policy of orientation to the southern states. However the budgetary dimension is resolved, it is clear that the Federal Government will put through more and more measures of financial support for farmers at the national level. This process of renationalization of agriculture had already begun in 1984 but all the signs are that it is now gathering pace. Most of the award made on 11 May 1986 was on a recurrent basis for instance. This is a partial reversal in the most integrated section of EC policy. It is an extremely paradoxical outcome for a state which has always prided itself on supporting integration. This renationalization of agriculture is likely to be strengthened by pressure from the United States on the EC for the CAP to have a less protectionist orientation.

Environmental policy

In the 1980s environmental policy has come to play an increasing role in both West German domestic politics and at the Community level. At the level of West German domestic politics the greater stress on environmental policy is a product of two factors. All opinion surveys in West Germany indicate a very high sensitivity towards environmental problems on the part of West German voters. This generalized sensitivity has been given added political thrust by the breakthrough of the Greens into the parliamentary arena. It is reinforced by incidents like that at Chernobyl. This has caused all the established German parties to compete for recognition as the champions of environmentalist issues.

The domestic pressure on environmental policy has translated into continuous efforts by the Federal Republic to transfer environmental policy-making to the European level. The perceptions and aims of the differing ministries in pushing for this transfer vary considerably and present new and challenging problems of co-ordination for the Federal Government. The *Auswärtiges Amt* sees environmental policy as a new route to integration, a route which would have the side-benefit of saddling West Germany's competitors with the same curbs on competitiveness as West Germany itself. In this context it should be noted that articles concerning environmental policy are among the treaty additions included in the Single European Act. The Interior Ministry had a long record of being committed to environmental policy and it was built into a policy network of environmental groups.[1] It was prepared to press ahead with environmental policy against vocal opposition from German industry which had been particularly annoyed by measures introduced by the present interior minister, Friedrich Zimmermann. Industrial opinion has been particularly hostile to the new rules on smoke emission codified in TA-Luft 1985 (see statement of DIHT 'Internationale Wettbewerbsfähigkeit Gefährdet', *Handelsblatt*, 6 February 1986).

The aims of the Economics Ministry reflect its role as *Anwalt* (attorney) for German industry and the 'industry-friendly' nature of its policies. It is much less concerned than the other ministries with the integrative potential of environmental policy. It is often in favour of using the European level to kill a domestic initiative or, as in the case of the chemicals law, to establish a directive which is probably less far-reaching than a directive generated inside the domestic political arena (see Chapter 7). The Agriculture Ministry is even more firmly against environmental policies than the Economics Ministry and it has, for instance, been able to use the resources of the domestic and European agricultural policy networks to block a Community approval procedure for pesticides first advanced by the Commission in 1976.

A further complication has been brought about by Chancellor Kohl's decision in early June 1986 to establish a new federal ministry for environmental affairs. This decision, taken in the aftermath of the Chernobyl nuclear accident in the USSR and in the run-up to elections in Lower Saxony, effectively transfers governmental responsibility away from the Interior Ministry. Its impact upon the *overall* policy-making framework is unlikely to be very great, especially given the importance of the *Länder* in environmental policy.

In the period since the 1972 Paris summit, at which the principle of EC activity on environmental matters was agreed, environmental legislation has gradually proliferated. Areas now involved include air and water pollution, waste disposal, nature conservation and the control of chemical materials. Most of these issues fell under the responsibility of the Interior Ministry, although some are compounded by the division of responsibility between the federal and *Länder* governments. This is the case for nature conservation and water pollution, for example (von Moltke, 1984; and see above, Chapter 8). As a policy area with considerable potential for further extension on an EC basis, it is essential to note that the FRG can be expected to be the key participant in policy-making. German distinctiveness will derive from the aforementioned differences of perception among the ministries and from the electoral sensitivity of environmental matters.

The EC debate concerning exhaust emission control has already provided evidence of both factors during the period 1983–5 (Turner, 1986; Kromarek, 1985). In July 1983 the Federal Government decided to proceed by requiring all new cars registered from 1986 in the FRG to be fitted with catalytic convertors to reduce lead emission.

This decision was taken by the Interior Ministry despite the reservations of the German automobile industry and the Economics Ministry. It reflected the long-standing commitment of the Interior Ministry to environmental policy improvements.

It also reflected the central place in West German discussion of 'the dying forest' issue. A very high proportion of West German forests are now in a parlous condition. There is a great deal of controversy about the extent and causes of '*Waldsterben*' but there is a general perception that car emissions play a major role. Zimmermann would have been likely to take a pro-environmental line as interior minister, but his resolve would have been strengthened by the potential damage to tourism in Bavaria caused by the dying forest issue and by the displacement of forest-owning interests in the CSU.

The Federal Government's unilateral declaration ahead of a decision in the Council of Ministers threatened to create a new problem, however. Through 'going it alone' the Federal Government risked prosecution by the European Court of Justice. The new requirement would have created a new non-tariff barrier by discriminating against foreign car manufacturers.

After heated negotiations in the Council of Ministers in March 1985 the Interior Minister eventually had to fall in line with a slower timetable acceptable to all EC ministers. This involved some loss of face for the government and there were continuing negotiations about the permissible level of emissions. As far as the FRG's European policy is concerned, the important conclusions are that environmental matters are assuming increasing importance, are difficult to co-ordinate and constitute a likely area for conflict with other governments.

The Federal Republic and European Union

This examination of public and party opinion, the nature of policy-making in this area and the difficulties connected with the agricultural and environmental sectors illustrate both the utility of the domestic politics approach and the difficulty the Federal Government will have in transforming West German economic strength into a sustained and clear leadership role in the EC. As the EC becomes more obviously an arena of competition, so West German policy-making machinery looks less and less appropriate. The fragmentation of West German policy-making machinery is also, as we have seen (Chapter 7), something of a disadvantage at the implementation stage.

In recent years major efforts have been made by those committed to the EC to escape these limiting conditions by attempting to change the agenda of the EC to include new areas like advanced technology and, more dramatically, to revise the institutions of the Rome Treaty in a more integrative direction. The FRG has played a leading role in these moves. In this area responsibility lies with the pro-integrationist *Auswärtiges Amt* rather than with the technical ministries embedded in a dense network of domestic interests. Chancellor Kohl is also, in principle, a supporter of these initiatives. Public opinion, while mistrustful of any initiative which appears to cut deeply into domestic prerogatives, in practice is very much in favour of the rhetoric of union. Parliamentary opinion, with the exception of the Greens, is solidly in favour (Lenz, 1985, pp. 209–16). The following section looks at the West German input into Community decisions from the broader perspectives of European Union and EUREKA.

Concern with European Union emerged in the aftermath of the Fontainebleau European Council (June 1984), at which a medium-term solution was found for the issue of British contributions to the EC budget, a problem which had dogged the Community's work for some five years (Denton, 1984). The Fontainebleau decisions also involved some limited reforms to the CAP, approval in principle of Iberian enlargement, together with an agreement to establish two committees to look at aspects of European Union. One committee was to look at the idea of popularizing the EC's work. The other was to examine the possibility of institutional reforms. Its mandate was to 'make suggestions for the improvement of European co-operation' so that 'concrete decisions concerning progress in the direction of a European Union can be taken' (Hrbek and Läufer, 1986, p. 174).

The work of the so-called Dooge Committee was completed and was presented for consideration by the European Council. It joined the EP's Draft Treaty on European Union, which had been passed by a majority of MEPs. Together they formed an important basis for the European Council's session in June 1985 at Milan, where European Union was given extensive consideration by heads of government.

The final report of the Dooge Committee showed the limits of reform despite the hopes invested in its work. The report endorsed union as a goal but Danish and Greek objections and British inhibitions were also obvious in the margins and footnotes. By mid-1985 there was a rough consensus on the extension of the internal market, the creation of a technological community and the establishment of a Community environmental policy.

At the Milan Summit of June 1985 there were clear differences between the French and German positions and that of the British, Danes and the Greeks. A Franco-German initiative on European Union was submitted, dealing primarily with EPC. This joined another paper presented by the British government, along with various other submissions including a Commission paper on establishing an internal market by 1992. At the Milan meeting the Federal Government's position was weakened by contradictions. Support for closer European Union had been undermined by Kiechle's action in the Council of Agriculture Ministers, namely his use of the veto to prevent cuts in cereal price levels. Despite the emergence of differing views between governments – and, in the German case, within the government – it was agreed against the votes of Britain, Denmark and Greece to call an intergovernmental conference to consider concrete steps towards establishing a European Union.

The negotiations culminated in the Luxembourg Conference of the European Council in December 1985. Final agreement on the details was achieved at the end of January 1986 and the Single European Act was signed on 17 February 1986. Danish agreement was conditional on a majority in a referendum; this was duly forthcoming.

The Single European Act comprises alterations to the Rome Treaty as well as a new treaty basis for European Political Co-operation. The preamble also commits the member states to the realization of European Union.

The deepening and extension of the internal market occupies a central place in the act and the signatories are committed to creating a '*Raum ohne Binnengrenzen*' (space without internal barriers) by 31 December 1992. In principle most decisions about the realization of the internal market are to be taken by majority vote in the Council of Ministers. Both the British and the German governments have given priority to the creation of an internal market but with certain qualifications. The Federal Government was concerned about the implications of the projected internal market for social security provisions for migrant workers and for the organization of the professions (Corbett, 1986, p. 8). Bearing in mind West German attitudes it is important to note that among the EC enabling legislation where unanimity will still be required in the Council of Ministers is that on the right of establishment (*Niederlassungsrecht*), the regulation of the professions and indirect taxes. These are all central areas in the creation of a more complete internal market. Wolfgang Wessels (1986, p. 68) has suggested that these deviations from the majority principle were made at the behest of the Federal Government. Only about one-third of the enabling legislation will require a unanimous vote in the Council; the remaining two-thirds will be by qualified majority vote.

The Single European Act also attempts to do something to fill 'the democratic deficit' in the Community. The measures envisaged are extremely modest however. In only one area, that of association and membership treaties, is the European Parliament given the right of co-decision. In a number of specified areas including realization of the internal market, the strengthening of the economic and social cohesion, the improvement of the work environment and in the implementation of decisions in the areas of research and technology, provision is made for a two-stage process of decision in the Council of Ministers. The intention here is to make sure that the Council takes account of the opinions of the EP. For those who envisaged a real strengthening of the EP these changes are merely procedural and may well not significantly increase the power of the EP (Hänsch, 1986, pp. 191–201). There was criticism of the limited nature of the measures in German political circles, including in the European movement.

The Federal Government's attitudes to two other parts of the Single European Act are worth noting. In the section on 'monetary capacity' there was criticism of the Commission's proposal to include EMU as a goal of the EC. For example, finance minister, Herr Stoltenberg, pointed out that there were problems in referring to central banks in the Single European Act because of the Federal Bank's autonomy (Corbett, 1986, p. 11). Although British and German opposition to including references to monetary co-operation were overruled, it is worth noting that provisions have been inserted noting the need for member states to promote convergent economic policies. This suggests that the Federal Government had to safeguard its position by ensuring that any future closer monetary co-operation must be matched by economic convergence. There are distinct shades of the government's 'economist' viewpoint on EMU here.

The second area worthy of comment concerns the related section of the Single European Act on 'cohesion' (economic convergence). The Federal Government's position showed a cautious attitude, perhaps reflecting a wish not to be saddled with contributing to any new redistributive policy instruments.

On EPC the Single European Act enshrines the Stuttgart Solemn Declaration of 1983. In general it merely gives legal form to existing practice. The major novel element is the creation of a small permanent secretariat in Brussels to aid whoever has the presidency.

One major area of concern which has run parallel to the negotiations on the Single European Act is the whole complex of advanced research and technology. The French have been very keen to push this as a counter to SDI. This has also been the view of the *Auswärtiges Amt* who see it both as an avenue for integration and as an alternative to SDI. The Research and Economics Ministries see it now from the perspective of the internal market (Riesenhuber, 1986, pp. 185–90).

In his important article in *Europa Archiv*, the Research Minister, Heinz Riesenhuber, describes a single unified market as the main goal (1986, p. 188). His diagnosis is that Europe suffers from fragmented markets. The solution suggested in the Hannover Founding Declaration of EUREKA is threefold,[2] i.e. the creation of common European standards (*Industrienormen*), to remove technical barriers to trade by mutual recognitions of tests and test certificates, to open up public procurement channels. EUREKA, which is not limited to EC member states, involves three kinds of joint projects:

1 Industrial projects for the European consumer, e.g. informatics and telecommunications.
2 Research and Development ventures in 'hitech' areas to deal with transnational problems such as the environment.
3 Projects for the creation of a modern European infrastructure.

The German response to EUREKA indicates difficulties. It failed to realize how important it was to the French. It also became part of an ongoing interministerial battle between the Chancellor's Office and the Foreign Office. Technological co-operation is important to the Federal Republic but, if it fails, German industry will lose less than its partners. The Single European Act envisages technological co-operation outside the framework of EUREKA on the basis of majority voting within the EC (*géometrie variable*).

The Single European Act has also created tensions within the FRG. It includes for the first time environmental protection as a Community task, thereby *formally* encroaching upon the competences of the *Länder* in a policy area where authority is disputed. This was one reason why the conclusion of the Single European Act raised problems for the relationship between the federal and the *Länder* governments. The Bavarian government complained that the *Länder* had not been sufficiently informed of the negotiations and conclusion of the Single European Act. There was a danger than *Länder* would thus lose powers indirectly – but formally – on the detour to Brussels without having adequate consultation. They also served notice that they would want to alter Article 24 Basic Law in order to gain a greater formal say in European policy-making (Hrbek and Läufer, 1986, p. 183).

This Bavarian *démarche* may have been partly prompted by longstanding rivalry between Strauss and Genscher and between the CSU and FDP but it does illustrate the continuing difficulties that flow from the federal structure of West Germany in attempting to play a leadership role. There is some evidence to show that discontent is much wider than Bavaria and that other *Länder* worried about the threat to their prerogatives and standards posed by the act will join with Bavaria at the Bundesrat stage (*Financial Times*, 8 May 1986).

The precise significance of the Single European Act remains to be determined in practice. The optimists point to the rhetoric, especially of the Federal Government. The pessimists point to the use of the veto by Kiechle, to the fact that unanimity appears to have been preserved in relation to important parts of the internal market at the urging of the Federal Government. These views are strengthened by rulings of German public opinion on supranationalism and its dislike of the paymaster role.

An overall view of these three policy sectors indicates that the Federal Government still finds it very difficult to transform the strength of the West German economy into an equally strong political position. In the area of European policy the contrast is not so much between the status of the Federal Republic as economic giant and political pygmy as between an economy which dominates Western Europe and a government which is only the second most influential in the Community.

Jonathan Story has argued that this is part of a wider pattern, 'that the essential condition of the German predicament is not dominance so much as dependence' (Story, 1981, p. 56). The FRG has a major and overriding interest in the maintenance of the EC framework for both political and economic reasons, since it arguably benefits more than any other member from its existence. This means that it has to be very careful about change. 'West Germany's paradox, then, is to be conservative by disposition and interest but revisionist by dint of its industrial pre-eminence' (Story, 1981, p. 56). The balance between leading change and defending the status quo is further complicated by the fact that the pre-eminently industrial character of West Germany coexists with a very influential agricultural sector. The difficulties of choosing a strategy are heightened for the FRG by the fragmented nature of decision-making. The changing of the rank order to make West Germany's political power coincide with its economic power is thus likely to prove a very intractable task.

Note

1 On the long-term commitment of the Interior Ministry to environmentalism, see the article by Günter Hartkopf, who was *Staatsekretär* from 1969–83, in *Die Zeit*, 14 February 1986.
2 Participation in EUREKA is not restricted to EC member states.

References

Ackermann, P. (1970), *Der Deutsche Bauernverband im politischen Kräftespiel der Bundesrepublik* (Tübingen: J. C. B. Mohr).

Adenauer, K. (1967), *Erinnerungen 1955–59* (Stuttgart: Deutsche Verlagsanstalt).

Allen, D., Rummel, R. and Wessels, W. (eds) (1982), *European Political Co-operation* (London: Butterworths).

Allison, G. and Halperin, M. (1972), 'Bureaucratic politics: a paradigm and some policy implications', in R. Ullmann and R. Tanter (eds) *Theory and Policy in International Relations* (Princeton: Princeton University Press), pp. 40–79.

Andrlik, E. (1981), 'The farmers and the state: agricultural interests in West German politics', *West European Politics*, vol. 4, no. 1, pp. 104–19.

Armstrong, H. W. (1985), 'The reform of the European Community regional policy', *Journal of Common Market Studies*, vol. 23, no. 4, pp. 319–43.

Averyt, W. F. (1977), *Agropolitics in the European Community* (New York: Praeger).

Balfour, M. (1982), *West Germany: a Contemporary History* (London: Croom Helm).

Baring, A. (1969), *Aussenpolitik in Adenauers Kanzlerdemokratie: Bonns Beitrag zur EVG* (Munich: Oldenbourg Verlag).

Bayne, N. (1986) 'International economic policy co-ordination', in Morgan and Bray, *Partners and Rivals in Western Europe*, pp. 175–83.

BDI (1978), 'Stellungnahme zu Problemen der "Erweiterung nach Süden" anlässlich der Anhörung des Auswärtigen Ausschusses des Deutschen Bundestages', Cologne.

BDI (1982), *Jahresbericht 1980-82 des Bundesverbandes der Deutschen Industrie e.V.* (Cologne: BDI).

BDI (1984), *Jahresbericht 1982–84 des Bundesverbandes der Deutschen Industrie e.V.* (Cologne: BDI).

BGA (1978), 'EG-Protektionismus', Dokumentation des BGA, Bonn, June.

BGA (1979), *Jahresbericht 1978–79* (Bonn: BGA).

Birke, H. E. (1972), *Die deutschen Bundesländer in den Europäischen Gemeinschaften* (Berlin: Duncker & Humblot).

Blaschke, D. (1977), 'Gemeinschaftsaufgabe und EG-Politik', in F. W. Scharpf, B. Reissert, F. Schnabel (eds), *Politikverflechtung II: Kritik und Berichte aus der Praxis* (Kronberg/Taunus: Athenäum Verlag), pp. 44–7.

Bogulanski, A. (1982), 'Rückzug aus Europa? Das europapolitische Bewusstsein der Deutschen im Spiegel der Demoskopie', *Europa Archiv*, vol. 37, no. 1, pp. 9–21.

Brandt, W. (1968), *Aussenpolitik, Deutschlandpolitik, Europapolitik* (Berlin: Berlin Verlag).

Brandt, W. (1969), *Bundeskanzler Brandt: Reden und Interviews* (Bonn: Hoffmann & Campe).

Braunthal, G. (1965), *The Federation of German Industry in Politics* (Ithaca, NY: Cornell University Press).

Bulmer, S. (1983a), 'Do parties matter? – West German political parties and policy output', paper to annual conference of the Political Studies Association, Newcastle University, April.

Bulmer, S. (1983b), 'Domestic politics and EC policy-making', *Journal of Common Market Studies*, vol. 21, no. 4, pp. 349–63.

Bulmer, S. (1983c), 'West German political parties: structures without function', *Political Studies*, vol. 31, no. 4, pp. 566–83.

Bulmer S. (1985), 'The European Council's first decade: between interdependence and domestic politics', *Journal of Common Market Studies*, vol. 24, no. 2, pp. 89–104.

Bulmer, S. (1987), *The Domestic Structure of European Policy-Making in West Germany* (New York: Garland).

Bulmer, S. and Paterson, W. E. (1986), 'The Federal Republic of Germany' in J. Lodge (ed.), *Direct Elections to the European Parliament 1984* (London: Macmillan), pp. 190–210.

Bulmer, S. and Wessels, W. (1987), *The European Council: Decision-Making in European Politics* (London: Macmillan).

Burkhardt-Reich, B. and Schumann, W. (1983), *Agrarverbände in der EG* (Kehl am Rhein: N. P. Engel Verlag).

Butt Philip, A. (1985), *Pressure Groups in the European Community* (London: UACES).

Caporaso, J. (1974), *The Structure and Function of European Integration* (Pacific Palisades, Calif.: Goodyear).

Carr, J. (1985), *Helmut Schmidt, Helmsman of Germany* (London: Weidenfeld & Nicolson).

Casper, U. (1979), 'Background notes to regional incentives in the Federal Republic of Germany', in K. Allen (ed.), *Balanced National Growth* (Lexington: D. C. Heath), pp. 97–129.

Cohen, C. D. (ed.) (1983), *The Common Market: Ten Years After* (Oxford: Philip Allen).

Collins, L. (1984), *European Community Law in the United Kingdom*, 3rd edn (London: Butterworths).

Corbet, R. (1986), 'The 1985 intergovernmental conference', unpublished paper.

Cox, R. and Jacobson, H. (1974), *The Anatomy of Influence: Decision-Making in International Organisation* (New Haven: Yale University Press).

Czempiel, C.-O. (1980), 'The Atlantic Community, Europe, Germany: options, objectives or contexts of German foreign

policy?', in Kohl and Basevi, *West Germany: a European and Global Power*, pp. 89–108.
Denton, G. (1984), 'Re-structuring the EC Budget: implications of the Fontainebleau agreement', *Journal of Common Market Studies*, vol. 22, no. 2, pp. 117–40.
Dettke, D. (1984), 'Gemeinsame Europäische Sicherheitspolitik – mehr Unabhängigkeit gegenüber den Vereinigten Staaten?', in Hrbek and Wessels, *EG-Mitgliedschaft*, pp. 413–42.
Deubner, C. (1984a), 'Die westdeutsche Industrie in der EG – Vorteile für traditionelle und moderne Branchen', in Hrbek and Wessels, *EG-Mitgliedschaft*, pp. 127–51.
Deubner, C. (1984b), 'Change and internationalization in industry: towards a sectoral interpretation of West German politics', *International Organization*, vol. 38, no. 3, pp. 501–35.
Deutsch, K. *et al.* (1957), *Political Community and the North Atlantic Area* (Princeton: Princeton University Press).
DGB (1978), *Dokumentation zur Entwicklung der Europapolitik des DGB nach 1945* (Dusseldorf: DGB).
Dyson, K. (1977), *Party, State and Bureaucracy in West Germany* (Beverley Hills: Sage Publications).
Dyson, K. (1981), 'The politics of economic management in West Germany', *West European Politics*, vol. 4, no. 1, pp. 35–55.
Dyson, K. (1982a), 'West Germany: the search for a rationalist consensus?' in Richardson, *Policy Styles in Western Europe*, pp. 17–46.
Dyson, K. (1982b), 'The politics of economic recession in West Germany', in A. Cox (ed.), *Politics, Policy and the Economic Recession* (London: Macmillan) pp. 32–64.
Dyson, K. H. F. and Wilks, S. (eds) (1983), *Industrial Crisis: a Comparative Study of the State and Industry* (Oxford: Martin Robertson).
Economist Intelligence Unit (1983), *West Germany: a structural forecast to 1990* (London: The Economist Intelligence Unit).
Eisner, E. (1975), *Das europäische Konzept von F.-J. Strauss – die gesamteuropäischen Vorstellungen der CSU* (Meisenheim am Glan: Anton Hain).
El-Agraa, A. (ed.) (1983), *Britain within the EC* (London: Macmillan).
Ertl, J. (1985), *Agrarpolitik ohne Illusionen. Politische und persönliche Erfahrungen* (Frankfurt: Verlag Alfred Strothe).
Esser, J., Fach, W., with Dyson, K. H. F. (1983), '"Social market" and modernization policy: West Germany', in Dyson and Wilks, *Industrial Crisis*, pp. 102–27.
Everling, U. (1976), 'Die allgemeine Ermächtigung der Europäischen Gemeinschaft zur Zielverwirklichung nach Artikel 235 EWG-Vertrag', *Europarecht*, Sonderheft, pp. 23–6.
Farrands, C. (1983), 'External relations: textile politics and the Multi-Fibre Arrangement', in Wallace *et al.*, *Policy-Making in the European Community*, pp. 295–319.
Feld, W. (1981), *West Germany and the European Community: Competing Interests and Competing Policy Objectives* (New York: Praeger).

Fendel, F. (1981), *Industriepolitik der Europäischen Wirtschaftsgemeinschaft* (Frankfurt: Peter Lang).

Franzmeyer, F. (1984), 'Mehr Gemeinsamer Markt bei verschärftem Aussenschutz der EG – die Bundesrepublik im handelspolitischem Dilemma?' in Hrbek and Wessels, *EG-Mitgliedschaft*, pp. 71–96.

Gleske, L. (1980), 'Die Zusammenarbeit der Notenbanken in Europa', in H. Hahn (ed.), *Integration und Kooperation im Europäischen Währungssystem* (Baden-Baden: Nomos), pp. 87–101.

Grant, W., Paterson, W. E. and Whitston, C. (1985), 'Government–industry relations in the chemical industry: an Anglo-German comparison', paper to the ESRC conference on government–industry in the major OECD countries, Cambridge, December.

Gregory, F. (1983), *Dilemmas of Government: Britain and the EC* (Oxford: Martin Robertson).

Grewlich, K. (1984), 'EG-Forschungs- und Technologiepolitik – eine besondere Verantwortung fur das wirtschaftliche-technologische "Flaggschiff" ', in Hrbek and Wessels, *EG–Mitgliedschaft*, pp. 221–68.

Haas, E. (1958), *The Uniting of Europe* (London: Stevens).

Haas, E. (1976), 'Turbulent fields and the theory of regional integration', *International Organization*, vol. 30, no. 2, pp. 173–212.

Haftendorn, H. *et al.* (eds) (1978), *Verwaltete Aussenpolitik: sicherheits- und entspannungspolitische Entscheidungsprozesse in Bonn* (Cologne: Verlag Wissenschaft und Politik).

Hager, W. (1980), 'Germany as an extraordinary trader', in Kohl and Basevi, *West Germany: a European and Global Power*, pp. 3–43.

Hanrieder, W. (1967), *West German Foreign Policy 1949–1963: International Pressure and Domestic Response* (Stanford: Stanford University Press).

Hanrieder, W. (1982), 'Germany as number two? The foreign and economic policy of the Federal Republic', *International Studies Quarterly*, vol. 26, no. 1, pp. 57–86.

Hanrieder, W. and Auton, G. (1980), *The Foreign Policies of West Germany, France and Britain* (Englewood Cliffs: Prentice-Hall).

Hansard Society for Parliamentary Government (ed.) (1977), *The British People: their Voice in Europe* (Farnborough: Teakfield).

Hänsch, K. (1986), 'Europäische Integration und parlamentarische Demokratie', *Europa Archiv*, vol. 41, no. 7, pp. 191–201.

Henig, S. (1980), *Power and Decision in Europe* (London: Europotentials).

Hennings, K. H. (1982), 'West Germany', in A. Boltho (ed.), *The European Economy: Growth and Crisis* (Oxford: Oxford University Press), pp. 472–501.

Herz, T. A. (1977), *Europa in der öffentlichen Meinung – zur politischen Mobilisierung in Deutschland und Frankreich zwischen 1962 und 1977* (Bonn: Europa Union Verlag).

Heumann, H.-D. (1980), *Europäische Integration und nationale Interessenpolitik* (Königstein/Taunus: Forum Academicum).

Hine, R. C. (1985), *The Political Economy of European Trade* (Brighton: Wheatsheaf).

Hodges, M. (1983), 'Industrial policy: hard times or great expectations?', in Wallace *et al.*, *Policy-Making in the European Community*, pp. 265–93.
Hrbek, R. (1973), *Die SPD, Deutschland und Europa. Die Haltung der Sozialdemokratie zum Verhältnis von Deutschlandpolitik und Westintegration 1945–57* (Bonn: Europa Union Verlag).
Hrbek, R. and Läufer, T. (1986), 'Die Einheitliche Europäische Akte. Das Luxembourger Reformpaket: eine neue Etappe im Integrationsprozess', *Europa Archiv*, vol. 41, no. 7, pp. 173–84.
Hrbek, R. and Wessels, W. (1982), *Das vitale Interesse der Bundesrepublik Deutschland an EG und EPZ. Ein Plädoyer für eine (Rück-) Besinnung auf die grundlegende Bedeutung des EG-Systems für die Bundesrepublik* (Bonn: Institut für Europäische Politik).
Hrbek, R. and Wessels, W. (eds) (1984a), *EG-Mitgliedschaft: ein vitales Interesse der Bundesrepublik Deutschland?* (Bonn: Europa Union Verlag).
Hrbek, R. and Wessels, W. (1984b), 'Nationale Interessen der Bundesrepublik Deutschland und der Integrationsprozess', in Hrbek and Wessels, op. cit., pp. 29–69.
Hu, Y.-S. (1981), *Europe Under Stress* (London: Butterworths).
Hull, C. and Rhodes, R. A. W. (1977) *Intergovernmental Relations in the European Community* (Farnborough: Saxon House).
Jansen, B. (1977), *EWG und DDR nach Abschluss des Grundlagenvertrages* (Baden-Baden: Nomos).
Jaspert, G. (1982), 'Der Bundesrat und die europäische Integration', *Aus Politik und Zeitgeschichte*, no. 12 (27 March), pp. 17–32.
Jenkins, R. (ed.) (1983), *Britain and the EEC* (London: Macmillan).
Jeutter, P. (1986), *EWG – kein Weg nach Europa. Die Haltung der Freien Demokratischen Partei zu den Römischen Verträgen 1957* (Bonn: Europa Union Verlag).
Katzenstein, P. (1976), 'International relations and domestic structures: foreign economic policies of advanced industrial states', *International Organization*, vol. 30, no. 1, pp. 1–45.
Keohane, R. O. (1984), *After Hegemony, Cooperation and Discord in the World Political Economy* (Princeton: Princeton University Press).
Keohane, R. O. and Nye, J. S. (1977), *Power and Interdependence: World Politics in Transition* (Boston: Little, Brown).
Klein, L. (1981), 'The European Community's regional policy', *Built Environment*, vol. 7, nos. 3/4, pp. 182–9.
Kloten, N. (1980), 'Germany's monetary and financial policy and the European Community', in Kohl and Basevi, *West Germany: a European and Global Power*, pp. 177–99.
Knott, J. (1981), *Managing the German Economy* (Lexington: D. C. Heath).
Kohl, W. and Basevi, G. (eds) (1980), *West Germany: a European and Global Power* (Lexington, Mass.: D. C. Heath).
Kohler, B. (1980), 'Germany and the enlargement of the European Community', in Kohl and Basevi, *West Germany: a European and Global Power*, pp. 151–75.

Kramer, H. (1982), 'Bundesrepublik Deutschland', in Weidenfeld and Wessels, *Jahrbuch der Europäischen Integration 1981*, pp. 409–20.
Kramer, H. (1983), 'Bundesrepublik Deutschland', in Weidenfeld and Wessels, *Jahrbuch der Europäischen Integration 1982*, pp. 312–20.
Kramer, H. (1985), 'Bundesrepublik Deutschland', in Weidenfeld and Wessels, *Jahrbuch der Europäischen Integration 1984*, pp. 330–9.
Krause, J. and Wilker, L. (1980), 'Bureaucracy and foreign policy in the Federal Republic of Germany', in Krippendorf and Rittberger, *The Foreign Policy of West Germany*, pp. 147–70.
Kreile, M. (1978), 'West Germany: the dynamics of expansion', in P. Katzenstein (ed.), *Between Power and Plenty, Foreign Economic Policies of Advanced Industrial States* (Madison: University of Wisconsin Press).
Krippendorf, E. and Rittberger, V. (eds) (1980), *The Foreign Policy of West Germany* (Beverly Hills: Sage Publications).
Kromarek, P. (1985), 'Umweltschutzpolitik', in Weidenfeld and Wessels, *Jahrbuch der Europäischen Integration 1984*, pp. 177–82.
Kunze, R. (1968), *Kooperativer Föderalismus in der Bundesrepublik* (Stuttgart: Fischer Verlag).
Lange, H. C. (1983), 'Transnationale Politik in Europa: der Beitrag von Verbänden zur europäischen Zusammenarbeit', *Europäische Integration* (Mitteilungen des Arbeitskreises Europäische Integration), no. 4, April, pp. 3–10.
Lankowski, C. (1982a), '*Modell Deutschland* and the international regionalization of the West German state in the 1970s', in Markovits, *The Political Economy of West Germany*, pp. 90–115.
Lankowski, C. (1982b), *Germany and the European Communities: Anatomy of a Hegemonial Relation*, Columbia University PhD thesis (Ann Arbor, Mich.: University Microfilms International).
Lawrence, P. (1980), *Managers and Management in West Germany* (London: Croom Helm).
Lenz, C. O. (1985), 'The Draft Treaty establishing the European Union: report on the Federal Republic of Germany', in R. Bieber, J.-P. Jacqué, J. Weiler (eds), *An Ever Closer Union: a Critical Analysis of the Draft Treaty Establishing the European Union* (Luxembourg: Commission of the EC/European University Institute), pp. 209–16.
Leonhardt, H. A. (1984), 'Zur Europapolitik der Grünen', *Zeitschrift für Politik*, vol. 31, no. 2, pp. 192–207.
Littlechild, M. B. (1982), 'Regional policy in Germany', *Town and Country Planning*, vol. 51, no. 5, pp. 155–9.
Loewenberg, G. (1966), *Parliament in the German Political System* (Ithaca: Cornell University Press).
Ludlow, P. (1982), *The Making of the European Monetary System* (London: Butterworths).
Mahant, E. (1969), 'French and German reactions to the Common Market', unpublished PhD thesis, University of London.
Markovits, A. S. (ed.) (1982a), *The Political Economy of West Germany* (New York: Praeger).

Markovits, A. S. (1982b), 'Introduction: Model-Germany – a cursory overview of a complex construct', in Markovits, op. cit., pp. 1–11.

May, B. (1982), *Kosten und Nutzen der deutschen EG–Mitgliedschaft* (Bonn: Europa Union Verlag).

May, B. (1984), 'Der deutsche Beitrag zum Gemeinschaftshaushalt – die "Nettozahler"-diskussion', in Hrbek and Wessels, *EG–Mitgliedschaft*, pp. 357–87.

Mayntz, R. and Scharpf, F. (1975), *Policy-Making in the German Federal Bureaucracy* (Amsterdam: Elsevier).

Menke, K. (1985), 'Germany', in K. H. Reif (ed.), *Ten European Elections: Campaigns and Results of 1979/81 First Direct Elections to the European Parliament* (London: Gower), pp. 67–84.

Mény, Y. and Wright, V. (1985), *La crise de la sidérurgie européenne 1974–84* (Paris: Presses Universitaires de France).

Menyesch, D. and Uterwedde, H. (1982), 'Partner oder Konkurrenten? Wirtschaftsbeziehungen zwischen nationalen Strategien und internationalen Abhängigkeiten', in R. Picht (ed.), *Das Bündnis im Bündnis – deutsch-französische Beziehungen im internationalen Spannungsfeld* (Berlin: Severin und Siedler), pp. 105–39.

Merritt, A. and Merritt, R. (eds) (1970), *Public Opinion in Occupied Germany: the Omgus Surveys 1945–49* (Chicago: University of Illinois).

Mintzel, A. (1972), *Die CSU, Anatomie einer konservativen Partei* (Cologne: Westdeutscher Verlag).

Mintzel, A. (1977), *Geschichte der CSU – ein Überblick* (Cologne: Westdeutscher Verlag).

Monthly Report of the Bundesbank (1977), 'The growing importance of the European Communities for the public budgets of the Federal Republic of Germany', no. 1, pp. 15–22.

Morawitz, R. (1981), *Die Zusammenarbeit von Bund und Ländern bei Vorhaben der Europäischen Gemeinschaft* (Bonn: Europa Union Verlag).

Morgan, R. (1978), 'West Germany's foreign policy agenda', *The Washington Papers*, vol. 6, no. 54 (Beverly Hills: Sage Publications).

Morgan, R. (1981), 'The Federal Republic of Germany', in C. and K. Twitchett (eds), *Building Europe: Britain's Partners in the EEC* (London: Europa Publications), pp. 60–79.

Morgan, R. and Bray, C. (1982), 'Berlin in the post-detente era', *The World Today*, vol. 38, no. 3, pp. 81–9.

Morgan, R. and Bray, C. (1986), *Partners and Rivals in Western Europe: Britain, France and Germany* (Aldershot: Gower).

Müller-Roschach, H. (1974), *Die deutsche Europapolitik, Wege und Umwege zur politischen Union Europas* (Baden-Baden: Nomos).

Nass, K. O. (1976), 'Der "Zahlmeister" als Schrittmacher', *Europa Archiv*, vol. 31, no. 10, pp. 325–36.

Neville-Rolfe, E. (1984), *The Politics of Agriculture in the European Community* (London: Policy Studies Institute).

Noelle-Neumann, E. (1980), 'Phantom Europe: thirty years of survey research on German attitudes toward European integration', in L. Hurwitz (ed.), *Contemporary Perspectives on European Integration* (Westport, Conn.: Greenwood Press), pp. 53–74.

Noelle-Neumann, E. and Herdegen, G. (1983), 'Die Europäische Gemeinschaft in der öffentlichen Meinung: Informationsdefizite und enttäuschte Erwartungen', *Integration*, vol. 6, no. 3, pp. 95–105.

Oberthür, K. (1978), 'Die Bundesländer im Entscheidungssystem der EG, *Integration*, vol. 1, no. 2, pp. 58–65.

Oetting, U. (1973), *Bundestag und Bundesrat im Willensbildungsprozess der Europäischen Gemeinschaften* (Berlin: Duncker & Humblot).

Paterson, W. (1974a), *The SPD and European Integration* (Farnborough: Saxon House).

Paterson, W. (1974b), 'The making of European policy in West Germany', University of Warwick, Department of Politics Working Paper no. 3.

Paterson, W. (1975), 'The Ostpolitik and Regime Stability in West Germany', in R. B. Tilford (ed.), *The Ostpolitik and Political Change in Germany* (Farnborough: Saxon House), pp. 23–44.

Paterson, W. (1977), 'The German Social Democratic Party', in W. Paterson and A. Thomas (eds), *Social Democratic Parties in Western Europe* (London: Croom Helm), pp. 176–212.

Paterson, W. E. (1981), 'Political parties and the making of foreign policy – the case of the Federal Republic', *Review of International Studies*, vol. 7, no. 4, pp. 227–35.

Paterson, W. E. (1985a), 'The Union parties', in H. Wallach and G. Romoser (eds), *West German Politics in the Mid-Eighties* (New York: Praeger), pp. 60–80.

Paterson, W. E. (1985b), 'European elections in the Federal Republic of Germany', paper at the European Consortium for Political Research workshop on European elections, Barcelona.

Pearce, J. and Sutton, J. (1986), *Protection and Industrial Policy in Europe* (London: Routledge & Kegan Paul/RIIA).

Pfetsch, F. R. (1981), 'Wie abhängig ist die Bundesrepublik?', *Politische Vierteljahresschrift*, vol. 22, no. 2, pp. 144–67.

Platzer, H.-W. (1984), *Unternehmensverbände in der EG – ihre nationale und transnationale Organisation und Politik* (Kehl am Rhein: N. P. Engel Verlag).

Pöhle, K. (1984), 'Die Europa-Kommission des Deutschen Bundestages: ein politisches und geschäftsordnungsmässiges Novum', *Zeitschrift für Parlamentsfragen*, vol. 15, no. 3, pp. 352–9.

Pridham, G. (1980), 'The European policy of Franz-Josef Strauss and its implications for the Community', *Journal of Common Market Studies*, vol. 8, no. 4, pp. 313–32.

Priebe, H. (1980), 'German agricultural policy and the European Community', in Kohl and Basevi, *West Germany: a European and Global Power*, pp. 139–50.

Puchala, D. J. (1983), 'Worm cans and worth taxes: fiscal harmonization and the European policy process', in Wallace *et al.*, *Policy-Making in the European Community*, pp. 237–64.

Puchala, D. J. and Lankowski, C. (1976), 'The politics of fiscal harmonisation in the EC', *Journal of Common Market Studies*, vol. 15, no. 3, pp. 155–79.

Pünder, T. (1970), 'Die Gemeinden und die europäische Integration', *Archiv fur Kommunalwissenschaften*, vol. 10, I. Halbjahresband, pp. 148–58.

Putnam, R. and Bayne, N. (1984), *Hanging Together: the Seven-Power Summits* (London: Heinemann).

Rausch, H. (1976), *Bundestag und Bundesregierung* (Munich: C. H. Beck).

Regelsberger, E. and Wessels, W. (1984a), 'Entscheidungsprozesse Bonner Europapolitik – verwalten statt gestalten?' in Hrbek and Wessels, *EG–Mitgliedschaft*, pp. 469–99.

Regelsberger, E. and Wessels, W. (1984b), 'Die Europäische Politische Zusammenarbeit (EPZ) – Emanzipationsvehikel, Koalition oder Integrationsrahmen fur die Aussenpolitik Bonns', in Hrbek and Wessels, *EG–Mitgliedschaft*, pp. 389–412.

Regelsberger, E. and Wessels, W. (1985), 'National paper on the Federal Republic of Germany', in C. O. Nuallain (ed.), *The Presidency of the European Council of Ministers* (London: Croom Helm), pp. 73–100.

Ress, G. (1984), 'Die Auswirkungen des europäischen Gemeinschaftsrechts auf die deutsche Rechtsordnung', in G. Rüther and A. Panlik (eds), *Der Beitrag des Rechts zum europäischen Einigungsprozess* (Melle: Verlag Ernst Knoth).

Richardson, J. (ed.) (1982), *Policy Styles in Western Europe* (London: Allen & Unwin).

Richardson, J., Gustafsson, G. and Jordan, A. G. (1982), 'The concept of policy style', in Richardson, op. cit., pp. 1–16.

Richonnier, M. (1984), 'Europe: decline is not irreversible', *Journal of Common Market Studies*, vol. 22, no. 3, pp. 227–43.

Rideau, J. *et al.* (1975), *La France et les Communautés Européennes* (Paris: Librairie Générale).

Riesenhuber, H. (1986), 'EUREKA – ein neues Element europäischer Technologiepolitik', *Europa Archiv*, vol. 41, no. 7, pp. 185–90.

Rosenthal, G. G. (1975), *The Men Behind the Decisions* (Lexington, Mass.: D. C. Heath).

Rummel, R. (1980), 'Bonn and European Political Cooperation', in Kohl and Basevi, *West Germany: a European and Global Power*, pp. 73–87.

Rummel, R. and Wessels, W. (1983), 'Federal Republic of Germany: new responsibilities, old constraints', in C. Hill (ed.), *National Foreign Policies and European Political Cooperation* (London: Allen & Unwin), pp. 34–55.

Saeter, M. (1980), *The Federal Republic, Europe and the World* (Oslo: Universitetsforlaget).

Sasse, C. (1974), 'Bundesrat und Europäische Gemeinschaft' in *Der Bundesrat als Verfassungsorgan und politische Kraft* (Bad Honnef: Neue Darmstädter Verlag), pp. 335–63.

Saase, C. *et al.* (1977), *Decision-Making in the European Community* (New York: Praeger).

Schlupp, F. (1980), 'Modell Deutschland and the international division of labour', in Krippendorf and Rittberger, *The Foreign Policy of West Germany*, pp. 33–100.

Schmidt, G. (1984), 'Die Durchführung des Europäischen Gemeinschaftsrechts in der Bundesrepublik Deutschland und anderen Mitgliedstaaten', *Integration*, vol. 7, no. 4, pp. 205–16.

Schmidt, H. (1985), 'The European Monetary System: proposals for further progress', *The World Today*, vol. 41, no. 5, pp. 87–91.

Schmitz-Wenzel, H. (1969), 'Die deutschen Länder und ihre Stellung im europäischen Einigungsprozess', PhD dissertation, University of Bonn.

Schmuck, O. and Wessels, W. (1985), 'Die Mailänder Tagung des Europäischen Rats – weder Fehlschlag noch Durchbruch zur Europäischen Integration', *Integration*, vol. 8, no. 3, pp. 95–102.

Schumacher, H. H. (1980), 'Die Eingliederung von Berlin (West) in den Hoheitsbereich der Europäischen Gemeinschaft', *Europarecht*, vol. 15, no. 2, pp. 193–9.

Schüttemeyer, S. (1978), 'Funktionsverluste des Bundestages durch die europäische Integration', *Zeitschrift für Parlamentsfragen*, vol. 9, no. 2, pp. 261–78.

Schwarz, H.-P. (1975), 'Die Bundesregierung und die auswärtige Beziehungen', in H.-P. Schwarz (ed.), *Handbuch der deutschen Aussenpolitik* (Munich: Piper), pp. 43–112.

Schweitzer, C. C. (1978), *Die nationalen Parlamente in der Gemeinschaft – ihr schwindender Einfluss in Bonn und Westminster auf die Europagesetzgebung* (Bonn: Europa Union Verlag).

Simonian, H. (1981), 'France, Germany and Europe', *Journal of Common Market Studies*, vol. 19, no. 3, pp. 203–19.

Simonian, H. (1985), *The Privileged Partnership: Franco-German Relations in the European Community 1969–84* (Oxford: Clarendon Press).

Smith, E. O. (1983), *The West German Economy* (London: Croom Helm).

Smith, G. (1976), 'West Germany and the politics of centrality', *Government and Opposition*, vol. 11, no. 4, pp. 387–407.

Smith, G. (1979), *Democracy in Western Germany* (London: Heinemann).

Smith, G. (1980), *Politics in Western Europe*, 3rd edn (London: Heinemann).

Stadlmann, H. (1985), 'Der Europäische Rat', in Weidenfeld and Wessels, *Jahrbuch der Europäischen Integration 1984*, pp. 33–41.

Steinherr, A. (1980), 'German industrial and labor policy and the European Community', in Kohl and Basevi, *West Germany: a European and Global Power*, pp. 111–38.

Story, J. (1981), 'The Federal Republic – a conservative revisionist', *West European Politics*, vol. 4, no. 1, pp. 56–86.

Strauss, F.-J. (1965), *The Grand Design* (London: Weidenfeld and Nicolson).
Strauss, R. (1983), 'Economic effects of MCAs', *Journal of Common Market Studies*, vol. 21, no. 3, pp. 261–81.
Talbot, R. B. (1977), 'The European Community's regional fund', *Progress in Planning*, vol. 8, part 3, pp. 183–281.
Taussig, A. (1970), 'European integration and German ministries', unpublished PhD thesis, Harvard University.
Tsoukalis, L. (1977), *The Politics and Economics of European Monetary Integration* (London: Allen & Unwin).
Tsoukalis, L. (1983), 'Money and the process of integration', in Wallace *et al.*, *Policy-Making in the European Community*, pp. 115–41.
Turner, I. D. (1986), 'Interest group activity and EC policy-making: a case study of the 1985 car exhaust emission control decisions', unpublished paper, Henley Management College.
Ungerer, W. (1983), 'Europa-Politik under deutscher Präsidentschaft', *Aussenpolitik*, vol. 34, no. 1, pp. 3–16.
Vannicelli, P. (1974), *Italy, NATO and the European Community: the Interplay of Foreign and Domestic Politics* (Harvard: Harvard Studies in International Affairs, no. 31).
VCI (1976), *Jahresbericht 1975–6* (Frankfurt: VCI).
Veen, H. J. (1983), *Politische Einstellungen zur Europäischen Gemeinschaft im Herbst 1983* (Sankt Augustin: Konrad Adenuaer Stiftung).
Veen, H. J. *et al.* (1984), *Europa im Spiegel der Umfrageforschung, November 1978 bis Oktober 1983* (Sankt Augustin: Konrad Adenauer Stiftung).
von Moltke, K. (1984), 'Die EG-Umweltpolitik – notwendige Ergänzung nationaler und internationaler Massnahmen', in Hrbek and Wessels, *EG–Mitgliedschaft*, pp. 299–320.
von Urff, W. (1985), 'Agrar- und Fischereipolitik', in Weidenfeld and Wessels, *Jahrbuch der Europäischen Integration 1984*, pp. 99–112.
Wadbrook, W. P. (1972), *West German Balance-of-Payments Policy* (New York: Praeger).
Wallace, H. (1973), *National Governments and the European Community* (London: Chatham House/PEP).
Wallace, H. (1977), 'The establishment of the regional development fund: common policy or pork barrel?', in H. Wallace, W. Wallace, and C. Webb, *Policy-Making in the European Communities*, 1st edn (Chichester: John Wiley), pp. 137–63.
Wallace, H. (1980), *Budgetary Politics: the Finances of the European Communities* (London: Allen & Unwin).
Wallace, H. (1981), 'National politics and supranational integration', in D. Cameron (ed.), *Regionalism and Supranationalism* (London: Policy Studies Institute), pp. 111–26.
Wallace, H. (1986a), 'Bilateral, trilateral and multilateral negotiations in the European Community', in Morgan and Bray, *Partners and Rivals in Western Europe*, pp. 156–74.
Wallace, H. (1986b), 'The conduct of bilateral relationships by govern-

ments', in Morgan and Bray, *Partners and Rivals in Western Europe*, pp. 136–55.

Wallace, H., Wallace, W. and Webb, C. (eds) (1983), *Policy-Making in the European Community*, 2nd edn (Chichester: John Wiley).

Wallace, W. (ed.) (1980), *Britain in Europe* (London: Heinemann).

Wallace, W. (1983), 'Political cooperation: integration through intergovernmentalism', in Wallace *et al.*, *Policy-Making in the European Community*, pp. 373–402.

Wallace, W. (1986), 'Foreign policy: the management of distinctive interests', in Morgan and Bray, *Partners and Rivals in Western Europe*, pp. 205–24.

Webb, C. (1983), 'Theoretical perspectives and problems', in Wallace *et al.*, *Policy-Making in the European Community*, pp. 1–41.

Weber, J. (1977), *Die Interessengruppen im politischen System der Bundesrepublik Deutschland* (Stuttgart: Kohlhammer).

Weidenfeld, W. (1979), 'Die Europapolitik Konrad Adenauers', *Politische Studien*, Sonderheft 1, pp. 33–40.

Weidenfeld, W. and Wessels, W. (eds) (1982), *Jahrbuch der Europäischen Integration 1981* (Bonn: Europa Union Verlag).

Weidenfeld, W. and Wessels, W. (eds) (1983), *Jahrbuch der Europäischen Integration 1982* (Bonn: Europa Union Verlag).

Weidenfeld, W. and Wessels, W. (eds) (1985), *Jahrbuch der Europäischen Integration 1984* (Bonn: Europa Union Verlag).

Weiler, J. (1983), 'The Genscher–Colombo draft European Act: the politics of indecision', *Journal of European Integration*, vol. 6, nos 2/3, pp. 29–53.

Welch, D. (1983), 'From "EuroBeer" to "Newcastle Brown", a review of EC action to dismantle divergent "food" laws', *Journal of Common Market Studies*, vol. 22, no. 1, pp. 47–70.

Wessels, W. (1986), 'Die Einheitliche Europäische Akte – Zementierung des Status quo oder Einstieg in die Europäische Union?, *Integration*, vol. 9, no. 2, pp. 65–79.

Wilks, S. and Dyson, K. H. F. (1983), 'The character and economic context of industrial crises', in Dyson and Wilks, *Industrial Crisis*, pp. 1–25.

Ziller, G. (1979), *Der Bundesrat*, 5th edn (Dusseldorf: Droste Verlag).

Zimmermann, M. (1981), 'Struktur und Einfluss der Chemieindustrie auf die Umweltpolitik', Diplomarbeit, Berlin.

Index

Authors' Note

Institutions and policies at the *European level* are indexed under European Community. *West German* institutions and policies are dispersed throughout the index rather than all being listed under Germany.

Act of Ratification of the Treaties of Rome Article 2 167–8, 171; 192, 193
Adenauer, K. 5, 7, 9, 10, 28, 45, 109, 111, 124–8, 129, 132, 136, 142–3, 156, 163, 223, 225, 226, 239, 240–1
Aerssen, J. van 144, 148, 164
agriculture 13, 20, 31, 35, 52, 89–90, 156, 158–61, 233
  Agricultural Act (1955) 157
  agricultural lobby 73; *see also* German Farmers' Union
  agricultural policy 71–2
  agricultural structures 19, 74–5, 190, 196, 197
  Central Committee of German Agriculture 156
  cereals sector 158
  compensation payments to farmers 72, 76, 82, 158–9, 242
  EEC adjustment plan 158, 159
  Lübke Plan (1953) 157
  part-time farming 75
  social insurance provisions 105, 242
  south Germany 74–5
Agriculture Ministry 13, 19, 23, 35, 40, 41, 42, 71–7, 81, 82, 92, 105, 154, 157, 160
  dismantling of MCAs 75–7
  EC Budget contributions 68–9
  environmental policy 245
  structural policy 35, 74–5
allied powers 5, 7, 18, 110, 124–5, 166, 223
  and Berlin 198–9
Amrehn, F. 216
anti-terrorism 37
Apel, H. 114, 147
  finance minister 36, 115, 139, 207
  junior Foreign Office minister 32, 38, 67, 115, 206–7, 211, 216
  SPD commission on CAP 147, 160
Argentine 26
Association of German Chemical Industry (VCI) 92, 99–100, 176–9
  and CEFIC 99, 176
  and Economics Ministry 105, 176–8
Atlantic Alliance 6, 8, 78; *see also* NATO
Australia 50, 88
automobile industry 89, 245

Baden Württemberg 75
Bahr, E. 138
Bangemann, M. 146, 150, 151
banks 91, 93
Barre, R. 65, 228
BASF 99
Basic Law 223, 233
  Article 24 5, 166, 180, 188, 250
  Article 32 191
  Article 38 190
  Article 53 193
  Article 65 27, 214
  Article 70 187
  Article 73, 185, 189
  Article 91a 189, 206
Bavaria 73, 75, 129, 131, 144, 246
  Bavarian interests 144, 192

Bavarian government 192, 201, 250–1
state election (1986) 242
Bayer 99, 178
Belgium 88, 94, 156
Benelux countries 64; *see also* individual countries
Berlin 224, 232
allied powers 198–9
Berlinförderungsgesetz 200
Berlin crisis 136
Berlin Wall 112
East Berlin 199
Quadripartite Agreement 186, 198, 199, 200
West Berlin and EC 23, 186, 198–200, 206
Biedenkopf, K. 82
bio-ethanol 242
Bismarck, O. von 18
Bismarck, P. von 144
Blücher, F. 132
Bonn government; *see* Federal Government
Brandt, W. 41, 137
Brandt-Scheel coalition; *see under* Federal Government
chancellorship 1, 32, 212, 226
European policy of 38, 62, 67, 79, 137–8, 140, 210, 211, 227
Ostpolitik 37, 44, 78, 115, 137, 138
SPD European policy 137–8, 140, 147, 148, 149, 162
Bremen 55, 189
Bretton Woods system 13, 62, 63
Brentano, H. von 31
brewing industry 47, 105
Brück, A. 216
Britain; *see* United Kingdom
Bund-Länder co-operation; *see* federalism
Bundesrat 154, 166–73
Act of Ratification of the Treaties of Rome 167–8, 171, 192, 193
Agriculture Committee 144, 171, 172, 214
attitude towards EC 171, 251
chemicals legislation 178, 179
Committee for EC Affairs 171, 195, 214–15
division of EC policy responsibilities 171
ERDF 206, 214–15
expertise of committees 171, 172, 195
powers in EC policy-making 165, 171–2, 186, 187, 191, 192–3, 194, 195, 239
Bundestag 140, 143, 148, 154, 155, 163, 166–73, 200, 226
Act of Ratification of the Treaties of Rome 167–8, 193
adjournment debates on EC 172
Agriculture Committee 73, 105, 145, 157–8, 168–70
Budgetary Committee 169–70, 178
committee system 73, 168–71
Council of Elders for Integration 168
Economics Committee 169, 178, 212, 215
Employment and Social Affairs Committee 169
ERDF 215–16
Europa-Kommission 170–1
expertise 168–9, 170
Foreign Affairs Committee 96, 169
plenum 170, 172, 178
powers in EC policy-making 148, 165, 166–71, 192, 239
questions on EC affairs 172
Transport Committee 169
Youth Family and Health Committee 169, 178
Bundesumweltamt 179

Cabinet 18, 21, 28, 32, 40–1, 65, 68, 69, 160, 220; also *see under* Federal Government
decisions on ERDF 207, 210, 212, 213, 216, 219
Callaghan, J. 213, 214
Canada 50, 88, 176
capital goods industries 44, 89
capital markets 58
Carstens, K. 128
cartels 90
crisis cartels in steel industry 90–1
Carter, J. 64
Carter Administration 65, 228
Catholics 123, 124, 127, 128, 129
CDU 36, 38, 43, 70, 82, 109, 115, 123–8, 133
agriculture 101, 143, 156, 158–60
European policy 124–8, 132
federal committees 143

federal party headquarters 142–3
'Gaullists' and 'Atlanticists' debate 10, 28, 127, 128, 153
impact on European policy 153
Mittelstandsvereinigungen 144
organization 124, 142–4
Wirtschaftsrat 144
CDU/CSU parliamentary group 142, 143, 144, 145
and ERDF 216
and MEPs 148–50
Central Committee of German Agriculture 156
chancellor 21, 27, 32, 36; *see also* Federal Government and individual chancellors
and European policy 21, 27, 28, 37–9, 68, 73, 76, 81
Chancellor's Office 21, 32, 66, 128, 160
EC budgetary contributions 68–9
European policy 37–9, 40, 240, 241, 250
chemical industry 19, 89, 92, 99, 105, 106; *see also* German Chemicals Law
Chernobyl nuclear accident (1986) 236, 245
China 130
Chirac, J. 231
Churchill, W. 109
City of London 48
clothing industry 51, 52, 89, 91, 106
coal 110, 166
coal industry 5, 55, 94, 125
coalition governments 18, 28, 74; *see also under* Federal Government
1982 change of coalition 25, 43, 81, 149, 154
Cold War 6, 7
collective bargaining 92, 97
Committee of Commercial Organizations of the EC (COCCEE) 99
Committee of Professional Agricultural Organizations (COPA) 102, 103
Committee of State Secretaries for European Affairs 32, 40, 211
Concerted Action 19, 87, 92
Confederation of German Employers' Associations (BDA) 19, 92, 93, 97–8, 100, 103
Confederation of Socialist Parties 151
Conference on Security and Co-operation in Europe (CSCE) 11, 78
consumer interests 107
Corterier, P. 32, 147
Council of Chemical Industry Federations (CEFIC) 103, 176
Council of Europe 6, 125
courts: *see under* legal system
CSU 35, 43, 73, 82, 109, 115, 123, 127, 246; *see also* CDU/CSU parliamentary group
agriculture 99, 101, 131, 144, 156, 158–9
in the Bundestag 144
EC policy-making 144–5
European integration 129–31, 132
impact on European policy 153
currency reform (1948) 62, 86
Czechoslovakia 138

Dahrendorf, R. 152
Davignon, E. 54, 56
defence policy 5, 8
Dehler, T. 132, 133
Denmark 49, 64, 88, 177, 234, 247, 248
detente 5, 78, 126
Deutsche Mark (DM) 19, 62, 65, 76, 116
undervaluation 86, 87
Deutscher Brauer Bund 105
Deutschlandplan 136
Deutschlandpolitik 4; *see also* German-German relations
Dohnanyi, K. von 32, 54, 69, 147
dollar 64, 65
Dooge Report 121, 247
Douglas-Home, Sir A. 211
Dulles, J. F. 136

East Germany; *see* German Democratic Republic
East-West relations 5, 9, 11, 128
Economics Ministry 19, 31, 33, 34–5, 40, 41, 42, 44, 45–58, 59, 60–1, 65, 66, 72, 91, 105, 106, 134, 250
Division E 34, 167, 212
environmental policy 176–9, 244–5
ERDF 206, 207, 208, 209–10, 211, 212, 215, 218, 219
social market economy 45, 53, 60–1

electoral law 37
employment policy 92
environmental policy 19, 99, 155, 175–9, 244–6
Equalization of Burdens Law (1951) 125
Erhard, L. 10, 28, 31, 45, 94, 126, 127, 129, 226
Ertl, J. 35, 73, 75, 102, 133, 159, 161
EUREKA 32, 60, 229, 247, 250
Eurobarometer 113
EUROFER 56
European Atomic Energy Community (Euratom) 8, 94, 110, 126, 132, 136, 167
European Coal and Steel Community (ECSC) 5–8, 34, 87, 94, 95, 110, 125, 132, 166, 188, 192
  Assembly 6
  High Authority 94, 166
  Treaty of Paris 6, 54, 56, 188
European Community
  aerospace 34, 53
  Budget 2, 4, 20, 33, 36, 41, 72, 82, 194; German contributions 12, 13, 14, 36, 38, 60, 67–70, 76, 139, 203, 220, 243; own resources 67, 69, 70, 71, 79, 95; Value Added Tax 70, 71, 243
  co-determination policy 97, 131, 195
  Commission of the EC 3, 20, 30, 32, 38, 47, 51, 54, 56, 60, 74, 80, 91, 99, 102, 103, 104, 126, 139, 152, 167, 168, 175, 191–2, 194, 197, 236, 240, 243, 248
    ERDF 205, 206, 208, 209, 210, 211, 213, 215, 217, 219, 222; German commissioners 82, 83, 126, 152, 240
  Committee of Permanent Representatives (COREPER) 18, 54, 168
  Common Agricultural Policy (CAP) 12, 14, 17, 20, 23, 35, 62, 71–7, 82, 98, 105, 131, 140–1, 167, 205, 231, 241–4
    annual price review 74, 96, 105, 240, 241, 243; cereals 21, 77, 101, 102, 158, 159, 242, 243, 248; dairy quotas 72, 75, 76, 82, 131, 158, 159, 162, 242; EAGGF 233; German attitudes to creation 13, 101, 110, 156, 158, 159; Mansholt Plan 74–5, 101–2, 131, 144; MCAs 66, 75–7, 102, 160–1, 228–9, 241–2; reform 2, 13, 37, 69, 70, 71, 81, 102, 147, 160, 231, 247; structural policy 35, 74–5, 190, 194, 197; surpluses 72, 98, 119, 121, 157
  Common Commercial Policy 49
  competition policy 17, 34, 54, 58–61, 167
  Council of Ministers 21, 26, 31, 32, 33, 36, 38, 39, 47, 48, 56, 67, 69, 75, 76, 104, 152, 165, 166–7, 168, 170, 171, 176, 194, 195, 196, 233, 234, 240, 246, 248
    ERDF 204, 205, 207, 211, 212, 216, 219; German presidency 1978 228; German presidency 1983 41, 70, 78, 81, 237; presidency 20, 26, 54, 78; secretariat 167; veto in 21, 82, 187, 242, 248–9
  Court of Auditors 71
  Court of Justice 134, 179, 180, 181, 182, 246; *Cassis de Dijon* case 47; Leberpfennig Judgement (1970) 181
  Economic and Monetary Union 13, 62–5, 79, 95, 203, 205, 210, 212, 215, 217, 221, 226, 228, 249; the Snake 39, 63; Werner Report 63
  Economic and Social Committee 104
  education 189, 196
  empty chair crisis (1965) 114, 136, 216
  energy policy 44, 80, 203, 212, 221
  enlargement (1973) 38, 95, 205, 210
  enlargement, southern 70, 81, 82, 95, 146, 222, 247
  environmental policy 17, 37, 83, 140, 155, 188–9, 197–8, 244–6, 247
    chemicals legislation 175–9; Foreign Office 244; exhaust emission control 37, 83, 155, 245–6
  ESPRIT 59
European Council 33, 37, 41, 65, 66, 68, 69, 80, 152, 227, 229, 240
  Copenhagen (1978) 64, 65–6, 228; Brussels (1983) 38, 70; Stuttgart

(1983) 9, 33, 38, 70, 78, 135; Brussels (1984) 76; Fontainebleau (1984) 70, 76, 82, 83, 243, 247; Milan (1985) 21, 82, 159, 242, 247, 248; Luxembourg (1985) 121, 248
European Monetary Fund 66
European Monetary System (EMS) 4, 13, 14, 15, 39, 64–7, 93, 131, 143
Franco-German relations 66, 80, 228–9, 230; Monetary Compensatory Amounts (MCAs) 76, 160–1, 228–9; H. Schmidt 13, 21, 28, 37, 38, 64–7, 80, 228–9, 230
European Parliament 95, 104, 136, 148, 155, 162, 168, 193, 200, 206, 211, 212, 213, 215, 219, 249
direct elections 37, 79, 80, 116–17, 134, 137, 143, 148, 152, 227; Draft Treaty on European Union 121, 247; election (1979) 116, 118, 140, 148, 162, 170; election (1984) 23, 75, 76, 120, 134, 140, 146, 149, 151, 159, 162, 242; Liberal Group 135; links with German parties 148–50, 171; MEPs 147–50, 247; Rainbow Group 150, 151
European Regional Development Fund (ERDF) 23, 190, 197, 202–22
creation 18, 67, 80, 114, 202–17; Economic and Monetary Union 203, 205, 212, 215, 217, 221; management 200, 217–19; Regional Policy Committee 215
European Social Fund 200
external relations 48–53
fiscal harmonization 71
fisheries policy 35
foodstuffs legislation 39
German disillusionment with 13–14
German economic 'domination' of 1, 8, 15
harmonization policy 36, 47, 190, 196
importance to West Germany 2, 5–14
industrial policy 12, 34, 48, 53–8, 60
institutional reform 136
internal market policy 12, 24, 44, 45, 46–8, 50, 52, 54, 58, 62, 95, 229, 247, 248
labour market policy 97, 140
law 167, 174, 196
directives 173, 181, 182, 190, 197; German law 165, 167, 179–83, 191; regulations 173, 181, 190
monetary co-operation 13, 36, 39, 44, 61–7, 93, 249
Protocol on Interzonal Trade 231–7
research policy 58–61
shipbuilding 34, 53
Single European Act (1986) 37, 95, 200–1, 229, 244, 248–51
Sixth VAT Directive 174, 181, 182
social policy 97, 140
steel policy 34, 48, 53–7, 60, 90–1, 197
manifest crisis procedure 56, 57; steel quotas 55–7
summit meetings 227
The Hague (1969) 1, 62, 67, 95, 138, 205, 210; Paris (1972) 38, 80, 202, 205, 210, 245; Copenhagen (1973) 211; Paris (1974) 213
synthetic fibres 53
tariffs 44, 46, 50, 167
telecommunications 53
Thomson Report 209
trade policy 12, 17, 34, 46–7, 54, 99, 167, 229
transport policy 190
tripartism 97
Vredeling proposal 101
wine-growing 192, 194
European Defence Community (EDC) 6, 126, 132, 136, 166, 225
European Democratic Union 151
European Economic Community (EEC) 8, 45, 49, 87, 94, 95, 110, 126, 132, 137, 158, 167
Treaty of Rome 46, 94, 132, 139, 166, 180, 189, 190, 192, 193, 205, 211, 246, 248
European Free Trade Association (EFTA) 49–50, 95
European Investment Bank 209
European Liberals and Democrats (ELD) 151

European Payments Union (EPU) 7
European People's Party (EPP) 151
European Political Co-operation (EPC)
  Conference of Foreign Ministers 33
  Franco-German draft treaty (1985) 82, 229, 247
  German policy 8–11, 30–1, 77–9, 229, 247
  Gymnich agreement 78
  Luxembourg (Davignon) Report 31, 77
European Trade Union Confederation (ETUC) 101, 103
European Union 2, 24, 38, 79, 82, 138, 227
  Solemn Declaration on (1983) 9, 20, 30, 33, 78, 82, 135, 237
  West Germany and 241, 246–51
Europrotectionism 47, 51–2, 87
Everling, U. 212, 215
exporters 19, 74

Falkland Islands 26
Federal Bank 3, 18, 19, 26, 27, 36, 61–2, 87, 154, 249
  EMS 39
  European policy 39, 62, 66
  Federal Bank Act (1957) 39
  functions 39, 66
Federal Cartel Office 55, 59, 90
Federal Constitutional Court; *see* legal system
Federal Government, *see also* individual ministries
  bureaucratic politics 21, 29–30, 155
  coalitions
    Brandt–Scheel (1969–74) 10, 67, 79, 224, 226; Centre-Right (1982–) 46, 81; Grand Coalition (1966–9) 128, 131, 133, 136, 137, 153; Social–Liberal coalitions (1969–82) 35, 43, 46, 74, 87, 101, 114, 128, 147, 153, 159
  constitutional principles 3, 27–8, 36, 37, 68, 73, 160, 214, 241
  European policy co-ordination 1, 21, 27, 28, 29, 32, 34, 40–1, 83, 221
  European policy style 27–31
  ministerial bureaucracy 25, 29–30, 41, 104, 106, 174, 175
  sectorized nature 16, 23, 25–42, 67, 72–4, 79, 83, 85, 90, 91, 104, 105, 212, 217, 230, 240–1
federalism 1
  European 6, 126, 129–30, 166
  West German 18, 185
    Bund-Länder committees 187, 191, 193; *Bund-Länder* procedure (1980) 191, 193–4, 195; co-operative federalism 187–8, 192, 193, 196, 201; finance reform (1969) 187; Troeger Commission 187
Federation of European Wholesale and International Trade Associations (FEWITA) 99, 103
Federation of German Industry (BDI) 19, 92, 93–7, 98, 99, 100, 102, 103, 105, 106
  branch associations 19, 95, 96–7
  EC policy-making 95
  UNICE 96
Federation of German Trade Unions (DGB) 48, 92, 97, 100–1
Federation of German Wholesale and Foreign Traders (BGA) 92, 98–9, 105
Finance Ministry 36–7, 40, 41, 45, 61–71, 72, 82
  CAP 36, 73, 75, 76, 220, 242–3
  EC Budget 36, 44, 53–4, 61, 67–71, 80, 83, 207, 220
  ERDF 36, 206, 207–9, 210, 217–19, 220, 221, 222
  Federal Budget 36, 68, 69, 70, 79, 81, 206
Focke, K. 32, 38, 139
foreign affairs 27
foreign economic policy 86
Foreign Office 134, 240
  EC Budget 68–9, 70
  EC environmental policy 244
  EPC 19, 31, 77–9
  ERDF 205–7, 208, 209, 210, 212, 214, 215, 218, 222
  European policy-making 18, 19, 20, 21, 26, 30–4, 36, 38, 40, 41, 42, 45, 60, 79–83, 96, 121, 134, 135, 171, 192, 206, 207, 247, 250
  minister of state 32–3, 40, 54, 147, 153, 206, 207, 213
foreign policy 3, 5, 8, 11, 19, 26, 124, 126, 129, 133, 136, 147, 185

forests 246
Four-Power Agreement, *see* Quadripartite Agreement
France 2, 7, 8, 9, 10, 11, 13, 72, 76, 78, 88, 91, 94, 110, 130, 132, 136, 158, 160, 175, 177, 183, 198, 208, 224, 225, 240, 243
  Assemblée Nationale 126, 225
  balance of payments problems 63
  colonies 44, 156
  Conseil d'Etat 181
  Franc 76
  Franc zone 49
  government and internal market 46–7
  government and international trade 46–7, 49, 52, 87
  government's memorandum on EC trade 49, 57
Franco-German relations 5, 7, 14, 24, 38, 80, 124, 125, 126, 139, 223–31, 237, 247
  European Council 80, 227
  EMS 66, 80, 228–9, 230
  Franco-German Treaty (1963) 127, 224, 225, 226
Franconia 131, 192
Free Democratic Party (FDP) 22, 35, 43, 45, 46
  agriculture 35, 73, 102, 155–61
  electoral support 134, 160
  EC policy-making structures 145–6
  European policy 110, 132–5, 162
  impact on European policy 150–5
  MEPs 146, 148–50
  parliamentary group 145–6, 154

GATT 26, 50, 53, 59, 229
Gaulle, C. de 9, 10, 126–7, 136, 225–6
Genscher, H.-D. 31, 41, 78, 80, 81, 133, 150, 206, 213
  Genscher-Colombo 'European Act' 28, 30, 32, 33, 38, 78, 81, 117, 134–5, 237
German Chemicals Law (1980) 175–9
German Conference of Chambers of Industry and Commerce (DIHT) 93, 217, 244
German Democratic Republic (GDR) 9, 22, 24, 75, 135
  interzonal trade and EC 231–7
German Farmers' Union (DBV)
  Agriculture Ministry 19, 73, 75, 92, 105, 106, 157, 159, 160
  Bundestag 157–8
  CAP 74, 101, 158–60, 242
  membership 92, 157
  organization 101
  political parties 101, 131, 143, 144, 145, 154, 156–60
Germany, division of 5, 11, 126, 232
Germany, Federal Republic (FRG)
  bilateral relations 223–38
  contributions to EC Budget 12, 13, 14, 36, 38, 60, 67–70, 76, 139, 203, 229, 240
  de-centralized political system 3, 17–18, 22, 23, 26–7, 43, 76, 204, 246
  economic reconstruction 7, 8, 44, 85–7
  economic strength 44–5
  economy 1, 16, 23, 85–93, 110, 114
  establishment of 5, 18, 86
  European movement 100, 249
  European 'policy style' 14–22, 25, 79, 219
  European Union 241, 246–51
  export dependence 3, 11–12, 44–5, 87, 89, 98, 112
  federal election (1957) 161
  federal election (1976) 139, 162
  federal election (1980) 132, 162
  federal election (1983) 41, 148
  forests 246
  German–German relations 10, 77, 223, 225
    and EC 3, 225, 231–8; interzonal trade 132, 232–7
  importance to EC 2, 14
  legal system and EC 165, 179–83, 191
  national interests 14, 18, 22
  paymaster of EC 32, 67–8, 114–15, 119, 211, 251
  Permanent Representation to EC 34, 41, 167
  role in EC 1, 2, 15, 239–41, 246
  social market economy 8, 12, 22, 34, 42, 45, 60, 71, 98, 100, 110, 207
Germany, nationalism 18
Germany, reunification 5, 7, 111–12, 125, 132, 232, 236
Germany, Third Reich 157, 239

Germany, Weimar Republic 6, 12, 61, 157
Germany, Western zones 5, 108
Giscard d'Estaing, V. 38, 64, 65, 212, 213, 224, 227, 228
Greece 12, 88, 183, 196, 226, 231, 232, 247, 248
Greens 13, 22, 23, 105, 121, 142, 146, 151
  agricultural policy 72, 140–2
  European policy 43, 140–2, 152, 162, 163, 169, 240, 244, 247
  Karlsruhe Declaration (1984) 140–1
  MEPs 148–50
Group of European Specialists 40
Grundig 59
Grünewald, A. 212
Guillaume, F. 231
Guttenberg, K. T. Freiherr von und zu 128, 130

Haferkamp, W. 82
Hallstein, W. 126, 152, 223, 240
Hamburg 189, 192
Haniel-Niethammer, F. von 130
Hänsch, K. 164
Hasinger, Dr A. 178
Hassel, K.-U. von 127, 129
Hauenschild, K. 149
Heath, E. 226
Heereman, C. Freiherr von 158
Hesse 219
Heuss, T. 132
Hitler, A. 18
Höcherl, H. 73
Hoechst 99, 177
human rights 228
Humber Bridge 210
hyperinflation 61

Iberian enlargement, *see* EC enlargement
IG Chemie 149
IG Metall 149
implementation 20, 23, 173–9
importers 174–5
industrialists 19, 45, 65; *see also* Federation of German Industry
inflation 12, 13, 63, 86, 87
Infratest 120
integration *passim*
  variable geometry 121, 250
integration policy 25–6, 30–1, 43–4, 69, 79–83, 159, 185
interdependence 8, 9, 10–11, 15–16, 24, 27, 65, 223, 237
interest groups 15, 17, 19, 20, 21, 23, 25, 26, 77, 85–107, 170, 239, 240; *see also under* individual groups
  central organizations 19
  contacts with Federal Government 104
  ERDF 217
  implementation of EC policy 175
  institutional interest groups 34
  organization of EC policy 94–102, 104–7
  transnational interest groups 48, 102–4
Inter-German relations; *see* German–German relations
intergovernmentalism 15, 16, 38, 77, 236
Interior Ministry 37
  environmental policy 92, 177–8, 244, 245, 246
  exhaust emissions 245–6
international economy 3, 15, 44, 106, 227
International Labour Organization 98
international monetary system 45, 62, 64–5
international relations 17
  power politics theory of 9, 10, 15
International Ruhr Authority 7
Iranian hostage crisis 26
Ireland 88, 177, 231, 232
  and ERDF 205, 209, 211, 213, 218
Israel 11
Italy 2, 52, 88, 91, 183, 196, 198
  and ERDF 209, 211, 213, 218
  government 56, 135, 230

Japan 46, 50, 57, 58, 78, 87, 88, 176
Jeutter, P. 134
joint task legislation 19, 74, 189, 206, 208, 219

Kennedy Administration 111, 126
Kiechle, I. 21, 35, 73, 82, 131, 145, 154, 158, 159, 231, 242, 243, 248, 251
Kiesinger, K.-G. 128
Klöckner 55
Kohl, H. 11, 31, 37, 41, 128, 158, 245

and CAP 76–7
chancellor 22, 33, 43, 128, 229, 241
European policy 18, 38–9, 58, 69, 70, 79, 81, 128, 163, 247
Milan European Council 82, 229
Köhnen, H. 148
Konrad Adenauer Foundation 119
Korean War 8

Lahnstein, M. 135
Lambsdorff, O. Graf 35, 51–2
Länder 3, 25, 55, 90, 145, 185–201; *see also* individual states
agricultural policy 74, 143, 144, 185, 193
Bundesrat 171, 172–3, 191, 192–3
civil servants 21, 171, 182, 193
Conference of *Länder* Prime Ministers 193–4
EC Commission 191–2
EC educational and vocational training 189, 196
EC environmental policy 185, 189–90, 197–8, 201, 245
EC harmonization policy 190, 196
EC occupational law 189, 196
EC policy-making 70, 166, 185, 186, 191–8
EC regional policy 185, 190, 193, 206, 214–15
EC transport policy 190
ECSS membership 188, 192
impact of EC on powers 23, 175, 185–91, 194–5, 200
joint task legislation 19, 74, 189, 193, 206, 219
Länder Observer 34, 191, 193, 194, 195
parliaments 143
representatives on EC committees 194, 215
Single European Act (1986) 200–1, 250–1
Lange, E. 164
Langes, H. 164
Lautenschlager, H. 33
legal system 165, 179–83, 191
administrative courts 179, 180, 182
Bundesfinanzhof 180, 181, 182, 183
Bundesrechnungshof 174, 179, 183
Bundesverfassungsgerichtshof 23, 180–3
legislature; *see* Bundestag and Bundesrat
Lenz, C.-O. 171
local authorities
and EC 196, 198
Loderer, E. 149
Lomé Convention 50
Lower Saxony 182
election (1986) 242, 243, 245
Luxembourg 88

Marshall aid 86
Marx, W. 216
Matthöfer, H. 36, 69, 135, 139, 208
McCloy, J. 126
Mertes, A. 32
Middle East 11, 77
migrant labour 189, 196
mining 89
Ministry for Inter-German Affairs 206, 218
Ministry for Youth, Family and Health 39, 105, 178
Ministry of Economic Co-operation 39
Ministry of Justice 39
Ministry of Labour and Social Affairs 39
Ministry of Research and Technology 39, 54, 59–60, 250
Ministry of Transport 39
Mitterrand, F. 46, 59, 229–30
Mollet, G. 126
monetary policy
control of money supply 12
monetary stability 4
Monnet, J. 136
Multi-Fibre Arrangement 50–2, 91, 97, 100

Narjes, K.-H. 82, 152
National Liberals 132
Nazi regime 9, 10, 11, 111, 223, 224
Nazi atrocities 11, 77
neo-functionalism 15, 16
neo-Nazis 101
Netherlands 49, 88, 233, 237
newly industrializing countries (NICs) 46, 50
North Atlantic Treaty Organization (NATO) 7, 9, 78, 126
North-Rhine Westphalia 188

North-South dialogue 50
Norway 64, 177

occupying powers 5, 223; *see also* allied powers
Oder-Neisse line 233
oil crisis 17, 65, 114, 211, 213, 221
Organization for European Economic Co-operation (OEEC) 7, 45, 94, 132
Organization for Economic Co-operation and Development (OECD) 88, 98
Ostpolitik 10, 37, 44, 128, 131, 137, 138, 216, 226, 237
  Basic Treaty (1972) 234
own resources; *see* EC Budget

parliament; *see* Bundestag and Bundesrat
Parliamentary Council 5
pesticides 245
Petersberg Agreement 7
Pfeiffer, A. 82
Pius XII, Pope 124
policy analysis
  domestic policy-making 2–4, 15–22
  foreign policy-making 3, 15–16, 17
policy making
  consensual relations 21, 22, 25, 104–6
  incrementalism 20–1
  institutional pluralism 17, 18, 22
  sectorization 16, 19, 20, 25, 43, 65, 77, 104–8, 219–22
  standard operating procedure 16, 20–1
policy style
  concept 16–17
  FRG's European policy 14–22, 25, 79, 219
political parties 1, 22, 23, 123–64; *see also* individual parties
  consensus on European policy 21, 23, 25, 28, 30, 34, 41, 43, 72, 110, 123, 150, 163, 169, 183, 188, 239, 240
  impact on European policy 150–61
  transnational parties 151–2, 162
Pompidou, G. 64, 212, 226, 227
Portugal 12, 146
post-materialism 13
Probst, Dr M. 130
protectionism 46, 50, 51, 87, 98, 243
protestantism 127, 129, 131
public opinion 1, 13, 65, 138, 152
  European integration 108–22, 123, 239–40, 251
  European Parliament 119–20
  Europe's international role 120
  membership of EC 23, 72, 112–22, 243, 246, 247
public purchasing 58

Quadripartite Agreement (1971) 186, 198, 199, 200
quotas 94

raw materials 89
Reagan, R. 229
refugees 6, 86, 125, 129, 157
regional policy 61, 197, 219
  as joint task 19, 193, 197, 208
Rehwinkel, E. 101
Rhine 124, 189, 198
Riesenhuber, H. 250
Ritz, Dr B. 145
Ruhr 90

Saar 55, 90, 125, 132, 135, 188
Scandinavia 108
Scheel, W. 31, 133, 134, 206
Schiller, K. 45–6
Schleswig-Holstein 190
  local elections (1986) 242
Schmid, G. 164
Schmidt, H. 32, 36, 115, 206, 207
  CAP 74, 81, 160
  chancellor 14, 80, 114, 115, 138–9, 193, 212, 226, 239
  European policy 38, 69, 79, 80, 138–9, 147, 202, 224, 240
  monetary co-operation 13, 21, 28, 37, 38, 64–7, 228–9
Schröder, D. 145
Schröder, G. 127, 128, 129, 216
Schulmann, H. 66
Schulz, K.-P. 137
Schumacher, K. 135, 139
Schuman, R. 125
  Schuman Plan 5, 109–10
Second World War 5, 44
security co-operation 9
security policy 6, 78, 237
shipbuilding 55
shoe industry 52

small businesses 91, 94, 106
social policy 61, 92
songbird conservation 26, 189, 197–8
South Tyrol 133
sovereignty
  national sovereignty 5, 6, 9, 11, 15, 110, 113, 133, 165–6, 174, 188, 223, 224, 225, 232, 237
  parliamentary sovereignty 165, 183
Spain 12, 146
SPD 32, 36, 43, 54, 69, 82, 109, 124, 128, 132, 142, 206
  CAP 141, 156, 158, 159–61
  ERDF 216
  European policy 8, 110, 115, 135–40, 162
  impact on European policy 150–5, 156
  MEPs 148–50
  parliamentary party 136, 138, 146, 147–8
  policy-making structures 146–8
Stability and Growth Act (1967) 86
Stavenhagen, L. 32
steel industry 5, 8, 22, 50, 90–1, 94, 125, 197
  West German subsidies 55
  EC steel quotas 54–7
Stoltenberg, G. 36, 70, 243, 249
Strategic Defence Initiative 229, 250
Strauss, F. J. 22, 127, 129–31, 144, 192
supranationalism 10, 79, 80, 108, 115, 118, 126, 127, 130, 166, 225, 226, 227, 240, 251
Susset, E. 145
Sweden 64, 176

tariffs 94
taxation 194
  beer tax 47, 190
  motor vehicle tax 190
  VAT 190
taxpayers 107
textile industry 50–2, 89, 106
  industrialists 51, 91, 100
  outward processing 52
  trade unions 51, 91
Thatcher, M. 68, 117
Thomson-Brandt 59
Thyssen 56
Tindemans, L.
  Tindemans Report 30, 80, 227
trade liberalization 12, 46–7, 48, 49–53, 89, 98, 100, 106, 132
trade unions 87, 91, 136; *see also* Federation of German Trade Unions
  textile sector 51, 91
Tuesday Committee 40
Turkey 232

Union of Industries of the European Community (UNICE) 96, 98, 103
Union of Soviet Socialist Republics (USSR) 77, 111, 124, 125, 126, 130, 199, 200
United Kingdom 2, 8, 9, 11, 14, 33, 44, 52, 67, 88, 91, 122, 175, 224, 226, 229, 232, 235, 248, 249
  application for membership 79, 95, 109, 127
  British government 36, 49, 117, 241
  CAP 13, 72, 98, 241, 243
  EC Budget 33, 68, 69, 70, 194, 247
  ERDF 205, 209, 211, 212, 217, 218, 220
  Labour Party 149, 155, 214
  party politics and EC 123, 155, 163
  reservations on integration 108, 139, 165, 166, 183, 188, 225, 230
  Trades Union Congress 49
United Nations 8, 77
United States of America 47, 49, 50, 57, 58, 62, 78, 87, 88, 129, 130, 136, 177, 228, 244
  Carter Administration 65, 228
  Kennedy Administration 111, 126
  security ally 6, 7, 8, 64, 120, 124, 126–7, 130, 224, 225

Value Added Tax (VAT) 36
  EC Budget 70, 71, 243
  Sixth EC VAT directive 174, 181, 182
vocational training 94

watch industry 52
Wehner, H. 136
Weimar Republic; *see* Germany, Weimar Republic
West Germany; *see* Germany, Federal Republic
Western economic summits 65, 227

Western European Union (WEU) 9
Westpolitik 42, 44, 128, 138
Wettig, K. 164
Wilson, H. 214
Wischnewski, H.-J. 32, 206–7, 213

Zimmermann, F. 246
Zonal Border Area 215, 217, 218

For Product Safety Concerns and Information please contact our EU
representative GPSR@taylorandfrancis.com
Taylor & Francis Verlag GmbH, Kaufingerstraße 24, 80331 München, Germany

www.ingramcontent.com/pod-product-compliance
Ingram Content Group UK Ltd.
Pitfield, Milton Keynes, MK11 3LW, UK
UKHW020015200926
475702UK00014B/1892
9781138849167